D0026589

Psychoanalysis and the Scene of Reading

The Clarendon Lectures in English Literature 1997

Henri Matisse, *The Silence Living in Houses*
(*Le Silence habité des maisons*) 1947

Psychoanalysis and the Scene of Reading

MARY JACOBUS

OXFORD

UNIVERSITY PRESS

418.4019
J159p

OXFORD

UNIVERSITY PRESS

Great Clarendon Street, Oxford OX2 6DP

Oxford University Press is a department of the University of Oxford.
It furthers the University's objective of excellence in research, scholarship,
and education by publishing worldwide in

Oxford New York

Athens Auckland Bangkok Bogotá Buenos Aires Calcutta
Cape Town Chennai Dar es Salaam Delhi Florence Hong Kong Istanbul
Karachi Kuala Lumpur Madrid Melbourne Mexico City Mumbai
Nairobi Paris São Paulo Singapore Taipei Tokyo Toronto Warsaw

with associated companies in Berlin Ibadan

Oxford is a registered trade mark of Oxford University Press
in the UK and in certain other countries

Published in the United States
by Oxford University Press Inc., New York

© Mary Jacobus 1999

The moral rights of the author have been asserted
Database right Oxford University Press (maker)

First published 1999

All rights reserved. No part of this publication may be reproduced,
stored in a retrieval system, or transmitted, in any form or by any means,
without the prior permission in writing of Oxford University Press,
or as expressly permitted by law, or under terms agreed with the appropriate
reprographics rights organization. Enquiries concerning reproduction
outside the scope of the above should be sent to the Rights Department,
Oxford University Press, at the address above

You must not circulate this book in any other binding or cover
and you must impose this same condition on any acquiror

British Library Cataloguing in Publication Data

Data available

Library of Congress Cataloging in Publication Data

Data available

ISBN 0–19–818434–4

1 3 5 7 9 10 8 6 4 2

Typeset in Dante
by Graphicraft Limited, Hong Kong
Printed in Great Britain
on acid-free paper by
Bookcraft Ltd,
Midsomer Norton, Somerset

a profitable return from grey theory
to the perpetual green of experience
Sigmund Freud

Acknowledgements

I AM grateful to the English Faculty of Oxford University for inviting me to give the Clarendon Lectures during the autumn of 1997, and to Oxford University Press for supporting the Clarendon Lecture series. It was a great pleasure to return to my former faculty. I owe a special debt to Kim Scott Walwyn of Oxford University Press for her friendship and encouragement over the years, as well as to those responsible for the final editing and production of this book. I would also like to thank the Fellows of New College, Oxford, and particularly the Warden, Alan Ryan, and Kate Ryan, for their generous hospitality during my stay. It would be impossible to acknowledge everyone who commented on the lectures and essays on which this book is based, but their responses often helped me to improve them and take my thinking further. Among the many friends and colleagues who heard, read, or took time to comment on different chapters included in this book, I would especially like to thank the following: Isobel Armstrong, Gillian Beer, Rachel Bowlby, Cathy Caruth, Ian Donaldson, John Felstiner, Kate Flint, Marianne Hirsch, Biodun Jeyifo, Cora Kaplan, Jill Matus, Juliet Mitchell, Andrew Motion, Neil Saccamano, Jon Stallworthy, Riccardo Steiner, and Margot Waddell.

In addition, I would like to thank the Tavistock Clinic, London, for allowing me to be a non-clinical visiting fellow during the spring of 1997. What I learned there coincided with the writing of the Clarendon Lectures and continues to inform my thinking and affect me in important ways. My thanks to Margaret Rustin for making this visit possible, and to the clinicians whose seminars and lectures I attended. Among these, I am particularly grateful to Anne

Alvarez, David Bell, Cyril Couve, Alberto Hahn, and Priscilla Roth; Caroline Garland and Linda Young gave me invaluable insight into clinical aspects of trauma. I am also grateful to have had the opportunity to participate in John Steiner's theoretical and clinical seminar on the psychoanalytic setting. The members of our Bion reading group provided support for a reading project of a different kind. My greatest single debt is to Miss Betty Joseph, without whom this would have been a different book.

A year as Faculty Fellow at the Society for the Humanities, Cornell University, gave me time to revise and rewrite lectures originally written under pressure. I am grateful to all my colleagues there, and to the Director, Dominick LaCapra, for our stimulating discussions during an entire year devoted to the theme of psychoanalysis and trauma. My particular thanks for their generous comments on drafts of the Clarendon Lectures go to Jonathan Elmer, Max Hernandez, Petar Ramadanovic, Herman Rapaport, and Lyndsey Stonebridge. Maria Antonia Garcés, Susan Buck-Morss, and Biddy Martin offered timely information and pertinent questions. I am indebted to the members of our reconstituted Bion reading group for their willingness to keep going. As always, the staff of the Society for the Humanities contributed in innumerable and invisible ways to creating a congenial working environment; my special thanks to Mary Ahl, Linda Allen, and Lisa Patti for their practical support of the year's work and its activities.

Last of all, I would like to thank my family—my husband, Reeve Parker, and my children Frances and Josiah Jacobus-Parker—for travelling hopefully, tolerating my absences from time to time, and welcoming me back on my return. This book is for them.

M. J.

Ithaca
July 1998

Contents

Henri Matisse, *The Silence Living in Houses* (1947)
(*Le Silence habité des maisons*, Private
Collection, Paris)   *frontispiece*
© Succession H. Matisse/ARS New York

PART III. ROMANTIC WOMEN

Abbreviations

BSWM	Frantz Fanon, *Black Skin, White Masks* (1952), trans. Charles Lam Markmann (London, 1986)
E	Jean-Jacques Rousseau, *Eloisa, or a Series of Original Letters*, trans. William Kenrick (1803) (2 vols., Oxford, 1989)
EC	Mary Hays, *Memoirs of Emma Courtney* (1796), ed. Eleanor Ty (Oxford, 1996)
Essays	*The Essays of Virginia Woolf*, ed. Andrew McNeillie (4 vols., London, 1986)
F	Binjamin Wilkomirski, *Fragments: Memoirs of a Wartime Childhood*, trans. Carol Brown Janeway (New York, 1996)
FP	J.-B. Pontalis, 'Places and Separation', *Frontiers in Psychoanalysis: Between the Dream and Psychic Pain*, trans. Catherine Cullen and Philip Cullen (London, 1981)
IJP-A	*International Journal of Psycho-Analysis*
IW	*The Inner World and Joan Riviere: Collected Papers 1920–1958*, ed. Athol Hughes (London, 1991)
Journals	*The Journals of Mary Shelley 1814–1844*, ed. Paula R. Feldman and Diana Scott-Kilvert (2 vols., Oxford, 1987)
M	Mary Shelley, *Matilda*, ed. Janet Todd (Harmondsworth, 1991)
MP	Jane Austen, *Mansfield Park*, ed. Tony Tanner (Harmondsworth, 1966)
O	Claire de Duras, *Ourika*, trans. John Fowles, introd. Joan DeJean and Margaret Waller (New York, 1994)
SE	*The Standard Edition of the Complete Psychological Works of Sigmund Freud*, ed. James Strachey (24 vols., London, 1953–73)
Strachey	James Strachey, 'Some Unconscious Factors in Reading', *International Journal of Psycho-Analysis*, 11 (1930)
T	William Cowper, *The Task, A Poem* (London, 1785)

WMK   Melanie Klein, *The Works of Melanie Klein* (4 vols., London, 1975)

WNS   Andre Schwarz-Bart, *A Woman Named Solitude*, trans. Ralph Manheim, introd. Arnold Rampersad (San Francisco, 1985)

INTRODUCTION

MATTISSE'S painting, *The Silence Living in Houses* (1947; in French, more ambiguously, *Le Silence habité des maisons*, the inhabited silence of houses) is an image of interior space inhabited not only by silence, but by a reading couple and a book. An abstract, minimally perspectival representation of domestic space opens via a window on to a fluid natural landscape of tree, sky, and cloud. The flatness of the black interior background contrasts with the airily brushed vista outside. In this still life with figures, lines divide the window, frame it with curtains, scratch rudimentary building blocks on the walls, and compose the group itself: two readers at a table, with an open book in front of them and a vase of flowers to one side. But the book remains an empty space—a blank—for light to fall on, and for the viewer to fill with imaginary text or images; perhaps it is one of Matisse's own illustrated books, which he made by a process he considered analogous to that of painting. The cool blue of the figures, the vase, and the table, outlined with light against the sombre ballast of their background, provides both a tranquil focus and a visual connection with the distant blue of the sky. The non-visual (the book as more-than-object) is coded as the colour of intimacy, relationship, and silence, with a bit of distance thrown in. But the overlapping pose of the two human figures (two girls? a mother and child?) conveys as much about the mental activity of reading as the darkened interior. The painting constitutes a meditation on the relation of pictorial elements (volume, mass, perspective, depth, colour) to the mental representations that inhabit them. How effortlessly we 'read' this as an interior that leads the eye from the book to an inviting glimpse of a summer landscape seen through the window; and how easily, too, we understand its flat blackness and light-filled recession, not just as the contrast between darkness inside and the brightness of a summer day, but as a visual allusion to the peculiar mental absorption involved in the activity called 'reading'.[1]

It is tempting to read the intimacy of the two figures, with their overlapping edges and luminous yellow outlines, as a shorthand for what D. W. Winnicott, in 'The Location of Cultural Experience', calls 'the separation that is not a separation but a form of union'.[2] This might almost be a metaphor for the overall effect of a painting whose separations involve the play of eye and thought between a space that is neither inside nor outside—neither that of visual images nor of mental representations—but exists in the relation between them. Winnicott has in mind something that for him occurs between mother and child *at the point in time and space of the initiation of their state of separateness*. This, he says, is a relationship expressed by Marion Milner in pictorial terms when she writes of 'the tremendous significance that there can be in the interplay of the edges of two curtains, or the surface of a jug that is placed in front of another jug'.[3] In connection with her own experiments in drawing, Milner's introduction to *The*

---

[1] Eye problems at this period meant that Matisse was apt to pull the curtains against the sun and that 'the glare of black often has a tinge of melancholy'; see Hayden Herrera, *Matisse: A Portrait* (New York and London, 1993), 190; and cf. the darkened surround to the brilliant window of *Interior with an Egyptian Curtain* (1948). According to Alfred H. Barr, who also refers to *The Silence Living in Houses* as 'a nocturne interior made eerie by the bright summer day seen through the garden window', the year 1947 was 'marked in the history of Matisse's paintings by the brilliant variations on the theme of an interior with a window in the upper right-hand background and two girls seated behind a table'; see *Matisse: His Art and His Public* (London, 1975), 276, and cf. *Small Interior with Two Girls* (1947). Matisse's involvement with the creation of illustrated books and folios at this period provides an additional layer of reference in his depiction of the book as visual object; for this, and for Matisse's understanding of blackness as a colour in painting ('Black is a force: I used black as ballast to simplify the construction'), see Jack Flam, *Matisse on Art* (Berkeley and Los Angeles, 1995), 165–6, 166–8.

[2] See D. W. Winnicott, 'The Location of Cultural Experience' (1967), *Playing and Reality* (1971; repr. London, 1991), 98. For an intelligent and defamiliarizing account of Winnicott's ideas, and for transitional phenomena generally, see Adam Phillips, *Winnicott* (London, 1988), esp. 113–21.

[3] *Playing and Reality*, 97–8; Winnicott's italics.

Suppressed Madness of Sane Men refers to the ways in which her interest in perspective had originally brought her 'to face ideas to do with separation and distance while outline brought in the whole question of boundaries'.[4] Reproducing a sketch of two overlapping jugs from her earlier book, *On Not Being Able to Paint* (1950), she quotes her own comment that the drawing had been motivated by the dim fear stirred in her 'of what might happen if one let go one's mental hold on the outline which kept everything separate and in its place'.[5] But one morning, 'without any mental struggle', she was able to see the edges of the two jugs 'in relation to each other, and how gaily they seemed almost to ripple now that they were freed from this grimly practical business of enclosing an object and keeping it in its place'. This, she thought, was what painters meant by 'the *play* of edges', or the phrase 'freedom of line'. Clinging to the world of outlines had meant, for her, clinging to 'the world of fact, of separate touchable solid objects; to cling to it was therefore surely to protect oneself against the other world, the world of the imagination'.[6] The play of the line opened on to the inner world, a world of mental representations. Access to what she calls 'the world of the imagination' depended, she discovered, on blurring outlines and losing a sense of boundaries between objects and people; but the thought of crossing the boundary between the tangible, visible world and the inner world of feelings and ideas had brought with it (at least for one part of her mind) the fear of being mad. Her suppressed madness was freed by playing with line.

For Matisse, the line was inherently expressive of relationship, particularly when used to depict the human figure: 'Remember', he told his students, 'a line cannot exist alone; it always brings a companion along. Do remember that one line does nothing;

[4] Marion Milner, *The Suppressed Madness of Sane Men: Forty-four Years of Exploring Psychoanalysis* (London and New York, 1988), 7. See also 'Winnicott and Overlapping Circles' (1977), ibid. 279–86, where Milner reflects on Winnicott's interest in her drawing of the two overlapping jugs, seeing in the area of overlap 'an apt symbol for Winnicott's concept of the transitional area that he says is the place where all culture belongs' (ibid. 280).

[5] Marion Milner, *On Not Being Able to Paint* (2nd edn., New York, 1957), 16.

[6] Ibid. 16, 17.

it is only in relation to another that it creates a volume. And do make the two together.'[7] 'Making the two together' offers another way of thinking about Matisse's *The Silence Living in Houses*, where one figure brings a companion along to create volume 'in relation to another'. The reading couple becomes a symbolic expression of unity-in-duality, like Milner's gaily overlapping jugs. For Matisse, music provided a traditional analogy for such effects ('The lines must play in harmony and return, as in music'); a curved line was to be read in relation to the straight one that accompanied it. In his graphic lexicon, 'All the lines must close around a center' to contain the human form if the drawing was to exist as a unit and arrest the viewer's attention ('fleeing lines carry the attention away—they do not arrest it').[8] By emphasizing the constructive and containing aspects of line as well as its rhythmic expressiveness, Matisse puts a more robust, down-to-earth spin on Milner's eyes-closed opposition between linear freedom and imprisonment within the rigidity of objects. But both of them, in their different ways, may be seen as engaged in what Winnicott called 'the perpetual human task of keeping inner and outer reality separate yet inter-related'.[9] In 'The Location of Cultural Experience', Winnicott tells us that his own account of 'transitional phenomena' was—appropriately—crystallized by 'playing about' in 'a state of not-knowing'. He began with concepts that he did know, such as 'mental representations', phenomena located in 'the personal psychic reality, felt to be inside' (i.e. internal objects), and 'the effects of the operation on the mental mechanisms of projection and introjection'; that is, with the familiar lexicon of psychoanalysis he had inherited from Freud and Melanie

---

[7] Flam, *Matisse on Art*, 48; notes made in 1908 by Sarah Stein while studying with Matisse.

[8] Ibid. 48–9. Cf. Bion's observation, relevant to the three circular forms in Matisse's painting (two heads and a fan?) that 'The circle cut by the line offers a connection with point and line and a model for inside and outside'; elsewhere, Bion speaks of the circle as 'a visual image of "inside and outside"'. See W. R. Bion, *Transformations* (1965; repr. London, 1984), 96, 82.

[9] 'Transitional Objects and Transitional Phenomena' (1953); *Playing and Reality*, 2; as Phillips suggests, 'the paper . . . enacts the problem it attempts to describe' (see *Winnicott*, 120–1).

Klein.[10] But he went on to ask whether these discrete concepts, phenomena, and mental mechanisms might be relocated in what was, for him at least, a freer and less bounded 'potential' space between the individual and the environment. This, he says, is neither the space of inner psychic life nor the place of lived experience, but what he terms an intermediate area (just as the object used by the baby is neither created nor simply found lying around, but symbolizes 'the union of two now-separate things'). For Winnicott, this 'place that is at the continuity-contiguity moment, where transitional phenomena originate', is to be found not only in play (compare Milner's *play* of edges'), but in cultural experience.[11] It brings with it a further paradox that bears on Matisse's depiction of 'the silence living in houses': not only the presence of a trusted object, but the capacity to be alone in the presence of an object, whether the mother, the analyst, or the book. Matisse's painting can be understood as an attempt to render just such an inhabited solitude at the moment of continuity-contiguity. Because an open book provides its focal image, it identifies this moment with reading.

As a contrast to Matisse, I want to invoke another meditation on reading that is also based on a pictorial image and the book as icon. In his alarmed account of the impact of technology on reading, *The Gutenberg Elegies: The Fate of Reading in an Electronic Age* (1994), Sven Birkerts describes a painting that he carries in his mind's eye ('Either it really exists, or else I have conjured it up so often that it might as well'):

The painting belongs to a familiar genre—that of the pensive figure in the garden. I see a bench, a secluded bower. A woman in Victorian dress gazing away from a book that she holds in one hand. The image is one of reverie and privilege. But these attributions scarcely begin to exhaust its significance. If reverie or privileged leisure were the point, then the book would not figure so profoundly in my mental reconstruction. Indeed, it is the book that finally grips my attention. I have it placed, if not literally then figuratively, in the center of my visual field. At the vanishing point. The painting is, for me, about the book, or about the woman's reading

---

[10] *Playing and Reality*, 96.   [11] Ibid. 103.

of the book, and though the contents of the pages are as invisible as her thoughts, they (the imagined fact of them) give the image its appeal.[12]

Here the pensive image of a woman reading outdoors coincides not only with ideas involving the privileged relations between gender, reverie, and leisure, but with the idea of being in the grip of a book while simultaneously inhabiting an intangible landscape synonymous with reading: 'The whole point of my summoning her up is to fasten upon a state that is other than thinking. If she were thinking, she would be herself . . . but for me the power of the image lies precisely in the fact that she is planted in one reality, the garden reality, while adrift in the spell of another. That of the author's created reality.' What is this state that is 'other than thinking'? Birkerts implies that when a woman is reading, as opposed to thinking, she is not 'herself'. But perhaps it is Birkerts who is in the grip of the book (and who estranges her from herself), fictionalizing the scene of reading in the field of vision—'at the vanishing point', which is also the vanishing point of the woman reader. Birkerts's verbal equivalent of this unidentified Victorian genre painting emphasizes what escapes the visual, 'the most elusive and private of all conditions, that of the self suspended in the medium of language'. But what he evokes most powerfully is his own condition of being merged with another in the medium of fiction.

For Birkerts, the book is 'an icon representing an imagined and immaterial order'; it contains figments transformed by the reader 'into a set of wholly internal sensations and emotions'. In short, the book is not a material object but a transitional object (in the sense neither created nor found by Winnicott when 'playing

---

[12] Sven Birkerts, *The Gutenberg Elegies: The Fate of Reading in an Electronic Age* (New York, 1994), 77. For paintings depicting Victorian women reading both outdoors and indoors, see Kate Flint, *The Woman Reader 1837–1914* (Oxford, 1993). Although no obvious candidate exists for Birkerts's composite picture, Arthur Hughes's poignant *April Love* (1856) provides some of its ingredients—the pensive woman in Victorian dress, the bench, and the secluded bower. But Hughes's woman is gazing away from a lover, not a book. Cf. also Hughes's *The Tryst* (1860), which includes a book as well as a lover. Among other Victorian paintings depicting women reading in garden settings, probably the most striking is Dante Gabriel Rossetti's *The Daydream* (1880) depicting Jane Morris up a tree, with a book. I am indebted to Kate Flint for this suggestion.

about' with psychoanalytic concepts): 'I see the book. Inside the book are the words. They are themselves the threshold between the material and immaterial, the outward and the inward . . . This is the paradox of paradoxes: The word is most signifier when it least signifies.'[13] Reading the book, as opposed to seeing it, depends on not-seeing the words (or, for that matter, the woman reader). Birkerts's line of thought takes him out of himself, indeed, out of the imaginary book, to an enchanted 'threshold' (an intermediate or potential space) where signs mean something other than them-selves and what he calls 'the merely existing self' turns into this hypostatized self-as-reader. The threshold—like Milner's boundary —is associated with crossing the line between outside and inside, and (since it depends on Winnicott's 'mental mechanisms of projection and introjection'), with abolishing what Birkerts refers to as 'the problematic boundary line that separates the one self from the other'. Reading, therefore, implies a change of state or orientation, and even gender—a dynamic process of connection, linguistic possession, and vehicular movement 'as unconscious as highway driving', which tends to be experienced as 'inwardness' and virtual temporality, as opposed to 'garden reality' and real time. With books like these, who needs the virtual reality of the electronic age? The paradox that none the less exercises Birkerts is 'the paradox of the book itself, which is to be a physical object whose value is found in the invisible play of energies entrapped by its covers'.[14] At once an elegist of literary culture and an un-witting phenomenologist of the book-as-potential-space (a book whose play of energies bears a remarkable resemblance to a com-puter), Birkerts writes evocatively about some of the ways in which we think about reading, about what books signify to their readers, and even about what books mean to the characters inhabiting them. But the categories he invokes—boundaries between selves, a reality neither found nor created, transformations of material objects into a world of internal sensations and emotions, changes in our relation to temporality (to name only a few)—assume an unquestioned continuity between reading and the elusive, fictive

---

[13] *The Gutenberg Elegies*, 78.   [14] Ibid. 86.

realm to which they provide a threshold. What does this realm consist of?

For Birkerts, the experience of reading remains ultimately indescribable and immanent, while the materiality of the book all but disappears. Given his idealized and private eco-phenomenology of reading, no wonder the book is opposed to technology. Hence his down-playing of the iterable or mechanical dimensions of reading, and the less pleasurable compulsions and accidents of print culture (just as he averts his gaze from the attributions of gender and class—let alone the historicity—of the woman reading in the garden). But why should the figure of the reader in Birkerts's unnamed Victorian painting be female? Is reading unconsciously gendered, or is the rise of the woman reader (the product of the leisured bourgeois family) inseparable from the more recent history of reading?—a woman reader considered, that is, as a cultural phenomenon that defines the relation between private and public spheres (for instance, the relation of garden and house to a supposedly ungendered public sphere, or of the Victorian woman reader to an imaginary community of like-minded readers; even the woman's reverie implies an absent lover who occupies a larger world). Not all the subjects of the essays that follow are women, although, as it happens, the majority of them are either women, psychoanalysts, poets, Rousseau, or children. Nor are these essays intended primarily as a contribution to recent attempts to understand relations between gender, class, nation, and print culture in the modern period, let alone as a brief history of reading or its discontents.[15] Rather, they attempt to unpack some

---

[15] See Flint, *The Woman Reader 1837–1914*, whose chapters on 'Reading Practices' and 'Fictional Reading' (ibid. 187–249, 253–73) provide a valuable corrective to Birkerts's unspecific account of the Victorian woman reader. For a resourceful, personal, and panoptical account of the intricate histories of reading and reading practices, see also Alberto Manguel, *A History of Reading* (London and New York, 1996), whose opening section ('The Last Page') plunges the reader into a heady account of what reading has meant in times past and present (ibid. 3–23). Birkerts's elegy for the demise of reading is predicated on the book as an object that maintains stability, hierarchy, and privacy, and on the idea of a cultural transformation that spells the displacement of the book by 'the rush of impulses through freshly minted circuits', threatening to upset the fragile ecology of literacy and put an end to 'the private self—that of the dreamy fellow with an open book in his lap'; see *The Gutenberg Elegies*, 3–7.

of the implicit assumptions about reading, whether considered as a process, a representation, or an ideology, that involve concepts or unconscious phantasies of inner and outer, absence and boundaries, and the transmission of thoughts and feelings between one self (or historical period) and another. These are concepts that provide the foundation for much of our thinking about subjectivity, and that receive their fullest elaboration in the twentieth-century discourse of psychoanalysis. Hence, *Psychoanalysis and the Scene of Reading*.

In the course of this book, I draw on a range of ideas associated with British object relations psychoanalysis as it developed in Britain in the wake of Freud and Klein. The evolution of psychoanalysis has its own national and geo-political specificity, its own debates, and its own theory of practice.[16] My thinking is indebted not only to the writings of Freud—the most literary of all psychoanalytic thinkers—but to the alternate strands of psychoanalysis represented by Sándor Ferenczi and Klein, and to the rich and varied body of psychoanalytic writing by theorists and practitioners who learned from, developed, or transformed Klein's ideas from the middle decades of the century onwards. But just as this is neither an account of the rise of the woman reader nor a history of reading in the modern period, I make no attempt to chart the local vicissitudes of psychoanalysis, or to trace the development of its differing strands; nor do I engage in any sustained way with the range of alternate psychoanalytic theories available today (let alone enter what have come to be known as the Freud wars). Rather, I try to make an implicit case for the literary and critical uses of British object relations psychoanalysis, particularly the version of object relations associated with contemporary post-Kleinian thinking, and with some continental

---

[16] See, for instance, Stephen Mitchell and Margaret J. Black, *Freud and Beyond: A History of Modern Psychoanalytic Thought* (New York, 1995); Meir Perlow, *Understanding Mental Objects* (London and New York, 1995); Eric Rayner, *The Independent Mind in British Psychoanalysis* (London, 1991); and Peter Rudnytsky, *The Psychoanalytic Vocation: Rank, Winnicott, and the Legacy of Freud* (New Haven and London, 1991); for the British wartime controversies between Kleinians and Freudians, see also *The Freud–Klein Controversies 1941–45*, ed. Pearl King and Riccardo Steiner (London and New York, 1991).

theorists who have managed to sustain a dialogue with British object relations.[17] Literary theory in its psychoanalytic mode has tended to be largely informed by the reappropriation of Freudian psychoanalysis that took place in the wake of Lacan's 'return to Freud', a return now almost inseparable from informed post-structuralist theories of the subject, considered as the subject in and of language. Like other literary and feminist critics of my generation, I have been thoroughly influenced by the legacy of Lacanian post-structuralism—as well as by the psychoanalytic writers (both feminist and non-feminist) who took issue with Lacan, if only because of his comparative down-playing of issues involving affect and the realm of the imaginary, as opposed to language and the symbolic. But while I write as a feminist critic, this does not set out to be a specifically feminist book, nor do I read with a specifically post-structuralist agenda—let alone spend much time on (for instance) the struggle between the decline of deconstruction and the rise of cultural criticism. On the other hand, what often gets left out of Kleinian and post-Kleinian accounts of literature and aesthetics, along with the material interventions of books, are the specifically literary, linguistic, and cultural aspects of reading. Here the literary critic has something to say.

---

[17] For the current revival of interest in the psychoanalytic thought of Melanie Klein in literary and cultural theory, see especially the collection of essays in Lyndsey Stonebridge and John Phillips (eds.), *Reading Melanie Klein* (London and New York, 1998); see also Lyndsey Stonebridge, *The Destructive Element: British Psychoanalysis and Modernism* (London and New York, 1998), and Jacqueline Rose, *Why War?—Psychoanalysis, Politics, and the Return to Melanie Klein* (Oxford, 1993). For literary responses to Winnicott, see Peter L. Rudnytsky (ed.), *Transitional Objects and Potential Spaces: Literary Uses of D. W. Winnicott* (New York, 1993). In general, I have had in mind the body of psychoanalytic work that includes not only Winnicott in England, but the writing of Wilfred Bion or, in France, that of André Green, whose theoretical work has been influenced by both Winnicott and Bion (as well as Lacan); see for instance, W. R. Bion, *Learning from Experience* (London, 1962), and the papers collected in *Second Thoughts* (London, 1967), and the papers translated in André Green, *On Private Madness* (Madison, Conn., 1986). For more recent post-Kleinian psychoanalytic work in Britain that has a bearing on aesthetics, see Hanna Segal, *The Work of Hanna Segal: A Kleinian Approach to Clinical Practice* (Northvale, NJ, and London, 1981), and *Dream, Phantasy and Art* (London and New York, 1991); for attention to the fine grain of the psychic text, see Betty Joseph, *Psychic Equilibrium and Psychic Change: Selected Papers of Betty Joseph* (London, 1989).

For reasons that have more to do with my personal inclinations than anything else, I have tried in writing these essays to follow Freud's injunction to make 'a profitable return from grey theory to the perpetual green of experience'—if only because, as Freud puts it, a fresh hypothesis allows us 'to see what we already know from another angle'. Freud is alluding to lines from Goethe's *Faust*—'My worthy friend, gray is all theory, | And green alone Life's golden tree'.[18] In the highly theoretical (not to say over-theorized) arena that has become synonymous with literary studies, this realigned seeing feels both pleasurable and liberating, much like the play of edges or freedom of line. Milner's 'plunge into colour' (her phrase) confronted her with just such a renewed form of seeing. Differentiating between the vividness and intimacy of colour and what she calls 'the cold white light of consciousness', she started to notice things and colours before unnoticed, but also found that closing her eyes to recall colour combinations allowed her to watch the memory of colour and observe its changes more closely: 'here was a meeting of the conscious inner eye and the blind experience of colour which resulted from the willingness to watch and wait. And it was a meeting which neither destroyed the dark possibilities of colour nor dimmed the light of consciousness . . .'[19] The painter whom Milner goes on to quote is Cézanne—'To love a painting, one must first have drunk deeply of it in long draughts'. In the context of his 'coloured undulation', she mentions her own fear (again) of the madness that seemed proximate to change as opposed to the sanity associated with a fixed world. Supposing, she asks, 'it was not a picture but a person that was loved like this?' Such a plunge might be painful as well as dangerous. Milner reminds us that the prospect of 'see[ing] what we already know from another angle' can arouse anxiety as well as the expectation of pleasure. What she undertook in her experiments with drawing and painting, I suggest, the reader constantly undertakes in the plunge into observation,

[18] See Sigmund Freud, 'Neurosis and Psychosis' (1924), *SE* xix. 149 and n. Freud is referring to Mephistopheles' speech in *Faust*, I. iv: 'Grau, teuer Freund, ist alle Theorie, | Und grün des Lebens goldner Baum'.

[19] *On Not Being Able to Paint*, 22–4.

self-observation, and memory involved in reading, which is also
a plunge into something both known and not-known. This too
is both an experience and a practice (and, to be sure, a practice
with its accompanying theory). In the essays that follow, I try
to stay close to the text while proposing specific hypotheses that
offer to illuminate it in fresh or unexpected ways—bearing in mind
that what Milner calls 'a meeting of the conscious inner eye and
the blind experience of colour' keeps the reading experience
perpetually green.

A lecture series constitutes an invitation to reflect on what one
already knows, and to see it from another angle. It can also provide an opportunity to follow the trajectory of the unexpected.
The lectures on which these essays are based turned out to lead
in a direction I could not have predicted, although it traced the
line of pre-existing interests, from the scene of reading to trauma
theory. The first pair of chapters ('Scenes of Reading') ask what
psychoanalysis has to say about forms of interiority and memory
that seem to be bound up with the ways in which we think of
ourselves when we read and re-read. Chapter 1 explores unconscious and cultural aspects of reading as they are depicted by two
writers of the Bloomsbury circle, James Strachey and Virginia
Woolf, taking as a point of departure the tendency of spacial
metaphors to converge on metaphors of eating and incorporation
in representations of reading. Chapter 2 goes on to explore the
ways in which reading, rereading, and landscape—reflections in
a landscape—constitute ways of denying, modifying, or mourning specific forms of absence and confinement in the fictional
worlds of Jane Austen and Jean-Jacques Rousseau. The second
pair of chapters ('Reading Trauma'), ask how psychoanalytic
theory, especially trauma theory, contributes to an understanding
of colonial slavery, history, and Holocaust writing. Chapter 3 uses
Fanon as a lens for trans-racial representations of black female
colonial subjects during the French Revolutionary period, focusing on novels by Claire du Duras and André Schwarz-Bart that
depict the melancholia of the colonial subject, the politics of
madness, and the malady of historical repetition. Chapter 4 brings

Ferenczian and Kleinian understandings of trauma to bear on the fragmentation, figuration, and topoi of Holocaust memory in the 'memoirs' of a child survivor, Binjamin Wilkomirski, tracing the relation between attempts to narrate the experience of the Holocaust, traumatic reading, and the scene of weeping. The final pair of essays ('Romantic Women')—written earlier than the others, but anticipating some of their concerns—stem from my long-standing interest in women writers of the Romantic period. Chapter 5 attempts to understand Mary Shelley's 'unreadability' via the writing of trauma, in her case, the relation between an incest-narrative, an unrepresentable trauma of object loss, and her problematic relation to silence, poetry, and literary transmission. Chapter 6 addresses the relation between public and private spheres in the writing of Mary Wollstonecraft's contemporary, Mary Hays, speculating about her use of the epistolary mode as a vehicle for kinds of communication that anticipate both Freud's account of telepathy and modern concepts of unconscious communication. This and other essays dedicate Milner's 'idea of no boundary between one self and another self'—the temporary form of madness permitted by both reading and psychoanalysis—to understanding some of the ways in which we communicate with the writing of others, and the writing of others communicates with us. Among the many things it entails, reading is what we do when we make this commitment to otherness.

PART ONE

Scenes of Reading

ONE

The Room in the Book
Psychoanalysis and the
Scene of Reading

GEORGES Poulet, in an essay called 'Criticism and Interiority' (1970), opens his phenomenological account of the effect books have on us with a scene of reading—a book within a book, in an empty room: 'At the beginning of Mallarmé's unfinished story *Igitur* there is the description of an empty room, in the middle of which, on a table, there is an open book.'[1] Poulet's essay explores the idea of a literary criticism that is neither too close nor too distant from its object—neither absorbed completely into the text, to possess and inhabit it entirely; nor, alternatively, abstracting from it, to think its thoughts at a distance that precludes real engagement. But Poulet also poses another question. If a book is an object, how is it transformed into an equivalent subjectivity—into a place-holder for what he calls 'interiority'? Poulet's book awaits deliverance by human intervention, like a caged animal being mistreated as a mere object. The book's openness ('on a table, there is an open book') is what moves us and constitutes its invitation: 'It asks nothing better than to exist outside itself, or to let you exist in it. In short, the extraordinary fact in the case of a book is the falling away of the barriers between you and it. You are inside it, it is inside you; there is no longer

---

[1] Georges Poulet, 'Criticism and Interiority', in Richard Macksey and Eugenio Donato (eds.), *The Languages of Criticism and the Sciences of Man: The Structuralist Controversy* (Baltimore and London, 1970), 56.

either outside or inside.'[2] Let me be, the book seems to say, and
you too can be (in) me. For Poulet, then, the book exists, not on
paper, not in its materiality nor in any physically locatable space
(on a table, for instance), but in what he calls 'my innermost self'.
When the barriers come down, books are us. Which isn't to say
that we are books, although we may sometimes think so.

I begin with Poulet because he eloquently evokes the recurrent
figure that I'm going to refer to as 'the scene of reading'—a scene
in which imagining an open book in an empty room gives rise to
a series of equivalences, such as 'inside the book' and 'inside me'.
Needless to say, we come to this imaginary scene of reading with
an open book in front of us, the book that contains Poulet's essay;
some other reader has always been there beforehand—Poulet,
Mallarmé, the midnight reader in Mallarmé's *Igitur*.[3] But it's not
this readerly *mise-en-abyme* that intrigues me, nor our need to
imagine ourselves as alone in the company of a book (although
I think we often do). Rather, I want to explore the question of
how things get, so to speak, from the outside to the inside—
simultaneously establishing the boundary between them and
seeming to abolish it. What does it mean to call this 'interiority'?
Where is this place that has neither outside nor inside, and by what
process does it come into being? Poulet makes us wonder how
an 'object' (an unread book, an unknown person) can turn into
an equivalent subjectivity, imaginatively alive and communicated
with, registered as different yet in some way available to us for
the peculiar use we call 'reading' (or knowing, or loving). What
might psychoanalysis have to say about this strange phenomenon?
In contemporary psychoanalytic accounts of literature, particularly those with a Kleinian emphasis (I'm thinking, for instance,
of the recent dialogue about 'imagining characters' between the

---

[2] Poulet, 'Criticism and Interiority', 57.

[3] See Stéphane Mallarmé, *Œuvres complètes*, ed. Henri Mondor and G. Jean-Aubry
(Paris, 1945), 423–51. Igitur is a Hamlet figure; the unfinished story opens at midnight, with a scene that includes 'la pâleur d'un livre ouvert que présente la table;
page et décor ordinaires de la Nuit, sinon que subsiste encore le silence d'une antique
parole proférée par lui, en lequel, revenue, ce Minuit évoque son ombre finie et
nulle par ses mots: J'étais l'heure qui doit me rendre pur' (435).

novelist, A. S. Byatt, and the psychoanalyst, Ignes Sodre), the phrase
'internal world' is often used surprisingly unselfconsciously, given
the caution with which even minimally sophisticated psychoanalytic
readers use a term like 'self' (with or without—usually with—scare
quotes).[4] Poulet's beginning fiction, his open book, is an invitation
to speculate not only about the kind of interiority we associate with
reading, but also about how books 'think' us—about the nature
of their peculiar linguistic intervention and their relation to what
Alix Strachey, in a paper on the psychoanalytic use of the word
'internal', calls 'the idea of insideness' or 'inside things'.[5]

In the discussion that followed Poulet's paper, the psychoanalytic critic Norman Holland (one of a distinguished group of
interlocutors) struck a dissenting note by introducing 'into all
this Gallic logic and lucidity something dark and murky from
psychoanalysis'.[6] This 'something dark and murky' that comes
from psychoanalysis turns out to be a murkiness that still troubles
contemporary discussions of psychoanalysis today, as it troubled
Freud and the early Freudians—hypnosis. Here is Holland: 'in
hypnosis, the subject—oh, excuse me, I'd better not use that
word—the hypnotisand feels the personality of the hypnotist as
though it is a part of himself; and when the hypnotist says: "Your
hand feels cold": your hand does feel cold, which I think is rather
like the way we respond to a book'. (Note Holland's disavowal
of the 'subject'—dead-already?—and how the hypnotisand has
acquired a body instead.)[7] Why isn't reading like being hypnotized?
Holland goes on to question whether the term 'identification'
(used by Poulet) would really be 'the psychoanalyst's term for
our relationship with the book'. He suggests, instead, that the
psychoanalyst would speak of 'incorporation'—'a much more
primitive kind of mechanism; in fact related basically, ultimately,

---

[4] See A. S. Byatt and Ignes Sodre, *Imagining Characters: Six Conversations about Women Writers*, ed. Rebecca Smith (London, 1995); and see Ch. 2 below (p. 52), for Byatt's reflection on the relation between books, rooms, and what she calls 'the world in the head' or 'the world inside, in which everything can take place', 'a meaningful internal world' (ibid. 37–8).

[5] See Alix Strachey, 'A Note on the Use of the Word "internal"', *IJP-A* 22 (1941), 37–43.

[6] *The Languages of Criticism and the Sciences of Man*, 86.   [7] Ibid. 87.

to eating, as, for example, when we speak of a man as a voracious reader.'[8] Among other possible figures for reading, Holland cites the relation between two lovers, invoking the opening chapter of *Civilization and its Discontents* (1930), where Freud writes of the melting away of boundaries between ego and object at the height of being in love.[9] In response, Poulet objects that 'in psychoanalysis you can find some kind of incorporation or identification in more than one example and in particular in the identification of the patient with the doctor'. This is not what concerns him, he says, since it occurs on an unconscious level. For him, reading takes place 'at the fully conscious level' even if it has to be seen as 'a kind of confused consciousness, a sort of cloudy consciousness'. Confused and cloudy, but *not* dark and murky. Poulet needs a *cogito*—what Freud calls 'the activity of thought'—for his theory of reading.[10] Holland responds with a topographical model that puts 'your *cogito* [i.e. consciousness] at the top' and 'a very primitive level at the bottom'. But for Poulet, who has the last word, consciousness is 'at the bottom end also'.[11]

[8] *The Languages of Criticism and the Sciences of Man*, 87. Holland's move from identification to incorporation is sketched by Freud himself in *The New Introductory Lectures* (1933) when he defines 'identification' as 'the assimilation of one ego to another one, as a result of which the first ego behaves like the second in certain respects, imitates it and in a sense takes it up into itself. Identification has been not unsuitably compared with the oral, cannibalistic incorporation of the other person' (*SE* xxii. 63).

[9] In *Civilization and its Discontents* (1930), Freud writes that the main exception to our sense of having a distinct, autonomous, and unitary sense of self is the experience of being in love: '. . . towards the outside, at any rate, the ego seems to maintain clear and sharp lines of demarcation. There is only one state—admittedly an unusual state, but not one that can be stigmatized as pathological—in which it does not do this. *At the height of being in love the boundary between ego and object threatens to melt away. Against all the evidence of his senses, a man who is in love declares that "I" and "you" are one, and is prepared to behave as if it were a fact* . . . Pathology has made us acquainted with a great number of states in which the boundary lines between the ego and the external world become uncertain or in which they are actually drawn incorrectly' (*SE* xxi. 66; my italics). See also ch. VIII, 'Being in Love and Hypnosis', in *Group Psychology and the Analysis of the Ego* (1921)—especially relevant to Holland's objection that Poulet's account of reading sounds like hypnosis.

[10] See *New Introductory Lectures*, where Freud writes of the ego as interposing a postponement between need and action 'in the form of the activity of thought' (*SE* xxii. 76).

[11] *The Languages of Criticism and the Sciences of Man*, 87–8. Perhaps only recourse to Freud's thesis in *The Ego and the Id* (1923) that there is something unconscious in consciousness could resolve the impasse here.

This twenty-five-year-old exchange on the 'subject' of psychoanalysis coincides with two seemingly unconnected features often
associated with representations of reading. On one hand, we have
the room and the book, and the invitation (not always innocent)
to enter an imaginary interior.[12] This can be a quite quotidian,
domestic space, or a more venerable one (a library, for instance)
—a room with or without a view, overlooking the everyday
world of realist fiction or opening on to the world of fantasy.[13]
But as well as the room and the book, we often find a prolifera-
tion of Holland's incorporatory language: typically, metaphors of
eating, savouring, or devouring. As a way to explore this piquant
relation between rooms, books, and eating, I want to take a detour
back from the structuralist controversy of the 1970s to the time
when psychoanalysis and literary production were near neighbours
in England—the time, during the 1920s, when James Strachey's
and Joan Riviere's translations of Freud began to emerge from the
basement of the Woolfs' Hogarth Press (although Virginia Woolf
herself seems not to have read Freud seriously until later).[14] This

---

[12] Cf. André Green's Gallic version of the book's invitation, in 'The Unbinding
Process' (1971): 'The desire to see is patent in the act of reading. The book cover,
the binding, function as garments . . . which offer themselves fascinatingly to the
eye.' He goes on to depict the reader-as-*flâneur* entering the bookstore to browse:
'we pick up a book. Here the pleasure starts, as we open it, finger it, thumb through
its pages, probing it in various places' until finally 'we pay for the book and leave
the store arm-in-arm with it'. What is this but a pick-up? Green goes on to suggest
that 'In order to read, we'll need to lock ourselves up with the book—in a public
place or in more confined quarters—sometimes in the most unlikely or, shall we
say, the least propitious places for this kind of exercise' (his footnote on bathroom-
radiator libraries alludes to reading as 'a scatological ritual'). See *On Private Madness*
(Madison, Conn., 1986), 342–3 and n.

[13] Keats, for instance, pictures himself reading thus: 'I should like the window to
open onto the Lake of Geneva—and there I'd sit and read all day like the picture
of somebody reading—' (To Fanny Keats, 13 Mar. 1819); see *Letters of John Keats: A
Selection*, ed. Robert Gittings (Oxford, 1970), 203.

[14] Hermione Lee suggests in her biography that Woolf did not actually read Freud
until the late 1930s, although she used psychoanalytic terminology and had a con-
versational knowledge of Freudian concepts; Leonard Woolf was, of course, familiar with the primary texts prior to the 1920s, and had reviewed *The Psychopathology
of Everyday Life* in 1915. See Hermione Lee, *Virginia Woolf* (London, 1996), 191, 197,
713, and esp. 722–6. Strachey records Woolf making 'a more than usually ferocious
onslaught upon psycho-analysis and psychoanalysts, more particularly the latter',
at a dinner party in 1925; see James Strachey to Alix Strachey (14 May 1925),

was also the time when shifts in Freud's own thinking replaced
Holland's topography of 'levels' with an emphasis on structure,
the so-called 'second topography'.[15] And partly as a consequence
of Freud's reorientation of psychoanalytic technique towards the
transference, attempts to disentangle the effects of psychoanalysis
from those of hypnosis took on renewed urgency.[16] Strachey's
lucid formulation of the problem in his foundational essay of
1934, 'The Nature of the Therapeutic Action of Psycho-Analysis',
asks how analytic understanding gets into the analysand, and why
psychoanalysis (unlike hypnosis) effects lasting change: questions
involving not only transference, but language.[17] For Strachey,
the immediacy of the transference interpretation (the so-called
'mutative interpretation') provided the lever for shifting the always
fluctuating, permeable, and inconstant boundaries between the

Bloomsbury/Freud: The Letters of James and Alix Strachey 1924–1925, ed. Perry Meisel
and Walter Kendrick (New York, 1985), 264. For other accounts of the relation
between Woolf and Freud, see also Elizabeth Abel, Virginia Woolf and the Fictions
of Psychoanalysis (Chicago, 1989), esp. ch. 1.

[15] See The Ego and the Id (1923), translated by Joan Riviere in 1927 (published by
the Hogarth Press).

[16] Freud's chapter on transference in the Introductory Lectures (1916–17; trans. 1929)
admits that the force within the patient to be mobilized on the side of recovery
is the familiar power of suggestion, then goes on to ventriloquize 'an objection boil-
ing up . . . so fiercely' that it has to be put into words: ' "Ah! so you've admitted it
at last! You work with the help of suggestion, just like the hypnotists! That's what
we've thought for a long time . . ." ' (SE xvi. 446). See Joseph Sandler and Anna Ursula
Dreher, What Do Psychoanalysts Want? (London and New York, 1996), 23–31, particularly for papers by Sachs, Alexander, and Rado which raised the problem of a
therapy based on transference and superego transformation as opposed to hypnosis.

[17] See James Strachey, 'The Nature of the Therapeutic Action of Psychoanalysis', IJP-A, 15 (1934), 127–59. Strachey builds on and refers to earlier papers such
as Rado's to make his own point about hypnosis but substitutes the idea of the
analyst as 'auxiliary super-ego', administering reality in 'minimal doses'. In his 1937
summary of his original paper, Strachey writes that the analyst hopes 'that he will
be introjected by the patient as a super-ego—introjected, however, not at a single
gulp . . . but little by little and as a real person' (IJP-A 18 (1937), 144). For the lasting
reputation and reassessment of Strachey's first paper, see also Herbert Rosenfeld,
'A Critical Appreciation of James Strachey's Paper on the Nature of the Therapeutic
Action of Psychoanalysis', IJP-A 53 (1972), 455–611. Side by side with Strachey's 1934
paper is an interesting paper by Richard Sterba, 'The Fate of the Ego in Analytic
Therapy', IJP-A 15 (1934), 117–26, which remedies Strachey's omission of the question
of language.

ego and the external world.[18] The mobile and overlapping concepts of incorporation, introjection, and projection—concepts to
be found in Freud's writing, but developed both from and in the
writings of Sándor Ferenczi, Karl Abraham, and Melanie Klein
—are indispensable to Strachey's account of the way in which
psychoanalytic understanding redraws this movable boundary.[19]
It's not surprising that representations of readerly interiority
should draw on the same dialectic of introjection and projection
which was for Freud himself the genesis of the crucial distinction
between subject (or ego) and object (or outside world); while for
Kleinians the interchange provides the very basis for the distinction between inside and outside (for Winnicottians, one might
add, the in-between space itself—the potential space—becomes
the site of imaginative and cultural activity).[20] The room is the
imaginary 'projective' space that allows us to think there is room
for a book inside us.

[18] See Strachey, 'Nature of Therapeutic Action', 142, 149–52. Cf. the passage in
Civilization and its Discontents (cited n. 8 above) which continues: 'There are cases
in which parts of a person's own body, even portions of his own mental life—his
perceptions, thoughts, and feelings—, appear alien to him and as not belonging to
his ego; there are other cases in which he ascribes to the external world things that
clearly originate in his own ego and that ought to be acknowledged by it. Thus even
the feeling of our own ego is subject to disturbances and the boundaries of the ego
are not constant' (*SE* xxi. 66).

[19] See, for instance, Sándor Ferenczi, 'Introjection and Transference' (1909),
First Contributions to Psycho-Analysis (1952; repr. London, 1994), 35–93; Karl Abraham,
'A Short Study of the Development of the Libido' (1924), *Selected Papers of Karl
Abraham*, trans. Douglas Bryan and Alix Strachey (1927; repr. London, 1979), 418–
501; Melanie Klein, 'Notes on Some Schizoid Mechanisms' (1946), *Envy and Gratitude*,
WMK iii. 1–24. For a Kleinian account of the evolution of introjection, projection,
and projective identification, see R. D. Hinshelwood, *A Dictionary of Kleinian Thought*
(London, 1991); for a post-Lacanian account of these concepts, see also J. Laplanche
and J.-B. Pontalis, *The Language of Psycho-Analysis* (New York, 1973).

[20] For this distinction in Freud's writing, see 'Negation' (1923): 'Expressed in the
language of the oldest—the oral—instinctual impulses, the judgment is "I should
like to eat this", or "I should like to spit it out"; and, put more generally: "I should
like to take this into myself and to keep that out." That is to say: "it shall be inside
me" or "it shall be outside me" ' (*SE* xix. 237). See also Joseph Sandler and Meir
Perlow, 'Internalization and Externalization', in Joseph Sandler (ed.), *Projection,
Identification, Projective Identification* (London, 1989), 1–11. For Winnicott's account
of 'potential space', see 'The Location of Cultural Experience' (1967), *Playing and
Reality* (1971; repr. London, 1991), 95–103.

This chapter in the history of psychoanalytic thought is helpful
for understanding both Poulet's phenomenology of reading and
Holland's objection to it. If indeed books change us (and many
readers have thought so), we could conceptualize reading—much
as Freud and Strachey conceptualize the therapeutic effects of
psychoanalysis—as a matter of widening the ego's field of perception. 'It is a work of culture,' Freud declared roundly in 1932.[21]
Both Strachey and Woolf say much the same thing about literacy:
where illiteracy was, there civilization shall be.[22] Freud refers to
his student passion for owning and collecting books ('I had become
a *book-worm*').[23] But for all his habitual use of literature to further
his thinking, he has remarkably little to say about reading itself,
as opposed to the collector's passion or the distinction between
thing-presentation and word-presentation which he derived from
nineteenth-century philology.[24] An exception is a youthful letter
written to Eduard Silberstein in 1875, when Freud was only 17:

[21] See *New Introductory Lectures* (*SE* xxii. 80): 'the therapeutic efforts of
psycho-analysis have chosen . . . to strengthen the ego, to make it more independent
of the super-ego, to widen its field of perceptions and enlarge its organizations, so
that it can appropriate fresh portions of the id. Where id was, there ego shall be. It
is a work of culture—not unlike the draining of the Zuder Zee.' Freud is repeating
an earlier passage from the *Introductory Lectures*, cited by Strachey in 'Nature of
Therapeutic Action', 132.

[22] Cf. Strachey in 'Some Unconscious Factors in Reading': 'Among the characteristics that distinguish the more advanced forms of civilization from the more
primitive perhaps the most outstanding are the arts of writing and reading. . . . even
today it is usual to estimate the relative degree of civilization in different countries
from the percentage of illiterates among their inhabitants' (*IJP-A* 11 (1930), 322; cited
thereafter as Strachey); and Virginia Woolf in 'How Should One Read a Book?'
(1926), who writes that it would not be surprising to find reading 'the reason why we
have grown from pigs to men and women, and come out from our caves, and dropped
our bows and arrows, and sat round the fire and talked and drunk and made merry
and given to the poor and helped the sick and made pavement and houses and erected
some sort of shelter and society on the waste of the world' (*The Essays of Virginia
Woolf*, ed. Andrew McNeillie (4 vols., London, 1986), iv. 399; hereafter cited as *Essays*).

[23] See *The Interpretation of Dreams* (1900), *SE* iv. 172–3. Freud suggests that his childhood memory of pulling a book to pieces like an artichoke was a 'screen memory'
for 'later bibliophile propensities'.

[24] See Sigmund Freud, *On Aphasia: A Critical Study* (London, 1953), esp. 72–8; 'The
Unconscious (1915), *SE* xiv. 201–2 and Appendix C. See also John Forrester, *Language
and the Origins of Psychoanalysis* (London, 1980), for Freud's relation to the 19th-
century philologists.

I recently read a chapter of Don Quixote and experienced an idyllic moment. That was at six o'clock and I was sitting alone in my room before a nourishing plateful which I devoured voraciously while reading the magnificent scene in which the noble Doctor Pedro Rescio de Tirteafuera, which must mean something dreadful in Spanish, has the food taken away from under poor Sancho's nose.[25]

Tantalizing as it is, however, this 'idyllic moment' does not prove to be a prelude to any sustained account of Freud's voracious reading habits. Instead, I want to explore the testimony of other writers, while trying to understand it in ways made possible by Freud's breakfast. In particular, I will be asking what Strachey and Woolf have to say about the scene of reading—the room, the book, and the meal. I will start with Strachey's miniature psychoanalytic squib, 'Some Unconscious Factors in Reading' (published in 1930), and then move back in time to Woolf's posthumously published essay, 'Reading' (probably written in 1919). For Strachey, the book-as-object is obsessively recovered, hung on to, recycled, trashed. For Woolf, by contrast, reading is at once the delirious feast that one of her essays calls, hyperbolically, 'this orgy of reading', and potentially melancholic.[26] Read together, Strachey's and Woolf's essays suggest how a phantasized identification with books may be a way to preserve or destroy what we love by consuming it. In this sense, both essays—consciously or not—are 'readings' of Freud's account of object-loss in 'Mourning and Melancholia' (1917). They invite us to think about our own relation to lost objects when we read, and even about the way our consumption of literature figures in ostensibly cultural accounts of reading.

The Psychopathology of Everyday Reading

if we turn from communities as a whole to the individual members of them, we may find that writing and reading

---

[25] *The Letters of Sigmund Freud to Eduard Silberstein, 1871–81,* ed. Walter Boehlich, trans. Arnold J. Pomerans (Cambridge, Mass., 1990), 87; I am grateful to Maria Antonia Garcés for drawing my attention to this Quixotic meal.

[26] 'Hours in a Library' (1916), *Essays,* ii. 55.

perform functions of some appreciable importance in the
economics of the mind of modern man . . . (James Strachey)[27]

As an adolescent, I used often to annoy my parents by bringing
a book to meals. Sometimes I got away with it. But mostly they
objected that if I read while I ate, I might not know what I was
eating. I could swallow anything, they pointed out. In retrospect,
it seems odd that neither parent thought of making the opposite
argument—that if I ate while I read, I might not know what I
was reading; after all, I could have been swallowing anything
. . . It was only much later, when I came across Strachey's 'Some
Unconscious Factors in Reading', that it occurred to me to think
of reading as connected with eating in other, less palatable ways.
Derrida, you may recall, alludes to Strachey's paper in the closing paragraphs of 'Freud and the Scene of Writing' (the essay my
title riffs on). Derrida's exploration of the role of repetition,
trace, and deferral in Freud's structural model of the mind as a
pictographic script uses his 1925 'Note on the Mystic Writing-Pad'
to uncover the systematic devaluation of writing in a logocentric
philosophical tradition.[28] But my concern isn't with the metaphysics
of presence and absence, let alone with deconstructive reading
as such (except to note that as soon as Poulet's *cogito* enters the
argument, *différance* comes in to challenge his phenomenological
approach; while Holland's top-to-bottom model gets redefined
by the magic writing-pad—in Derrida's words—as 'a depth without a bottom').[29] Rather, I'm interested in the end of Derrida's
essay, which sketches several directions his inquiry might take, and
among them, what he calls 'a new psychoanalytic graphology'.[30]
Derrida suggests that Melanie Klein 'opens the way' for such a
theory of writing with her account of the cathexis of signs in 'The

---

   [27] Strachey, 322. Strachey's paper was read to the British Psycho-Analytic Society
in Mar. 1930.

   [28] See Jacques Derrida, 'Freud and the Scene of Writing', *Writing and Difference*,
trans. Alan Bass (Chicago, 1978), 196–231.

   [29] See *Writing and Difference*, 224: 'the *depth* of the Mystic Pad is simultaneously
a depth without bottom, an infinite allusion, and a perfectly superficial exteriority:
a stratification of surfaces each of whose relation to itself, each of whose interior,
is but the implication of another similarly exposed surface.'

   [30] Ibid. 230–1.

Role of the School in the Libidinal Development of the Child'
(1923). This is the context for his parenthetical allusion to Strachey's
'Some Unconscious Factors in Reading'.

Strachey's essay resurfaces in Derrida's closing lines at the
point when he asks rhetorically how Artaudian excrement can
be put in relation to Ezekiel's 'son of man who fill his entrails
with the scroll of the law which has become as sweet as honey in
his mouth?'[31] Although Derrida doesn't say so, Strachey cites this
quotation from Ezekiel in the last footnote of his own paper—
making it a bit of unacknowledged recycling on Derrida's part
(a case of the subtext parasitically invading the host text). Like
Holland after him, Strachey had noted that the discourse of
reading is shot through with metaphors of oral consumption. We
speak (excessively) of voracious readers, of devouring books, of
browsing in a library, and so on. But Strachey, surprisingly, turns
out to have as much to say about the specific, materially located
scene of reading as about its unconscious aspects. No sooner does
the subject of reading (the subject in, or of, a book) enter the
picture than the scene gets (literally) set. The idea of reading a
book quickly ushers in the idea of being in a room—and sometimes eating at the same time. This movement is Strachey's version
of the structure of equivalences found also in Poulet's scene of
reading, between what's inside the book and what's inside the
reader. The difference is Strachey's cultural framing of the scene
—and (I want to insist) his humour. It's hard, in fact, not to read
his paper as something of a psychoanalytic *jeu d'ésprit*, aimed at
an audience of over-earnest British colleagues. 'Some Unconscious
Factors in Reading' is a miniature psychopathology of everyday
reading, with its dead-pan catalogue of modern reading practices
(reading in bed, in the bathroom, and even in London's public
lavatories).[32] Strachey also reminds us insistently that these private

---

[31] Ibid. 231.

[32] Strachey cites Edward Glover's 'Notes on Oral Character Formation', *IJP-A* 6
(1924), 139: 'Sleep can . . . be successfully wooed after a certain amount of reading
. . . in certain cases a fixed dose is ingested regularly before sleep, a "nightcap",
the directly oral equivalent of which is familiar to all' (quoted in Strachey, 325). The
first public conveniences were introduced into London in the 1850s, a technology
thereafter successfully exported across Europe and to the Empire.

and public spaces have as their cultural boundary that ubiquitous representative of the modern public sphere, the gutter press. He even manages to include in his serio-comic account the clown's indispensable prop, a custard pie.

Melanie Klein's 1931 essay, 'A Contribution to the Theory of Intellectual Inhibition', cites Strachey approvingly as having shown that 'reading has the unconscious significance of taking knowledge out of the mother's body'.[33] Her own position is characteristically unnuanced; there's taking out, and then there's taking in. Klein adds that it's essential for a satisfactory reading experience that 'the mother's body should be felt to be well and unharmed'. The inside of the child's body, too, must be felt as safe and non-persecutory if intellectual investigation is to take place—and, more importantly, if the child is to become acquainted with its own intrapsychic processes. Good mothering and good feeding set the scene for satisfying experiences of thinking, feeling, and introspection (remember Sendak's Mickey in *In the Night Kitchen*: 'I'm in the milk and the milk's in me'). Klein's model for the child's understanding of the relation between inner and outer worlds involves this constant two-way movement of introjection and what she here calls 'extrajection'— or (to use the more familiar term) projection, with its suggestion of purposive casting out, or the depositing of our own ideas or feelings into someone else, whence they may return to persecute us. Klein pairs the ability to absorb knowledge with the ability 'to give it out again, i.e. return it, formulate it, and express it'; that is, to put it into words and make it available for thought.[34] For her, the degree of freedom from anxiety accompanying this two-way process ultimately determines the capacity to order one's mind and to inhabit it peacefully. At the opposite extreme from

---

[33] See Melanie Klein, *Love, Guilt and Reparation, WMK* i. 241. Klein's essay on intellectual inhibition starts from mealtimes and from a little boy's difficulty in distinguishing between *poulet, poisson,* or *glace* (chicken, fish, and ice [-cream]). Mixing up *poulet* with *poisson* suggests to Klein that the child is warding off dangerous food for thought. Throughout, I follow the Kleinian usage of using the term 'phantasy', as opposed to 'fantasy', to refer to unconscious phantasy.

[34] Ibid. 244.

intellectual inhibition—the refusal to take in mental nourishment at all, or mental anorexia—Klein places indiscriminate appetite ('A craving to take in everything that offers itself, together with an inability to distinguish between what is valuable and what is worthless').[35] Intellectual binging, she implies, comes from the feeling of emptiness. An over-stocked mind is amassing secret reserves against phantasized attacks or the fear of inner impoverishment. So much for indiscriminate readers.

In Klein's book, incorporation—the subjective phantasy of actual bodily intake—provides the ground for the metaphor of introjection. Strachey's essay, however, posits a more material (not to say materialist) relation between the cultural consumption of books and food. As one might expect given his intellectual milieu, Strachey seems more interested in reading than eating, and he regards learning to read as much more arduous than learning to talk (which presumably came naturally to members of the Strachey family).[36] But although Strachey opposes talk to reading, the distinction quickly breaks down. Talking is for him 'a process of expulsion, a method of extruding something inside oneself (one's thoughts) into the outer world'. Talk gets one's thoughts out. Reading, by contrast, 'is actually a method of taking someone else's thoughts inside oneself. It is a way of eating another person's words' (Strachey, 326). Both talk and reading turn out to partake of the primitive, cannibalistic processes of incorporation. At times, Strachey comes close to making his colleagues eat their own words; for instance, when he footnotes Ernest Jones on 'the phallic significance of coprophagy' (Strachey, 329 n.) in a parody of collegial acknowledgement.[37] But his remarks on obsessional reading habits are close to home. Who hasn't recently defaced a book—succumbing to the temptation to mark a difficult or significant page, line by line, and paragraph by paragraph? Who

[35] Ibid. 246.

[36] See Lee, *Virginia Woolf*, 256, for Woolf's account of mealtimes at the Strachey family table.

[37] Compare the fun Strachey has when he refers to the gustatory impossibility of 'suck[ing] down the works of Bertrand Russell or chew[ing] up those of Miss Ethel M. Dell', or tough writers and sloppy ones (326).

hasn't mutilated a paperback by turning down the corner of a page, or read and re-read a particularly obscure passage (by Derrida, for instance—or even Freud)? Missed meanings haunt us. And surely everyone who has learned to read once went through the arduous transition from forming words in one's mouth to silent reading— the crucial difference, according to Strachey, between fast and slow readers, or what he calls *sotto voce* readers, 'persons who, though not reading aloud, always say each word to themselves as they go along', remaining for ever hindered by 'abortive movements of the tongue and lips' (Strachey, 324). We could call these *sotto voce* readers poetry-readers (or readers of prose that demands a hearing, if only by an inner ear). After all, the 'hindrance' of an auditory imagination is an essential ingredient in poetic pleasure and even understanding. Every silent reader contains a *sotto voce* reader, undoing the distinction between talk (putting out) and reading (taking in).

For Strachey, reading is a fragile form of sublimation, always liable to the hindrance of instinctual trends. Passing over scopophilia and anal eroticism, he moves quickly to orality. 'There is', he writes, 'a peculiar appearance of intense and continuous absorption in a person immersed in a book' (Strachey, 325). The absorbed reader is as irritated at being disturbed as an infant enjoying a meal. Readers may suck their fingers, or their pipes. But it's not just a matter of pre-ambivalent sucking (when 'everything seems to go smoothly and easily'), since reading has a tendency to pass into the later, ambivalent stage of orality, biting: 'There are the other, more solid books—the ones that we have to get our teeth into and chew up before we can digest them' (Strachey, 326). The 'blissful absorption' of the novel reader is only one side of the story. Reading has its aggressive and destructive aspects, like talk. When sublimation is unstable, writes Strachey, 'Each word is then felt as an enemy that is being bitten up . . . an enemy that may in its turn become threatening and dangerous to the reader.' The enemy is always 'lurking somewhere . . . between the lines', ambushing the reader with unsuspected meanings, causing him 'to turn back, to read and re-read, to read each word aloud, to fix each word with a tick, and yet never to be reassured' (Strachey, 327). Close readers, take note. But, Strachey reminds us, the same reader may also be engaged in an act of loving, incorporatory consumption—'simultaneously loving the words, rolling them round in his mouth and eventually making them a part of himself.' The scroll of the law can taste as sweet as honey; biting and loving may both be ways to repossess that elusive object, meaning.

Suppose, for a moment, that oral incorporation really is the unconscious aim of reading—the way we imagine putting the world inside us, disposing of its dangers by making its meanings ours, cannibalistically consuming it, recycling it, savouring its borrowed sweetness as our own. What does this make the literary object—the books, words, and printed pages that Poulet imagines as so many caged animals awaiting release? Or, as Strachey asks, what do they symbolize? He offers two answers—both reductive, and neither apparently of much interest to him (Strachey, 327 and n.). For Freud, books and paper are female symbols (hence the phallic pen that writes on them in the familiar, reductive binarism of gendered accounts of writing). For Ernest Jones, books are the symbol of faeces, an ingenious metonymy whereby the page stands in for the print ('by association with paper and the idea of pressing [smearing, imprinting]').[38] Rather than pursuing this line of argument, Strachey segues to the defecatory habits of the British reading classes, with their morning newspapers and specialized bathroom book collections; not to mention one obsessional patient—as we learn from Strachey's letters, a character called Enery—who spends much of his time in public and private lavatories, where he writes, reads (deriving his knowledge of current affairs from small squares of newspaper), and even eats; his greatest satisfaction, he confessed to Strachey, 'was to eat something (the specific food was a custard tart) at the very moment of defaecating' (Strachey, 328).[39] Strachey, straightfaced, moves from this symbolic act of coprophagy to a generalized coprophagic

---

[38] Freud, *Introductory Lectures on Psychoanalysis*, and Ernest Jones, 'Anal-Erotic Character Traits', *Papers on Psycho-Analysis* (1918); see also Otto Fenischel 'The Scoptophilic Instinct and Identification' (1935), *Collected Papers of Otto Fenischel* (2 vols., New York, 1953–4), i. 373–4, developing Strachey's ideas about reading.

[39] We could call him the Peppermint Man; see Strachey, 328 n.

theory of reading: 'The author excretes his thoughts and embodies them in the printed book: the reader takes them, and, after chewing them over, incorporates them into himself' (Strachey, 329). Don't give me that shit. Strachey is showing us how smoothly the symbolic equivalences go down if we are only willing to swallow them. But what, one wonders, is the real enemy lurking between his lines?

If literacy is the mark of modern civilization, as Strachey argues, then 'the economics of the mind of modern man' is a coprophagic economy of production and consumption, waste and recycling. Strachey invokes 'the orgies of newspaper reading which have accompanied the spread of literacy to the lower classes of the community. Inconceivably vast masses of ink-stained papers are ejected every day into the streets; there they are seized and devoured with passionate avidity, and a few moments later destroyed . . .' (Strachey, 329). The lives and breakfasts of the reading classes are lined with the evacuations of the gutter press, parodied by the voracious reading habits of the lower classes: 'no one can find enough abuse for the rags of this gutter Press, but no one feels he has breakfasted unless one of them is lying beside his coffee and his toast' (Strachey, 329). Class analysis of modern print culture could do worse than begin here, with a nation's ceremonial reading of the daily newspapers—an imaginary community of taste, built on the consumption of newsprint. Strachey pauses briefly to cite Karl Abraham as his authority for considering coprophagy 'a process of compensation for the loss of a loved object' (Strachey, 329), then turns reading into the type of ambivalent Oedipal rivalry (including 'feminine wishes directed towards the father': i.e. the wish to bear his faeces/children). A lurid primal-horde scene of reading culminates in the spectacle of 'the reader, the son, hungry, voracious, destructive and defiling', forcing his way into his mother 'to find out what is inside her, to tear his father's traces out of her, to devour them, to make them his own, and to be fertilized by them himself' (Strachey, 331). In case we should think this excited prose Strachey's own—after all, it's the kind of thing that has given psychoanalysis a bad name—Strachey goes on to give us the ambiguous footnote recycled by

Derrida at the end of 'Freud and the Scene of Writing', in which he cites 'the schizophrenic prophet Ezekiel': 'And he said unto me, Son of man, cause thy belly to eat, and fill thy bowels with this roll that I give thee. Then did I eat it, and it was in my mouth as honey for sweetness. And he said unto me, Son of man, go, get thee unto the house of Israel, and speak with my words unto them' (Strachey, 331 n.).[40] Can one doubt that in this moment of scriptural self-authorization, Strachey (a schizophrenic psycho-analytic prophet) is letting loose the belly-laughter of his own ambivalence about psychoanalysis?

On some level, the subject of Strachey's short history of read-ing is the gullible psychoanalytic reader. Confronted by the writings of Freud, Abraham, and Jones, and perhaps by the assembled members of the British Psycho-Analytic Institute, Strachey un-leashes the desublimatory effects of laughter. Psychoanalytic words are consumed, recycled, trashed; lovingly quoted, and sent outrageously over the top. The element of send-up depends on a too concrete, too literal reading of the 'roll' (the scroll) of psy-choanalysis. Strachey reminds us that every attempt to engage with another discourse—including psychoanalytic discourse—carries with it the ambivalent wish to appropriate, to make it one's own, but also to trash or destroy it; or at least to give it a bit of a chewing over. But in the last resort, the interest of Strachey's paper lies less in what it has to say about the unconscious factors in reading, or about Strachey's own relation to psychoanalysis, than in locating the scene of reading in the historically specific private and public spaces of his time, the spaces of modernity where the modern citizen comes into being. These are both the spaces of the middle-class household (bedroom, bathroom, and breakfast-room) and the urban spaces of modern public-sphere literacy (the gutter press that no breakfast table can be without)—not to mention the public lavatories of a relatively recently sanitized city

---

[40] Ezekiel 2: 9–10. See Derrida, 'Freud and the Scene of Writing', which ends: '. . . or what is said in Ezekiel about the son of man who fills his entrails with the scroll of the law which has become sweet as honey in his mouth' (*Writing and Difference*, 231). See also Alberto Manguel, *A History of Reading* (New York, 1996), 170–1, for this and other eating metaphors so richly present in the phenomenology of reading.

scape, inhabited by the guilty, custard-pie-consuming *flâneur*. We haven't lacked recently for histories of reading, or of the rise of literacy and the growth of print culture (or class- and gender-specific accounts of reading).[41] But Strachey reminds us that the rise of privacy in bourgeois life, with its separation of bodily, social, and mental functions, may have more to do than we realize with the form taken by Poulet's idealized scene of reading.[42] His paper invites us to consider, not only the instinctual aspects of reading (and the biting function of humour), but the relation between privacy and the management of a self, conceived as a bodily entity occupying a discrete space in a particular, historical, class-bound environment—a domestic and social setting where we eat together but for the most part read (and perform our bodily functions) alone; or, for that matter, where we may meet with an analyst in a private room in order to obtain access to our caged interiority through the intervention of language.

As a coda to Strachey's account of the psychic economy of reading, I'd like to contrast a different image of mass readership in the age of mechanical reproduction—what Benedict Anderson, in *Imagined Communities*, calls 'this extraordinary mass ceremony: the almost precisely simultaneous consumption ("imagining") of the newspaper-as-fiction'. Anderson goes on to link newspaper reading with the construction of fictional communities and ultimately with national identities:

The significance of this mass ceremony—Hegel observed that newspapers serve modern man as a substitute for morning prayers—is paradoxical. It is performed in silent privacy, in the lair of the skull. Yet each communicant is well aware that the ceremony he performs is being replicated simultaneously by thousands (or millions) of others of whose existence he is confident, yet of whose identity he has not the slightest notion . . . What more vivid figure for the secular, historically-clocked,

---

[41] See, most recently, Manguel, *A History of Reading*, as well as Kate Flint, *The Woman Reader 1837–1914* (Oxford, 1993); Flint's book contains an invaluable bibliography.

[42] Mary Wollstonecraft in her Enlightenment *Vindication of the Rights of Woman* singles out for special condemnation the habit of communal or non-private evacuation, as if the regulation of bodies and their separation has everything to do with her subject, women's education.

imagined community can be envisioned? At the same time, the news-paper reader, observing exact replicas of his own paper being consumed by his subway, barbershop, or residential neighbours, is continually reas-sured that the imagined world is visibly rooted in everyday life. . . . fiction seeps quietly and continuously into reality, creating the remarkable confidence of community in anonymity which is the hallmark of modern nations.[43]

This seepage of fiction into everyday life is a reminder that the private lair of the skull (like the room in the book) opens on to the streets; print capitalism turns an individual, psychic economy of reading into a way of relating to others—anonymously, as befits the subject of modernity. But if the room is imaginary, so too is the community. Notice how Anderson's scene of reading makes one reader indistinguishable from the next. Reading enters the public sphere at the cost of making readers, as well as newspapers, a visible fiction—exact copies of one another, a collectivity of reading heads replicating the same activity. The very move to figure the social and material dimensions of cultural consumption proves to be the point at which fiction enters most unmistakably and insidiously to shape our relations to ourselves, to others, and to reading.

A Room of Their Own

At this very late hour of the world's history, books are to be found in almost every room of the house—in the nursery, in the drawing room, in the dining-room, in the kitchen. But in some houses they have become such a company that they have to be accommodated with a room of their own—a reading room, a library, a study. (Virginia Woolf, 'How Should One Read a Book?')[44]

---

[43] Benedict Anderson, *Imagined Communities: Reflections on the Origin and Spread of Nationalism* (London, 1983), 39–40; Susan Buck-Morss first drew my attention to this striking passage. The issue of nationalism offers a different perspective on the Britishness of both Strachey's paper and his audience.

[44] 'How Should One Read a Book', *Essays*, iv. 388–9.

In March 1925, Strachey wrote: 'I've also once more during the week-end read Abraham's ['A Short Study of the Development of the Libido'], which as usual is extraordinarily illuminating, especially now that I see rather more deeply into Enery's story. But why, oh why, is Enery not a melancholic?'[45] Karl Abraham's study of obsession and melancholia (translated by Alix Strachey in 1927) provides the theoretical model for Strachey's interest in the economics of reincorporation. Abraham builds on Freud's thesis in 'Mourning and Melancholia' (1917) that the melancholic, 'after having lost his love-object, regains it once more by a process of introjection'.[46] Abraham had associated coprophagy with this melancholic phantasy of taking back an expelled love-object into the body by means of oral introjection ('The unconscious', he writes, 'regards the loss of an object as an anal process, and its introjection as an oral one').[47] But, alas, Enery is not a melancholic. The obsessional hangs on to his book in his own fashion—indeed, as Freud puts it, consideration for the (literary) object makes its first appearance here.[48] The melancholic, by contrast, consumes his object, and it in turn consumes him. But in the manic interval, Abraham

---

[45] *Bloomsbury/Freud*, 229–30.

[46] Abraham, *Selected Papers of Karl Abraham*, 419. Abraham recounts how he came to accept 'the idea of an introjection of the loved object' through his own experience of mourning the death of his father—when his hair turned grey, like his father's (ibid. 437–8).

[47] See ibid. 443–4; cf. also ibid. 481: 'In his unconscious he identifies the love-object he has lost and abandoned with the most important product of bodily evacuation —with his faeces—and reincorporates it in his ego by means of the process we have called introjection.'

[48] See Freud's commentary on Abraham in *New Introductory Lectures*, which clarifies the importance of this emergence of the object: 'Abraham showed in 1924 that two stages can be distinguished in the sadistic-anal phase. The earlier of these is dominated by the destructive trends of destroying and losing, the later one by trends friendly towards objects—those of keeping and possessing. It is in the middle of this phase, therefore, that consideration for the object makes its first appearance as a precursor of a later erotic cathexis. We are equally justified in making a similar subdivision in the first, oral phase. In the first sub-stage what is in question is only oral incorporation, there is no ambivalence at all in the relation to the object —the mother's breast. The second stage, characterized by the emergence of the biting activity, may be described as the "oral-sadistic" one; it exhibits for the first time the phenomena of ambivalence, which become so much clearer afterwards, in the following sadistic-anal stage' (*SE* xxii. 99).

writes, 'his ego no longer being consumed by the introjected object', the melancholic 'turns his libido to the outer world with an excess of eagerness'.[49] One patient calls this excess a 'gobbling mania'— 'a kind of intoxication or orgy', 'a wild excess'. He wants to devour 'every thing that comes his way', including impressions; the manic patient's 'flight of ideas, expressed in a stream of words, represents a swift and agitated process of receiving and expelling fresh impressions'.[50] This, according to Freud, is 'the festival of [the ego's] liberation'.[51] It would be a stretch to associate Abraham's manic patient with the aesthetic of literary modernism. None the less, Woolf's attempt to render the speed and mobility of impressions in her writing—the 'stream' of consciousness—can feel greedy and intoxicating in just this way.[52] Her account of her relation to books and reading is particularly orgiastic.

[49] *Selected Papers of Karl Abraham*, 472.

[50] Ibid. 472. Abraham goes on: 'In melancholia we saw that there was some particularly introjected object which was treated as a piece of food that had been incorporated and which was eventually got rid of. In mania, *all* objects are regarded as material to be passed through the patient's "psychosexual metabolism" at a rapid rate. And it is not difficult to see from the associations of the manic patient that he identifies his uttered thoughts with excrement' (ibid. 472).

[51] See ibid. 474.

[52] Woolf recorded that, as she wrote the last words of *The Waves*, she experienced such 'intensity & intoxication that I seemed only to stumble after my own voice, or almost, after some sort of speaker (as when I was mad). I was almost afraid, remembering the voices that used to fly ahead'; see *The Diary of Virginia Woolf*, ed. Anne Olivier Bell and Andrew McNeillie (5 vols., New York, 1976–84), iv. 10. For the vexed question of Woolf's own relation to manic depressive illness, see, for instance, Roger Poole, *The Unknown Virginia Woolf* (3rd edn., Cambridge, 1990); Poole is especially graphic on the treatment of Woolf's periodic collapses with forced rest and over-feeding by the conventional specialists whom Leonard Woolf consulted, initially over the post-marriage manic-depressive breakdown of 1913–14; see ibid. 148–58 for Woolf's problems with eating and the regime used to counter it. Leonard Woolf records that 'there was always something strange, something slightly irrational in her attitude towards food. It was extraordinarily difficult ever to get her to eat enough to keep her strong and well. Superficially I suppose it might have been said that she had a (quite unnecessary) fear of becoming fat; but there was something deeper than that, at the back of her mind or in the pit of her stomach a taboo against eating. Pervading her insanity generally there was always a sense of guilt, the origin and exact nature of which I could never discover, but it was attached in some peculiar way particularly to food and eating. In the early acute, suicidal stage of the depression, she would sit for hours overwhelmed with hopeless melancholia . . .'; see *Beginning Again* (London, 1964), 162–3, and, for accounts of mealtimes during these periods, ibid. 163–4.

Hermione Lee's rich and informative chapter on Woolf as reader, in her recent biography, points out how often, when Woolf is ostensibly writing about fiction, she is actually—or also— writing about herself as reader and how intimate and visceral her relation to books tends to be.[53] 'Indeed', writes Woolf, 'it is pre- cisely because we hate and we love that our relation with the poets and novelists is so intimate that we find the presence of another person intolerable.'[54] Alongside her experimental fiction, the Woolf of the 1920s was meditating the never-to-be-written book on 'reading' that became *The Common Reader* (1925 and 1932). Three years before *A Room of One's Own* (1929), in 'How Should One Read a Book?' (1926), a lecture given to a girls' school, Woolf had written that books, like women writers (and women readers), need 'a room of their own' (*Essays*, iv. 399 n. 1).[55] Woolf's imag- inary reader—by taste and breeding a bibliocrat—inhabits a country house; the pageant of history passes before her eyes. She demands solitude and freedom, and wanders off at will into a pastoral or urban landscape.[56] She can be greedy, gossipy, and frankly hedonistic—and critical of other fictional rooms, espe- cially those of psychoanalysis. Woolf's 1920 review of 'Freudian Fiction', for instance, complains about the scanty furnishings: 'The door swings open briskly enough, but the apartment to which

[53] See Lee, 'Reading', *Virginia Woolf*, 402–17.

[54] Woolf inserted this passage when she revised 'How Should One Read a Book?' for *The Common Reader* (1932): 'we may try to sink our own identity as we read. But . . . there is always a demon in us who whispers, "I hate, I love", and we cannot silence him. Indeed it is precisely because we hate and we love that our rela- tion with the poets and novelists is so intimate . . .'; see Rachel Bowlby (ed.), *Virginia Woolf: The Crowded Dance of Modern Life* (Harmondsworth, 1993), 67.

[55] Woolf initially found this subject 'a matter of dazzling importance and breath- less excitement', but subsequently became weighed down by the lecture ('I grind out a little of that eternal How to read, lecture'). Woolf's substantial revisions for the version republished in *The Common Reader* (1932) suggest her dissatisfaction with it as it stood when published in the *Yale Review* for Oct. 1926.

[56] See Lee, *Virginia Woolf*, 413, for an account of Woolf's street-haunting. Rachel Bowlby (who also writes of Virginia Woolf as *flâneuse*) notices how often Woolf uses gustatory metaphors for reading; see *The Crowded Dance of Modern Life*, p. xviii: 'They sometimes . . . imply an excess, a crude abundance that will need to be sorted out; and sometimes the stress is rather on eating as a basic need, an impulse or appetite that must be satisfied.'

we are admitted is a bare little room with no outlook whatever'
(*Essays*, iii. 197). Her own reading room, by contrast, has plenty of
books and a view of the garden: 'Let us imagine that we are now
in such a room: that it is a sunny room, with windows opening
onto a garden, so that we can hear the trees rustling, the gardener talking, the donkey braying, the old women gossiping at
the pump—and all the ordinary processes of life pursuing the[ir]
casual irregular way . . .' (*Essays*, iv. 388–9). But Woolf's relation
to the consumption of books is darker and more perplexing than
the casual irregularity of this bucolic scene allows. The reader who
lives in a book runs the risk of 'over-reading' in the face of too
much excitement, too much life; the book itself can turn into a
melancholic object.[57] This is especially clear in her earlier essay,
'Reading', whose gracefully constructed, country-house scene
of reading contains an inset scenario of intoxication, excitement,
and melancholic collapse. 'Reading' seems to point to an implied
understanding on Woolf's part of differing imaginative activities
—incorporatory, projective, introjective—involved in reading, but
also to an intensity of libidinal investment that Woolf links to
eating, to change, and ultimately to creativity.[58] I want to suggest
that this is, in part, a melancholic economy involving the consumption and destruction of a precious lost object, and that the

[57] 'Often the pages fly before us and we seem, so keen is our interest, to be living and not even holding the volume in our hands. But the more exciting the book,
the more danger we run of over-reading. The symptoms are familiar. Suddenly the
book becomes dull as ditchwater and heavy as lead' ('How Should One Read a Book?',
Essays, iv. 393).

[58] For an extensive but professedly 'anti-Freudian' study of Woolf and her
writing in relation to manic-depressive illness, see Thomas C. Caramango, *The
Flight of the Mind: Virginia Woolf's Art and Manic-Depressive Illness* (Berkeley, 1992);
Caramango, like Poole, argues against an old-fashioned view of Woolf's 'insanity',
but on the basis on a modern, neuroscientific understanding of manic-depressive
illness as bipolar affective disorder, throwing in his lot with Crews's revisionist
stance *vis-à-vis* Freud (equated with a psychoanalytic understanding of manic-
depressive illness), on the grounds that such psychoanalytic approaches pathologize
Woolf. Caramango basically endorses the rest-cure regimen administered by
Leonard Woolf under Savage's supervision, although his reading of Woolf's novels
is often illuminated by ideas drawn from post-Freudian object-relations and by his
thesis that her fiction allowed Woolf to find viable ways of surviving as a manic
depressive.

movement towards repair tends to be registered by Woolf as a saving or recuperative turn to poetry (or, perhaps one should say, to what poetry signifies in her writing).

Hermione Lee observes that it is hard to decide whether 'Reading' is 'an essay on reading—or dreaming—or an autobiographical reminiscence'.[59] What has reading, for instance, got to do with the capture and death of a splendid, drunken moth? The centre-piece of Woolf's essay is a memory based on the activities of the Stephen children's Entomological Society, a compressed version of which resurfaces in *Jacob's Room* (1922) as part of Jacob's childhood.[60] This narrative of a moth-hunting expedition occupies the night-time, or dream-space, of an essay unobtrusively structured by the passage from one day to the next, like *The Waves* (1931)—which, we know, Woolf originally thought of as *The Moths*.[61] 'Reading' opens with another country-house library, 'lined with little burnished books, folios, and stout blocks of divinity'; the carved shelves bear their procession of titles from Homer and Euripides to 'Wordsworth and the rest'. Outside, the gardener mows the lawn: 'One drew the pale armchair to the window, and so the light fell over the shoulder upon the page. The shadow of the gardener mowing the lawn sometimes crossed it . . .' (*Essays*, iii. 141). The hypnotic movement of the reader's eye (falling like light on the page, or crossed by a shadow that goes 'up and down' like lines of print) renders this outside scene as dream-like distance. The tall ladies and gentlemen play at tennis, butterflies and bees visit the flowers, birds hop, 'But they did not distract me from my book':

None of these things distracted me in those days; and somehow or another, the windows being open, and the book held so that it rested upon a background of escallonia hedges and distant blue, instead of being a book it seemed as if what I read was laid upon the landscape not printed, bound, or sewn up, but somehow the product of trees and fields and

---

[59] *Virginia Woolf*, 404.

[60] See ibid. 31–2 for the entomological activities of the Stephen family, and see also Virginia Woolf, *Jacob's Room*, ed. Kate Flint (Oxford, 1992), 26–7.

[61] See *The Waves: The Two Original Holograph Drafts*, ed. J. W. Graham (London, 1976), app. A, and see also Lee, *Virginia Woolf*, 417.

the hot summer sky, like the air which swam, on fine mornings, round the outlines of things. (*Essays*, iii. 142)

'These things' don't distract the reader from her book. 'Somehow', Woolf conveys, they render it transparent instead, 'laid upon the landscape not printed'; the book becomes the product of the land-scape, like the swimming air of summer. Somehow—but how? The book's transparency guarantees the solidity of the scene, yet its outlines too have a tendency to dissolve into the swimming air of summer. This mutual dissolving and resolidifying of book and landscape, like the movement into the past and back to the imaginary time present of reading, structures Woolf's essay so insistently that it becomes an inescapable aspect of its meaning as well as its principal technique of evocation.

I want to notice the persistent effect of transparency that attends Woolf's scene of reading, an effect which renders 'outside' the window fleetingly solid by virtue of the book's material irrelevance to what is seen by the reading eye. The 'past effect' in Woolf consists similarly of 'seeing things' (Queen Elizabeth I, for instance—'She flaunts across the terrace superbly and a little stiffly like the peacock spreading its tail', *Essays*, iii. 145). We note how easily Woolf's attention wanders from 'the broad yellow-tinged pages of Hakluyt's book' to 'the green shade of forests' (*Essays*, iii. 148). These green shades and greener thoughts, like the inaudible poetry of Elizabethan prose falling on some inner ear, lull us to sleep. Is this hypnosis? Are we hallucinating the past? After all, we hold no yellow-paged book; even *sotto voce* readers presumably hear nothing. Yet Woolf persuades us other-wise ('Let us imagine . . .'). In an essay called 'On Vivacity: The Difference between Daydreaming and Imagining-Under-Authorial-Instruction', Elaine Scarry similarly contrasts the sensory con-tent of 'the particular room one, at this moment, inhabits while reading', with the absence of actual sensory content represented by the book as object. A book's physical features (its print—'monotonous small black marks on a white page'; its texture and weight) are irrelevant to the mental images it tries to produce in us: '(steam rising across a window pane, the sound of a stone dropped in a pool, the feel of dry August grass underfoot).'[62] With this casual parenthesis, Scarry dissolves the book much as Woolf conjures with light and shadow, or puts us to sleep with unheard sentences. 'There is', Scarry observes, 'only *mimetic content*, the figural rooms and faces and weather that we mimetically see, touch, and hear, though in no case do we actually do so.'[63] Scarry asks how the writer persuades us that we are imagining rather than daydreaming. Her inquiry into the relation between 'vivacity' and the illusion of solidarity fascinatingly draws attention to the part played by what she calls 'the glide of the transparent over the surface of something', or the passing of a luminous film over solid walls at moments of fictional fragility (compare Woolf's swimming air round the outlines of things). Scarry's point is not so much that the fragility of the fiction gives rise to transparency. Rather, the transparency is what makes us 'see things' *as if* they were real.[64] As Scarry observes, only the 'fictional walls' of reading (the walls of the reading room) prevent us from '*sinking inward*' (her italics) and enable us to perform what she calls 'the projective act'—the projection of planes and solids, the perception of light or solidity at a distance from our eyes or touch; but also (in the other sense of projection) allowing us to 'lift the inhibitions on mental vivacity' which usually protect us, so that what we see is no longer what we (actually) see.[65]

[62] 'On Vivacity: The Difference Between Daydreaming and Imagining-Under-Authorial-Instruction', *Representations*, 52 (1995), 2. Scarry's essay bears on the old argument about whether, when we read, we occupy a world of words or images (Freud's 'word presentations' or the 'thing presentations' that he believed to be older than words); in this connection, see especially Ellen J. Esrock, *The Reader's Eye* (Baltimore, 1994), for a fascinating corrective to the idea that, when we read, we live in a world of words rather than images.

[63] 'On Vivacity', 3.   [64] Ibid. 12, 14.

[65] Ibid. 6; Scarry quotes Locke on perception (to Locke the idea of solidity 'hinders our further sinking downwards'). The thought-experiment Scarry conducts with her own readers involves, both predictably and appropriately, a scene of reading: 'If one looks at the surface on which this book is held—perhaps your hands, or a lamp-lit table, one will find that now . . . seven seconds later . . . the thing still sustains itself. If one instead imagines a lamp-lit table in some distant room, it is probably now . . . seven seconds later . . . already becoming lost to you . . .' (ibid. 19). Seven seconds is apparently the length of time the impression of an object seen remains on the retinal nerves. But here, which lamp-lit scene occupies

This 'risky projective space' of narrative that Scarry calls the 'mimesis of givenness' would be hallucinatory if we didn't happen to be reading a book.[66] What happens next in Woolf's 'Reading'? By now the author has read enough. She shuts her book—'So that, if at last I shut the book, it was only that my mind was sated'—and we recognize immediately that we are moving into the mimetic realm of the sensory writer. When 'the yellow page was almost too dim to decipher' and 'the book must be stood in its place' (*Essays*, iii. 149), then (writes Woolf) 'the moths came out, the swift grey moths of the dusk . . . It was, I supposed, nearly time to go into the woods' (*Essays*, iii. 149–50). The glide of the swift grey moths across the woods leaves imaginary solidity in its wake (just as the lantern leaves a wake of darkness, 'a fine black snow piling itself up in banks on either side of the yellow beam', *Essays*, iii. 150); even the hand sliding across the backs of books feels them swell with 'fullness and ripeness' (*Essays*, iii. 149). At this moment of unquestioned solidity and sensory life, the reader quits the room and the pace suddenly changes. Woolf slips into a remembered narrative of visceral excitement, primitive triumph, and its disquieting after-effects, rehearsed with all the checks and delays and shocks of animism, like a Wordsworthian 'spot of time'. This is the dream-time of her essay.[67] Roped

the more 'projective' space? Which book weighs heavier in our hands? Scarry illustrates the effect that Woolf sustains throughout 'Reading', that of using 'one in-itself-weightless image to calibrate and confirm the weightedness of a second in-itself-weightless image' (ibid. 16), while also introducing the 'visual' effects of a light-source.

[66] Ibid. 17.

[67] Woolf's original description of 'the Sugar campaign' is recorded in Aug. 1899 in Huntingdonshire, in *A Passionate Apprentice: The Early Journals of Virginia Woolf*, ed. Mitchell A. Leaska (London, 1990), 144–5: 'By the faint glow we could see the huge moth—his wings open, as though in ecstasy, so that the splendid crimson of the underwing could be seen—his eyes burning red, his proboscis plunged into a flowing stream of treacle. We gazed one moment on his splendor, & then uncorked the bottle. I think the whole procession felt some unprofessional regret when, with a last gleam of scarlet eye & scarlet wing, the grand old moth vanished'. Woolf's account reveals that she was 'the lantern-bearer' (Thoby Stephen was 'the leader') 'who lights the paths fitfully with a Bicycle lamp of brilliant but uncertain powers of illumination' (ibid. 144).

together by their beam of light, the children venture into the woods ('The little irregular beam of light seemed the only thing that kept us together, and like a rope prevented us from falling asunder and being engulfed', *Essays*, iii. 150). Woolf, bearing her light, guides us 'further and further into this unknown world' of heightened awareness, and 'As if we saw . . . through the lens of a very powerful magnifying glass', we too see the swarming of insect-life attracted by the lantern. Only when Woolf turns her lens (the light of authorial imagination) cautiously on to a bacchanalian orgy of drunken moths do we realize that we are in the presence of something resembling our own readerly absorption. Transfixed in the lantern beam, gorging on a moth-trap that consists of pieces of flannel soaked in rum and sugar, the moths are no longer 'whirring wings', but 'soft brown lumps' stuck in 'cataracts of falling treacle':

These lumps seemed unspeakably precious, too deeply attached to the liquid to be disturbed. Their proboscis were deeply plunged, and as they drew in the sweetness, their wings quivered slightly as if in ecstasy. Even when the light was full upon them they could not tear themselves away, but sat there, quivering a little more uneasily perhaps, but allowing us to examine the tracery on the wings, those stains, spots, and veinings by which we decided their fate. (*Essays*, iii. 151)

Strachey refers to the 'peculiar appearance of intense and continuous absorption' of readers immersed in their books (might he have seen a coprophagic subtext in these 'unspeakably precious' lumps, mired in their treacle?). The moths' ecstatic feeding—all plunged proboscis and quivering wings—is greedily consonant with our own readerly phantasy of oral ingestion, just as the scrambling insects ('greedy and yet awkward in their desire to partake of the light') pick up our fascination with the authorial eye.

In the syntax of Woolf's phantastic scene of reading, the young entomologists share both the mounting excitement of the hunters and the ecstatic absorption of their prey. We too are changed as we read, from moment to quivering moment, by the intensity of our own libidinal investment, our sense perceptions and palpating thoughts.[68] Woolf's central exhibit in 'Reading'—the prize specimen destined for the poison jar—is a single immobilized moth, a scarlet underwing:

Cautiously shielding the light, we saw from far off the glow of two red lamps which faded as the light turned upon them; and there emerged the splendid body which wore those two red lamps at its head. Great underwings of glowing crimson were displayed. He was almost still, as if he had alighted with his wing open and had fallen into a trance of pleasure. He seemed to stretch across the tree, and beside him other moths looked only like little lumps and knobs on the bark. He was so splendid to look upon and so immobile that perhaps we were reluctant to end him; and yet, when, as if guessing our intention and resuming a flight that had been temporarily interrupted, he roamed away, it seemed as if we had lost a possession of infinite value. (*Essays*, iii. 151)

The first thing we see is 'the glow of two red lamps', fading in the light. With its splendid, immobile body, its glowing under-wings, and its lamp-like eyes, the scarlet moth is at once the quarry of the lantern-bearing reader and her other. What meets her eyes in this moment of aesthetic rapport is the equivalent of the elusive, iridescent moment of being that Woolf attempted to capture in her writing.[69] Her reluctance to 'end' here is ours; we

---

[68] For the quivering wings, cf. 'Negation' (1923), where Freud writes of 'the post-ponement due to thought' as 'a motor palpating, with small expenditure of discharge. Let us consider where the ego has used a similar kind of palpating before, at what place it learned the technique which it now applies in its processes of thought. It happened at the sensory end of the mental apparatus, in connection with sense perception' (*SE* xix. 238). See also Freud's earlier account of thinking in 'Formulations on the Two Principles of Mental Functioning' (1911), *SE* xii. 221.

[69] In 'The Aesthetic Moment and the Search for Transformation', Christopher Bollas writes that 'The aesthetic experience occurs as a *moment*.' He describes such a 'moment' as a kind of trap, or 'A spell that holds self and other in symmetry and solitude, time crystallizes into space, providing a rendez-vous of self and other (text, composition, painting) that actualizes deep rapport between subject and object, and provides the person with a generative illusion of fitting with an object . . . Such moments . . . are registered through an experience of being, rather than mind'; Bollas links this experience of rapport between subject and object with the infant's experience of the maternal environment, but the aesthetic moment as he describes it is strikingly consonant, not only with Winnicott, but with the aesthetic of Woolf's modernism. See Peter Rudnytsky (ed.), *Transitional Objects and Potential Spaces* (New York, 1993), 40–1.

too want to prolong the graceful symmetries of identificatory reading, lost in our own trance of pleasure. A brief flight of the mind brings us to a second rendezvous, in the densest part of the breathing, sighing, alien, and inhuman forest ('No moth could have come as far as this'):

The scarlet underwing was already there, immobile as before, drinking deep. Without waiting a second this time the poison pot was uncovered and adroitly maneuvered so that as he sat there the moth was covered and escape cut off. There was a flash of scarlet within the glass. Then he composed himself with folded wings. He did not move again.
    The glory of the moment was great. (*Essays*, iii. 152)

But this glorious moment is marked, ominously, by 'a volley of shot'. An entire forest's death-rattle seems to salute the death of the moth: 'a hollow rattle of sound in the deep silence of the wood which had I know not what of mournful and ominous about it . . . An enormous silence succeeded. "A tree," we said at last. A tree had fallen' (*Essays*, iii. 152). What has happened?

    This mournful and ominous response to the moth's capture (displaced from hunters to forest) suggests that Woolf is registering some other, more disquieting triumph. What is 'the hostile alien force' against which the moth-hunters prove their skill? At the end of 'The Death of the Moth' (1942)—the posthumously published essay in which the writer, pencil in hand, watches an exhausted moth in its death throes—Woolf says: 'Death had triumphed.' In the closing lines of this later wartime essay, she uses the same word, 'composed', to describe the dead moth that she had used here of the scarlet underwing's graceful acquiescence in its death; her essay too has been 'composed' and must now come to its appointed end.[70] In 'Reading', after the moth's capture, Woolf asks, 'What is it that happens . . . ?'; and repeats,

---

[70] See Bowlby (ed.), *The Crowded Dance of Modern Life*, 181: 'The struggle was over. The insignificant little creature now knew death. As I looked at the dead moth, this minute triumph of so great a force over so mean an antagonist filled me with wonder. Just as life had been strange five minutes before, so death was now as strange. The moth having righted himself now lay most decently and uncomplainingly composed. O yes, he seemed to say, death is stronger than I am.'

'Something definitely happens' (*Essays*, iii. 152, 153). She marks the passage of time by registering 'the little shock' between the hour of midnight and dawn that is the shock of waking ('repeated shocks, the queer uneasy moment, as of eyes half open to the light'). Elsewhere, in 'How Should One Read a Book?', Woolf makes poetry a necessity for surviving aesthetic trauma and emotional turbulence—what she calls 'the intermittent but powerful shocks dealt us by beauty' and 'the incalculable impulses of our minds and body' (*Essays*, iv. 395). Here, in 'Reading', she wonders if 'repeated shocks' of experience, 'each unfelt at the time', have the effect of 'loosening the fabric' and 'breaking something away'. Is it the shock of 'collapse and disintegration', or is this a different process? A thought process, or a moment of emotional creativity? 'It is not destructive whatever it may be, one might say it was rather of a creative character' (*Essays*, iii. 152–3). Despite Woolf's swift conversion of collapse into creativity, the internal process ('whatever it may be') has certainly involved a destructive element. But Woolf moves quickly to bind 'Sorrow' at 'this sudden arrest of the fluidity of life' to a sense of aesthetic mastery: 'As with a rod of light, order has been imposed upon tumult; form upon chaos . . . one wakes, after heaven knows what internal process, with a sense of mastery' (note how the lamp has become an omniscient and omnipotent 'rod of light'). Repair comes, defensively as it were, in the wake of disintegration. Woolf turns adroitly to 'another sort of reading', poetry, resuming her unruffled literary progress through the poets of the past. No tremor of discomposure is allowed to shake her essay again, until the last lines when, instead of a tree falling, she turns the rose in its jar ('which, by the way, has dropped its petals', *Essays*, iii. 159), with an imagist turn all her own.

I have chosen to read Woolf's essay on 'Reading' as giving conscious literary form to unconscious phantasies that delineate the boundaries between psychic reality and reading, between instincts (both creative and destructive) and thoughts. It shouldn't need saying (nor, I think, does Woolf intend anything so pedestrian as an allegory of reading) that the most ancient symbol for the

psyche is a moth; the flight of the moth interests her more than
the moth itself. I want to end with Wallace Stevens's supreme
fiction of the scene of reading, 'The House was Quiet and the
World was Calm', as a way of drawing together the different strands
in both Strachey's and Woolf's essays, as well as saying something
about literary modernism's self-reflexive turn:

> The house was quiet and the world was calm.
> The reader became the book; and summer night
>
> Was like the conscious being of the book.
> The house was quiet and the world was calm.
>
> The words were spoken as if there was no book,
> Except that the reader leaned above the page,
>
> Wanted to lean, wanted much most to be
> The scholar to whom his book is true, to whom
>
> The summer night is like a perfection of thought.
> The house was quiet because it had to be.
>
> The quiet was part of the meaning, part of the mind:
> The access of perfection to the page.
>
> And the world was calm. The truth in a calm world,
> In which there is no other meaning, itself
>
> Is calm, itself is summer and night, itself
> Is the reader leaning late and reading there.

'The truth', for Stevens, is the absorbed reader, 'leaning late and
reading there.' Such truth depends on a fictional construction:
'summer night | Was like the conscious being of the book', 'like
a perfection of thought'; 'The words were spoken *as if* there was
no book'. By now, we should not be surprised at a form of consciousness rendered as a series of equivalences (as reader is to
poem, so reader in the poem is to book . . .); or at the fleeting
solidity of house and world in the wake of the adjectival glide of
'quiet' and 'calm'; or even at the *sotto voce* reading which makes us
hear the written word as if spoken aloud. The poem's hypnotic
repetitions-with-slight difference ('the world was calm', 'the world
was calm', 'And the world was calm', 'in a calm world', 'itself is
calm') insist that the poem, like the house, 'was quiet because it

had to be.' Quietness is at once the condition of its being and the way in which we internalize its meaning—'part of the meaning, part of the mind'. The unfolding, repeated sequence of nouns and adjectives at the end of each pair of lines—'calm', 'night', 'book', 'page', 'thought', 'mind', 'world'—work unobtrusively, like a half-heard, subliminal syntax, to reinforce this movement of internalization. The stealthy transfer of calm from world to book to thought is what persuades us of the poem's 'truth'.[71]

But the poem's meaning is ultimately its refusal of all refer-entiality other than the one it posits so insistently: 'there is no other meaning'. If 'the truth' of a calm world is 'itself' (three times repeated in the last three lines), it can only be found in the poem —in 'The access of perfection to the page.' The word 'access' implies the coming in from outside of something, as if the page (and the reader) have to be breached by what is other than itself, some differentiating desire. The book is open, like the mind, but it is entered by means of a powerful wish—the wish of the reader who emphatically 'Wanted to lean, wanted much most to be | The scholar to whom his book is true'. Does wishing alone make it so? Apparently. And what about the tell-tale mark of the negative—'as if there was no book', 'a calm world | In which there is no other meaning'? In his condensed but suggestive paper on 'Negation' (1923), Freud remarks that 'the content of a repressed image or idea can make its way into consciousness provided it is

---

[71] For one of the comparatively few critical discussions of Stevens's poem, see Charles Altieri, 'Why Stevens Must Be Abstract, or What a Poet Can Learn from Painting', in Albert Gelpi (ed.), *Wallace Stevens: The Poetics of Modernism* (Cambridge, 1985), 114–16. Altieri points to 'the brilliant syntactic shifts of the closing lines' where 'repetitions of single words (as opposed to the poem's earlier refrain effects) produce a sharp break with the dominant pattern of end-stopped lines. Syntax is suspended, only to speed up in very brief clauses. Then, as time turns back against itself, as reading self-consciously repeats its world and decides that it is good, it finds its culminating expression in a series of present participles transforming all that calm into a pure state for which the reading stands as its perfection. Confronting such a present, the sympathetic reader becomes absorbed in a corresponding activity. "There" and "here," the scene and the projected reader, become dialectical functions of one another, all as exponents of this single figure who proleptically represents one hundred eyes seeing at once, and finding that we must lean further into this enchanting site.'

negated' (*SE* xix. 235).[72] The 'truth' of Stevens's poem requires an immense effort of exclusion—*no* book, *no* unquiet house, *no* turbulent world; not even the language of what Freud (also in 'Negation') calls 'the oldest—the oral—instinctual impulse', expressed in the judgement ' "It shall be inside me" or "it shall be outside me" ' (*SE* xix. 237). Freud goes on to argue that, 'with the help of the symbol of negation, thinking frees itself' (*SE* xix. 236). How might thinking 'free itself' from material and even temporal contingencies in Stevens's poem? 'Negation' contains some of Freud's own subtlest and most speculative thinking about thought. He writes, for instance, that the function of judgement comes to apply to questions 'of *external* and *internal*'—'What is unreal, merely a presentation and subjective, is only internal; what is real is also there *outside*.' Freud continues:

The antithesis between subjective and objective does not exist from the first. It only comes into being from the fact that thinking possesses the capacity to bring before the mind once more something that has once been perceived, but reproducing it as a presentation without the external object having still to be there. (*SE* xix. 237)

The aim of reality-testing is not to '*find* an object in real perception which corresponds to the one presented', but rather—in its absence—'to *refind* such an object, to convince oneself that it is still there' (*SE* xix. 237).[73] Freud suggests that a precondition for reality-testing 'is that objects shall have been lost which once brought real satisfaction' (*SE* xix. 238); the strange shift of tense projects into the future the gains accrued from losses in the past. In effect, thinking is redefined as the representation to oneself of an absent object. 'The truth', for Stevens, is the reader 'reading there'; that is, elsewhere—not here, not now; perhaps not even yet. His poem, which appears to insist so calmly, so beautifully, and so metaphorically on the absolute adequacy to itself of the aesthetic experience of reading, can also be read as a meditation

---

[72] 'Negation' was translated by Joan Riviere in 1925.

[73] Freud's earlier remark that 'The finding of an object is in fact a refinding of it' provides a gloss on the nature of this lost object (ultimately, the mother's breast); see *SE* xix. 238 n.

on the impossibility of 'thereness', at least when it comes to symbolization. What Stevens has digested and cohabits with in the quiet house of his mind (the room in the book) is the inevitability of absence—that the object shall have been lost which once brought real satisfaction. This is why the world of the poem (a world in which privacy and privation are inseparable from reading) can be calm: it has become available to be thought.

TWO

A Whole World in Your Head
Rereading the Landscape of Absence

M Y title comes from a passage in which the novelist A. S. Byatt reflects on reading in her co-authored book, *Imagining Characters* (1995). Byatt is responding obliquely to a comment by the psychoanalyst Ignes Sodre about the relation between landscape and memory in Jane Austen's *Mansfield Park*:

And about reflection, I think the other thing that happens in all novels is that because you read a novel by yourself in a room, inner space in your own mind and outer space in novels become somehow equivalent, images of each other . . . There's a way in which the whole landscape is *inside* in a novel, even if it's said to be outside, which I find peculiarly exciting. I think to myself about the world in the head. And Mansfield at some level that I can't even quite explain is a very powerful image of that experience of having a whole world in your head . . .[1]

Byatt's reflection would be thought provoking even if she were not herself a novelist—here, a novelist reflecting on reading. For one thing, 'reflection' itself seems to mean both thinking *about* a novel (as an equivalent image of the mind) and the thinking that goes on *in* a novel, the sense that it has a mind and space of its own. But time comes into it too. Byatt draws a parallel between her younger reading self and the heroine of *Mansfield Park*, Fanny Price ('very much a reading person, she reads by herself in her

[1] A. S. Byatt and Ignes Sodre, *Imagining Characters: Six Conversations about Women Writers*, ed. Rebecca Smith (London, 1995), 37.

room'). She also alludes to Austen as a middle-aged woman, 'sitting on the sofa and observing the life and making sense of it.'[2] Byatt's reflection touches on the double temporality of the novel's writing and its reading—the division of consciousness, not only between reader and book, but between present and past, between living the life and observing it, that is constitutive of 'reflection' itself. Freud calls it the ability of one part of the mind to stand over against the other. Complex fictional worlds and psychoanalysis both rely on this benign, non-pathological form of splitting for their construction of meaning.[3] This division is also a function of memory, where the split has a temporal dimension, and (I'd argue) of reading. Reading, as Byatt implies, involves the double time of rereading and remembering.

Bearing in mind the relation between thinking *about* and thinking *in* fictional worlds, between reading and remembering, I want to explore an aspect of literary experience that is distinct both from imagining characters and from internalizing a fictional world such as Austen's. This mode of thought is partly induced in us by the way literature 'reflects' (and reflects on) itself— by the way it constructs what we sometimes refer to as its internal landscape. A bit arbitrarily, I want to locate such moments of reflection in specific uses of literary landscape—landscapes that seem to refer self-reflexively to the scene of reading. For Byatt, 'the world in the head' is associated with pleasurable readerly absorption. Landscape provides a metaphor for what goes on between the reader and the book, rather as landscape painting evokes not just the space of viewing, but also what goes on between

---

[2] Ibid. 37.
[3] See Richard Sterba, 'The Fate of the Ego in Analytic Therapy', *IJP-A* 15 (1934), 117–26. The ego, according to Freud's *New Introductory Lectures on Psycho-Analysis*, 'can treat itself like any other object, observe itself, criticize itself, do Heaven knows what besides with itself' (see ibid. 120 n.). Sterba ends his essay by quoting Herder on the origins of speech ('This first characteristic due to conscious reflection was a word of the mind'); he concludes: 'In the therapeutic dissociation which is the fate of the ego in analysis, the analysand is called on "to answer for himself" [in German: "put to speech"] and the unconscious, ceasing to be expressed in behavior, becomes articulate in *words*. We may say then, that in this ego-dissociation we have an extension of reflection beyond what has hitherto been accessible' (ibid. 126).

the viewer and the view.[4] We tend to think we know what
landscape means, just as we often take reading for granted. But
landscape in novels is a topos like any other—constructed in
terms of aesthetic categories such as the sublime, the beautiful,
or the picturesque, or composed of an ensemble of economic and
cultural meanings (e.g. that the wealth of a nation lies in its land,
or that the design of its parks and gardens bears some relation
to its political arrangements).[5] Needless to say, all representations
of landscape come aesthetically and ideologically freighted in
this way. But interior landscapes like the one invoked by Byatt
also bear looking at from a psychoanalytic perspective. They often
invoke not only internal space, but states of reverie, withdrawal,
or, in some cases, more questionable forms of psychic retreat.[6]
Looking at landscape involves ideas about absence and distance,
and can even imply looking away. In this sense, landscape is
less what we see in the mind's eye than what we don't see—our
peculiar, unconscious way of relating to an inner world and to its
internal objects. This is where psychoanalysis comes up against
(and goes beyond) the limits drawn by phenomenology.

[4] See Ernst van Alphen, 'De representatie van ruimte en de ruimte van representatie' ('The Representation of Space and the Space of Representation'), De Witte
Raaf, 70 (1997), 5–7 (forthcoming in English): 'The depiction of landscape . . . is not
an end in itself as a representation of space, but it is the way in which the space of
representation is being explored'; 'Landscape . . . becomes a metaphor for a mode
of looking . . . which draws the eye into the painting and makes the beholder
forget that the space is representational'. Van Alphen is especially interesting on
the way in which the space of landscape can be inviting, seducing, or promising.
By contrast, he argues, 'Architectural space engages by raising obstacles' which in
turn 'raise the desire of . . . doing something which is forbidden'. This distinction
has a bearing on the combination of landscape and architectural space in the design
represented by Austen's Sotherton in Mansfield Park, where access to landscape
involves overcoming physical and psychic obstacles. See also Jean-Philippe Antoine,
'Photography, Painting and the Real: The Question of Landscape in the Painting of
Gerhard Richter', in Gerhard Richter (Paris, 1995), 53–89, for a relevant discussion of
absence and memory in the painting of Caspar David Friedrich.
[5] See, for instance, Alan Liu, Wordsworth: The Sense of History (Stanford, Calif.,
1989) for the politics of the picturesque, and see also Ann Janowitz, England's Ruins:
Poetic Purpose and the National Landscape (Oxford, 1990).
[6] Cf. John Steiner's use of this term in relation to borderline patients, in Psychic
Retreats: Pathological Organizations in Psychotic, Neurotic and Borderline Patients
(London and New York, 1993).

Absence can be thought of in terms of its dictionary meaning
—being away from a place or person, but also the duration of
being away, and hence as bound up with temporality. I will be
arguing that the landscape of absence typically functions to deny
or make bearable spacial or temporal breaks between persons,
or even within ourselves. It can equally be a way to maintain
connection or preserve memory—a way to think. *Not* being
there can be as important as being there; what has gone may be
as significant as what remains. All this has a bearing on internal
topography. In an essay called 'The Unconscious Phantasy of an
Inner World Reflected in Examples from Literature' (1952), Joan
Riviere—one of Freud's early translators, but also a formidable
literary essayist in her own right—remarks on 'the suspicion and
intolerance' often aroused by 'the concept of internal objects'.[7]
She locates the source of this intolerance in the unwelcome idea
that we might have such internal objects within ourselves which
are somehow felt not to be our true 'selves' ('but are felt to
be *unknown* and therefore alarming', *IW* 304), and which disturb
us especially when they give us trouble (whereas, by contrast,
we tend to take good internal objects for granted). Like Klein,
Riviere founds this primitive splitting of good and bad on the
baby's 'bodily sensations of taking in and containing' (*IW* 308) the
prototype for the process of internalization. Sucking, looking,
perceiving, and registering all contain elements of the phantasy
process. In later life, Riviere suggests, our objects need not necessarily be people, but may equally be non-human, inanimate, or
abstract. By way of illustration, Riviere quotes a metaphysical
poem called 'Absence'. Misattributed by her to Donne, now
attributed to a minor metaphysical poet called John Hoskins,
the poem begins: 'Absence, heare my protestation | Against thy
strengthe | Distance and lengthe . . .'[8]

---

[7] First published in *IJP-A* 33 (1952), Riviere's essay was also included in Melanie
Klein, Paula Heimann, and R. Money-Kyrle (eds.), *New Directions in Psychoanalysis*
(London, 1955); quoted here from *The Inner World and Joan Riviere: Collected Papers
1920–1958*, ed. Athol Hughes (London, 1991), 303, cited hereafter as *IW*.

[8] Quoted from *The Poems of John Donne*, ed. Herbert Grierson (2 vols., Oxford,
1912), app. B: Poems Attributed to John Donne, ii. 428–9. Riviere quotes the first

The argument of Hoskins's 'Absence' is simple: 'To harts that cannot vary | Absence is present.' The idea of the beloved 'within' means that she (or he) can always be enjoyed privately (like a poem?), 'In some close corner of [the] braine.' The poem ends with a metaphysical paradox: 'There I embrace and there kiss her, | And so enjoye her, *and so misse her*' (my italics). Interestingly, and in keeping with her thesis, Riviere misquotes this closing couplet, subtly changing its meaning: 'There I embrace and kiss her, | And so enjoy her, *and none miss her*' (my italics again). Hoskins writes that to enjoy is always to miss; where the lover is concerned, the best kind of possession is absence. Riviere's misreading, by contrast, emphasizes the privacy, exclusiveness, and omnipotence of the lover's imaginative enjoyment of the beloved. This is the compensation for possessing an internal object in phantasy only. The poem's idealization of the loved one (always contained and available within the lover) banishes pain: 'Its message consists in a denial, a "protestation" against the plain emotional fact that the absence of the loved one is painful' (*IW* 310). Denial produces idealization, splitting off the fear of loss or erasing the lover's imperfections; a witty paradox distances the painful reality so that it becomes bearable. Interestingly, however, Riviere's argument is not simply that the reparative mode of the depressive position gives rise to literary creation (this would be the more orthodox Kleinian line).[9]

line as 'Absence, hear thou my protestation . . .'; this and other slight inaccuracies may suggest she is quoting the poem from memory or from another source. Later in her essay, Riviere gives an account of a comparable lover's experience drawn from Conrad's story, 'The Arrow of Gold' (see *IW*, 326–8) to illustrate 'the phantasy of self-*projection* into the object which appears to be bound up and simultaneous with the process of *introjection* of the object' (327).

[9] See, for instance, Hanna Segal's classic paper, 'A Psychoanalytic Approach to Aesthetics', in *The Work of Hanna Segal: A Kleinian Approach to Clinical Practice* (Northvale, NJ, and London, 1981), 185–205. Segal's example, inevitably, is Proust: 'Writing a book for him is like the work of mourning in that gradually the external objects are given up, they are reinstated in the ego, and re-created in the book. . . . all creation is really a re-creation of a once loved and once whole, but now lost and ruined object, a ruined internal world and self' (190). In her 1980 postscript, however, Segal adds that she would 'now emphasize more the role of idealization arising from the paranoid-schizoid position' citing Adrian Stokes on the artist's wish to 'maintain simultaneously an ideal object merged with the self and an object perceived as separate and independent, as in the depressive position' (204)—a crucial revision.

Rather, she implies that the narcissistic component of a poem like 'Absence', which defends against 'fear of the loss of and craving for possession of something outside oneself . . . on which one's life seems to depend' (*IW* 311), has a creative aspect. In psychoanalytic terms, the lost object (a missing breast) prompts reflection—Bion's first step towards thinking, Lacan's first step towards language—even if such thoughts give rise in the first instance to an evasive phantasy, or set in motion an unassuagable desire.[10] Absence does not only, or always, give rise to symbolization, or to only one kind of symbolic solution. As Riviere also points out, the absence of those we love 'can be equivalent, in our unconscious, to *lack of love*, hostility, hate, even malevolence, in them to us and in us to them' (*IW* 323). The negative of presence is not absence, but—surprisingly—hatred. We hate those who leave us because they seem not to love us, nor we them. This is the underlying, unstated, 'metapsychological' paradox of Hoskins's love-poem.

For Riviere, a missed mother provides us with our earliest experience of fear and craving; hence 'the phantasy of taking her into the self in order nevermore to be without her' (*IW* 311). In her view, the unconscious phantasy subtending 'Absence' is (once again) cannibalistic consumption of the loved object. Riviere finds in Hoskins's poem the overwhelming fear of loss that fuels our wish to incorporate inner objects. She links this fear not only

---

[10] See, for instance, W. S. Bion, 'A Theory of Thinking' (1962), *Second Thoughts* (London, 1984), 112: 'If the capacity for toleration of frustration is sufficient the "no-breast" becomes a thought and an apparatus for "thinking" it develops . . . The crux lies in the decision between modification or evasion of frustration.' See also Edna O'Shaughnessy's elegant, brief essay, 'The Absent Object', *Journal of Child Psychotherapy*, 1 (1964), 34–43: 'the absent object is a spur to the development of thought. It is not an accident that this is so, since there is a logical connection between thought and absence. You can be asked to think of something that is absent, a painting in a gallery (say), but you cannot be asked to think of a painting you are already looking at; perception shuts out thought, in this basic and simple sense. You can think about—in the sense of reflect upon—anything, things present as well as absent, but before you can "think about" you must develop the prior capacity to "think of". This latter is essentially linked to things absent; developmentally speaking, to the absent breast' (34). The Lacanian position—that lack hollows being into desire (i.e. gives rise to language)—is too well known to need further elaboration, but similarly implies the absence of the object and of immediate satisfaction.

with Jones's 'aphanisis' (loss of pleasure in life, especially sexual pleasure) but with Klein's emphasis on a deeper fear, the fear of losing life itself.[11] Riviere calls it 'the capacity for death in oneself' (*IW* 314). What one most fears, she writes, is 'the *loss of one's own identity*, by the disintegration and splitting of the ego' (*IW* 316). Here Freud's benign splitting of the ego tips over into the dread of disintegration and dying associated with the hidden workings of the death drive. Unexpectedly, Riviere's essay provides a return route to Byatt's reflections on rereading *Mansfield Park*. To Byatt, the excitement of discovering the landscape inside a novel is allied to the pleasure of finding that a novel can be (as Sodre puts it of Fanny's relation to landscape) 'the container of . . . past, good experiences' (i.e. the memory of a past, good experience of reading). What Sodre is saying about the world *in* the novel— its continuing meaning for Fanny—parallels what Byatt is saying about the world *of* the novel, which is that it continues to have meaning for her over time. For Riviere, the assumption of something '*still present* and available' is a phantasy relating to 'acts of absorption when alone in thoughts and memories of [the] *past*' (*IW* 320; her italics). By this, she doesn't just mean 'the banal fact that memories are always present with us, to be called up when required'. Rather, memories exist in the continuous time present of the inner world (the unconscious knows no time). All the more tantalizing, then, that we can never either be wholly self-possessed or magically repossess the past.

Later, I will return to *Mansfield Park* to suggest how pervasively Austen makes Fanny identify with what is absent in her own internal landscape. But first I want to look at the role of landscape in Jean-Jacques Rousseau's *La Nouvelle Héloïse*, where the lover typically struggles to sustain the phantasy that absence is really presence after all. What interests me is not so much the contrasts or resemblances between Austen and Rousseau (although they are striking). Rather, my concern is to emphasize the continuum

---

[11] See Melanie Klein, 'On the Theory of Anxiety and Guilt' (1948; *Envy and Gratitude*, WMK iii. 25–42), and Paula Heimann, 'Notes on the Theory of the Life and Death Instincts', in Melanie Klein, Paula Heimann, Susan Isaacs, and Joan Riviere, *Developments in Psycho-Analysis* (London, 1952), 321–37.

that links evading and modifying absence, and the differing part
played by a fictional landscape when it comes to denying or
mourning the loss of a loved object, or even to anticipating one's
own death. These subtly differentiated literary representations of
absence also bear on the relation between reading, rereading, and
memory.

Looking into a Mirror

> Another aspect of the inner world, its mysterious, inaccessible
> quality, is also commonly represented symbolically by *far
> away*, by *looking into space*, both not tangible, incapable of
> exploration; again, by *farthest away*, equivalent to nearest,
> one's own inside; by *looking into a mirror*, into one's own
> inside; or by *the sky, heaven high above*, inaccessible, unknow-
> able and again *above*. (Joan Riviere, *IW* 321)

In an essay called 'Places and Separation', the psychoanalyst
J.-B. Pontalis succinctly maps the psychoanalytic landscape inhabited
by Rousseau.[12] He points out that Rousseau's model for his own
life was one of traumatic separation, and that his autobiography
consists of repeated separations, dismissals, and exclusions—
journeys from one place to another, in search of a place where he
would belong. Apropos of Rousseau's internal exile, Pontalis has
this to say: 'The evidence of the importance of places to Rousseau
lies within ourselves, since two centuries later, we perceive them
as both real and fictitious places, literary and geographical places,
places of the memory and places of retreat' (*FP* 120). Rousseau's
contemporary readers were already travelling the same route

---

[12] J.-B. Pontalis, 'Places and Separation', *Frontiers in Psychoanalysis: Between the Dream
and Psychic Pain*, trans. Catherine Cullen and Philip Cullen (London, 1981), 112–25,
cited hereafter as *FP*; subsequent page references in the text are to this translation.
For object loss and separation anxiety considered particularly from a Kleinian
perspective, see also Jean-Michel Quinodoz, *The Taming of Solitude: Separation
Anxiety and Psychoanalysis* (London and New York, 1973). Quinodoz defines excessive separation anxiety as 'the tragic fear of finding oneself alone and abandoned—
the fount of psychical pain and the affect of mourning, as Freud showed in 1926 [in
Inhibitions, Symptoms, and Anxiety]' (ibid. 3).

between real and fictitious scenes when they visited the alpine settings of *La Nouvelle Héloïse* in search of this landscape of memory and retreat. Wary of associating place with an absent mother, Pontalis prefers the term 'local memory' to describe the process whereby the autobiographer can say: 'I find *myself* in this landscape' (*FP* 121). For Rousseau, he argues, places become a figure for himself. But they had to be places unthreatened by the intrusion of others—as we can see elsewhere, for instance, in his *Reveries of the Solitary Walker* (1782), where any sign of human commerce in landscape, however rustic, is experienced by him as a form of persecution.[13] Paradoxically sedentary in spite of his wanderings, Rousseau, writes Pontalis, '*self*-traveled'. He seems to be saying about Rousseau what Riviere has to say about the internal world —that we are disturbed by our difference from other people, especially when they seem to inhabit or divide us.

The Rousseauian landscape is a private space, equivalent to always being alone or ideally at one with oneself. Difference can only be accommodated as a minimal difference *within* the private space of the self:

what is dissimilar to me is myself. And let us add it *must* be myself so that my private space can offer (as in a well arranged landscape in which one does not know whether the effect is due to the gardener or to a natural order) enough disparity to move me and sufficient protection to ward off the savage violence of the outside, a radical otherness. The '*myself*' must remain. . . . (*FP* 122)

'Throughout his numerous periods of staying and fleeing . . .', Pontalis concludes, 'Rousseau remains the same.' Imagined intimacy ('*Two souls in the same body*, his body') is the other face of this minimal internal difference; compare the lover's wish for undisputed and undivided self-possession in Hoskins's 'Absence'. For Rousseau, according to Pontalis, only the self-referential world of *La Nouvelle Héloïse* (1761) could produce an equivalently gratifying fiction of intimacy. In his actual life, compulsive attachments

---

[13] See, for instance, Promenade VII, where Rousseau hears the clicking of a stocking mill in the midst of his imaginary solitude; Jean-Jacques Rousseau, *Reveries of a Solitary Walker*, trans. Peter France (Harmondsworth, 1979), 118.

alternated with the breaking of ties. But the cycle of loneliness and distress was at the same time one of triumphant uniqueness: 'He had to be *cast out* of the social space—the space of others— to be able to delimit his own space' (*FP* 124). Hence the proto-typical predicament of self-exile described by the *Confessions*: 'Rousseau never needed to *mourn* the lost object, for the object-person was above all in his eyes [a] figural representation.' Since no one but Rousseau is ever allowed to exist, he avoids experi-encing anything other than figural rejection or loss. Instead, he simply moves from one place to the next when each successive refuge gives rise, as it inevitably does, to a sense of claustro-phobic confinement. But, Pontalis urges, we shouldn't persecute Rousseau—the already persecuted paranoiac—by probing him too deeply. Instead, 'we should open ourselves to his space so as to expand our own' (*FP* 125). Reading Rousseau allows us to travel this figurative terrain, even if the only 'figure' we find there is Rousseau, our *semblable*—a figure whose narcissism we can recognize as uniquely 'literary', in the sense of relying on the fiction that memory is preserved by and speaks in landscape.

In *La Nouvelle Héloïse* separation is the precondition for the letters exchanged between Rousseau's two lovers, Saint-Preux (a bourgeois) and his pupil, Julie, or 'Eloisa' (the daughter of an aris-tocrat).[14] Rousseau ostensibly turns the pre-Enlightenment plot of seduction and castration—the story of Eloisa and Abelard— into an Enlightenment allegory of civilization and its discontents; passion is the sacrifice demanded by civilization, and the violence of sexuality must be tamed within the conjugal family in the interests of morality, transparency, and order. Or so it would seem, since, in reality, Rousseau tells a story of reason thwarted

[14] Quotations are from the Woodstock edition of William Kenrick's 1803 trans-lation, *Eloisa, or a Series of Original Letters* (2 vols., Oxford, 1989), in which Julie becomes 'Eloisa'; this was the much-reprinted edition available to Rousseau's late 18th-century and Romantic readers in England and is cited hereafter as *E*. References in the text are to the volumes and pages of this edition. For influential readings of Rousseau's novel which have shaped my own reading, see, for instance, Jean Starobinski, *Jean-Jacques Rousseau: Transparency and Obstruction*, trans. Arthur Goldhammer (Chicago, 1988), and Tonny Tanner, *The Novel of Adultery: Contract and Transgression* (Baltimore, 1979).

by transgressive and recalcitrant passions. The novel's pervasive
equation between landscape and an inner world makes the lover's
narcissistic experience of solitude and longing paradigmatic of the
fictional space itself. We are equally in the landscape and inside
the lover's head. In this imaginary space, separation can be overcome and losses made good in the lover's phantasy—but only up
to a point. As a repository for lost objects, Rousseauian landscape
is almost always eroticized or melancholy, seductive or potentially
fatal. Ultimately, however, it is inhabited by death. Rousseau's
Saint-Preux is a time-traveller, forever seeking the traces of past
emotions which haunt the landscape of absence, savouring a
form of affective and aesthetic experience that involves tantalizing distance rather than nearness. Landscape can function to
minimize anxieties about loss and neutralize troubling contact with
others, constituting a sort of no-go area or 'psychic retreat'—'an
area of the mind where . . . phantasy and omnipotence can exist
unchecked'.[15] Letter XXIII from Part I of *La Nouvelle Héloïse*,
written by Saint-Preux during a walking tour, delineates just
such a retreat where phantasy can flourish unchecked.[16] In the
aftermath of their first passionate encounter, Eloisa—ever the
educator—sends Saint-Preux to cool off in the mountains. He
describes himself as setting out on his journey 'suspended in a state
of languor that is not disagreeable to true sensibility' (*E* i. 117).
His account of his travels is aesthetically coded to suggest passions
contained and transcended ('stupendous rocks', 'drizzling cloud',
thundering cascades, yawning abysses, but also hanging woods and
flowery plains). This harmonious intermingling of the sublime
and the beautiful—ensuring that external and internal differences
are abolished—subsumes conflict into the peaceful coexistence
of opposites that Rousseau calls 'serenity of . . . mind' (*E* i. 118).
Serenity is associated not only with mountain solitude, but with
rising above the warring passions that define the lover.

---

[15] See Steiner, *Psychic Retreats*, 3.

[16] Earlier, Eloisa—staking out the scene of their first kiss—anticipates Saint-
Preux's experience during a ramble of her own: 'You, my amiable friend—you were
my companion—or rather, I carried you in my heart. I sought those paths which I
imagined we should have trod, and marked the shades which seemed worthy to
receive us' (*E* i. 95).

Riviere's aesthetics of the inner world uses the language of the sublime to evoke what is internal, inaccessible, and unknown; or, as Saint-Preux tells Julie, 'Having walked awhile in the clouds, I came to a place of greater serenity' (E i. 119)—a place where he no longer knows his own feelings. In this cloudy landscape, feelings and desires are evoked only to be idealized and disavowed ('Upon the tops of mountains, . . . our minds [are] more serene, our pleasures less ardent, and our passions much more moderate', E i. 119). Longing and looking—'the pleasure of gazing'—give way to 'gazing at an entire new scene', a 'new world' that Rousseau equates with unbreached self-possession and self-forgetfulness:

Imagine to yourself all these united impressions: the amazing variety, magnitude, and beauty, of a thousand stupendous objects; the pleasure of gazing at an entire new scene . . . another nature, and a new world . . . In short, there is a kind of supernatural beauty in these mountainous prospects which charms both the senses and the mind into a forgetfulness of one's self and of everything in the world. (E i. 120–1)

Saint-Preux's new-found serenity renders him immune to the painful realities of his situation (not just his distance from Eloisa, but his social and economic inferiority, and the seemingly immutable class hierarchy which separates them). We begin to see how the absence of others makes possible what Riviere calls 'the special compensatory connection between external loss and internal acquisition' (IW 322). If, as Saint-Preux claims, everything is 'connected with the idea of Eloisa', separation is just another form of togetherness; they need never be apart. The same tree shades the lovers, they recline on the same bank, gaze at the same landscape:

Is it possible for me to be one moment of my life alone, who exist only through her? O no! Our souls are inseparable . . . I did not take one step without you, nor admire a single prospect without eagerly pointing out its beauties to Eloisa. The same tree spread its shadow over us both, and we constantly reclined against the same flowery bank. Sometimes as we sat, I gazed with you at the wonderful scene before us, and sometimes on my knees turned with raptures to an object more worthy the contemplation of human sensibility. If I came to a difficult pass, I saw you skip over it with the activity of a bounding doe. When a torrent happened to cross our path, I presumed to press you in my arms, walked slowly through the water, and was always sorry when I reached the opposite bank. Everything in that peaceful solitude brought you to my imagination . . . every object that gave pleasure to the eye or to the heart, seemed inseparably connected with the idea of Eloisa. (E i. 127–8)

You're never alone in the mountains. In such a state of mind, nothing is missing, so nothing is missed; objects that give pleasure to the eye and the object of love are interchangeable. Obstacles magically dissolve, and crossing a torrent simply provides an opportunity for imaginary closeness.

But the post is about to leave: 'Why was I roused from my reverie? I was happy at least in idea.' The materiality of the letter—the fictional form of Rousseau's novel—intrudes on this prospect of unbroken self-possession as an insistent reminder of separation in time and space. Reality is allegorized as a rocky landscape, hostile, unyielding, and wintry. Just a few letters later, Rousseau shows us the phantasy breaking down (Letter XXVIII). Saint-Preux spends his days in 'a solitary cleft' from which he views, through a telescope, the house by the lake that contains the distant Eloisa. Although he believes that 'in spite of every obstacle, [he] can penetrate into [her] very chamber', he is forced to recognize that it is 'all a dream, the idle phantom of a projecting mind' (E i. 142). He imagines her reading the letters he writes on his rocky desk and melting into tears. Soon he is hurrying from rock to rock, contemplating a watery suicide ('The rock is craggy—the water deep—and I am in despair!', E i. 147). In this novel of self-seduction, the lover risks drowning in his own reflection. Ten years later, Saint-Preux revisits his rocky retreat in the company of Eloisa—now virtuously married to her middle-aged husband and mentor, Wolmar, who has taught her how to civilize passion by fencing it out or sequestering it within. Eloisa's crowning achievement as an Enlightenment gardener is her creation of a seemingly natural wilderness whose confines have been disguised by artful cultivation (Pontalis's 'well arranged landscape in which one does not know whether the effect is due to the gardener or to a natural order'). Here Saint-Preux learns that Eloisa inhabits marriage as a willing guest, and receives his own key from Wolmar so that he too can come and go freely. But when they venture outside, the lovers re-encounter the seductive, deathward drift of their former passion. During a boating expedition, a storm blows them across the lake, and they arrive at the same rocky cleft where Saint-Preux had once taken refuge with his telescope ('that lovely retreat, which served me as an asylum in the midst of ice', E iii. 215). Now this once-bleak retreat seems 'designed as an asylum for two lovers'. Calling it 'a spot which is full of [her]', Saint-Preux leads Eloisa 'toward the rock, and shewed her where her cypher was engraved in a thousand places, with several verses in Petrarch and Tasso, relative to the state [he] was in when [he] engraved them' (E iii. 216–17). But these multiple inscriptions of Eloisa's name have a devastating effect on the lover.

Rereading this lovely landscape, inscribed as it is with his memories of previous absence, reactivates the 'gloomy and greedy eye' of Saint-Preux's earlier suicidal melancholy:

Here is the stone where I used to sit, to reflect on your happy abode at a distance; on this I penned that letter which moved your heart; these sharp flints served me as a graving tool to cut your name; here I crossed that frozen torrent to regain one of your letters which the wind had carried off; there I came to review, and give a thousand kisses to the last you ever wrote to me; this is the brink, where, with a gloomy and greedy eye, I measured the depth of this abyss . . . (E iii. 218)

Fort/da . . . The 'here' and 'there' of an absence mastered, in this case, through letters recalls the repetitive strategies of Freud's little grandson in *Beyond the Pleasure Principle* (where a mirror also plays its part in the game of disappearance and return).[17] When Saint-Preux unexpectedly finds himself 'draw[ing] near the brink' again, the lovers leave in a hurry. As their melancholy increases on the return boat journey, Saint-Preux phantasizes a double suicide by water. Why the sudden brinkmanship and death-driven thoughts? What seems to intrude at this moment of rereading is not just the repetition of painful experience, but an intolerable sense of loneliness and fragmentation. Klein's

[17] See *Beyond the Pleasure Principle* (SE xviii. 15 and n.).

posthumously published essay 'On the Sense of Loneliness' (1963) calls it 'the feeling that one is not in full possession of one's self, that one does not fully belong to oneself or, therefore, to anybody else. The lost parts too, are felt to be lonely.'[18] To Petrarch and Tasso—devoted and maddened lover-poets respectively— add Saint-Preux, measuring the abyss with his self-destructive eye. Death by drowning appears the only means to reunite these lost parts that have been projected into others. But it is Eloisa rather than Saint-Preux who dies at the end of the novel, ostensibly from plunging into the lake to save her young son. On some level, she dies because only her death can heal the split in Saint-Preux (while making it finally possible for Eloisa herself to acknowledge her unextinguished passion for him). On the last page, we hear her plaintive voice calling, Echo-like, from 'the hollow tomb' in the certainty that 'she has not yet forsaken those haunts which she used to make so delightful' (E iv. 284–5). The landscape of absence becomes her speaking epitaph; the past returns, not as a textual fragment or a cypher written on the rocks, but as a ghostly presence—a voice. This trope of the speaking epitaph could be thought of as sustaining the entire novel. In order to read letters, after all, we have to imagine them as a form of prosopopoeia, spoken by a disembodied voice. Saint-Preux's phantasy about landscape—that absence is really presence—turns out to be the informing phantasy of Rousseau's epistolary novel. *La Nouvelle Héloïse* retells the story of a modern Narcissus seduced by his own reflection in terms of the haunting of landscape by echo.[19] Riviere's poetic phantasy of something '*still present* and available' allows Rousseauian reading to be redefined as the recovery of the past in the present ('acts of absorption when alone in thoughts and memories of [the] past', *IW* 320). You're never alone in a book, especially when the landscape of narcissistic reflection—the classically derived tropology that underlies *La Nouvelle Héloïse*— speaks with the voice of echo.

---

[18] See *Envy and Gratitude*, *WMK* iii. 303.
[19] Cf. Rousseau's mini-drama, *Pygmalion*, for his interest in the interplay between narcissism and artistic creation, and his articulation of something close to the Kleinian concept of narcissistic projective identification.

The Inequalities of Memory

If any one faculty of our nature may be called *more* wonderful than the rest, I do think it is memory. There seems something more speakingly incomprehensible in the powers, the failures, the inequalities of memory, than in any other of our intelligences. The memory is sometimes so retentive, so serviceable, so obedient—at others, so bewildered and so weak—and at others again, so tyrannic, so beyond control!—We are to be sure a miracle every way—but our powers of recollecting and forgetting, do seem peculiarly past finding out. (Jane Austen, *Mansfield Park*)[20]

Fanny Price's rhapsody on memory in *Mansfield Park* is as thought-provoking as Byatt's reflection on reading, which—generically speaking—belongs to the same line of descent. Austen's heroine is addicted not only to reading in her own room, but to retreating into an imaginary landscape (with or without a book).[21] The most Romantic as well as the most Evangelical of all Austen's heroines, Fanny turns to landscape for tranquillity, uplift, and a much-needed sense of continuity. Her attachment to place

[20] Jane Austen, *Mansfield Park*, ed. Tony Tanner (Harmondsworth, 1966), 222, cited hereafter as *MP*; subsequent page references in the text are to this edition. *Mansfield Park* has given rise to an exceptionally interesting group of critical essays in recent years, mostly, however, focused on the theatricals. See, for instance, David Marshall, 'True Acting and the Language of Real Feeling: *Mansfield Park*', *Yale Journal of Criticism*, 3 (1989), 87–106. For a subtle and relevant consideration of Austen's *Persuasion* in relation to the literary and to books, see Adela Pinch, 'Lost in a Book: Jane Austen's *Persuasion*', in *Strange Fits of Passion* (Stanford, Calif., 1996). See also Ruth Bernard Yeazell, 'The Boundaries of *Mansfield Park*', *Representations*, 7 (1984), 133–52, repr. in Judy Simons (ed.), *Mansfield Park and Persuasion* (New York, 1997), 69–92, for an interesting anthropological consideration of the structure of space that includes the Sotherton episode. A. S. Byatt and Ignes Sodre explore the novel's underlying concern with 'constancy' (including memory and constancy to place) in *Imagining Characters*, ch. 1; I am indebted to the many suggestive insights in their chapter, although choosing to place my own emphasis on the more problematic aspects of Fanny's psychic conservatism.

[21] See the passage from Sven Birkerts, *The Gutenberg Elegies: The Fate of Reading in an Electronic Age* (New York, 1994), 77, quoted on pp. 5–6 above, which suggests how strongly the image of a woman in a garden (or shrubbery) may be subliminally associated with the idea of reading.

preserves and overlays the memory of an earlier separation. Like Rousseau, she is a displaced person, uprooted from her crowded and chaotic family of origin in naval Portsmouth and transplanted to the spacious country house of a surrogate family. At once protected and excluded by her wealthy adoptive family, the landed and titled Bertrams, she lives alone among others—whether socially inferior or simply overlooked; there is no person, group, or place to which she really belongs. Her closest relationship, with her kind, serious cousin, Edmund Bertram (the younger son), replicates her enduringly affectionate childhood bond with her seagoing brother, Tom. But, for much of the novel, the privileged locus of her attachment is Mansfield Park itself. Despite her awareness of its subtle cruelties and manifest imperfections, Fanny comes to love the tranquillity and spaciousness of Mansfield and suffers from the noise when she revisits her cramped Portsmouth home. She alone, in fact, is loyal to the principles of her unbending uncle, Sir Thomas Bertram (whose deficiencies as a parent emerge during the course of the novel), while attending uncomplainingly to the needs of her inert and sofa-bound aunt, Lady Bertram. But it is Fanny herself—voicing Austen's own abolitionist sympathies— whose discreetly placed question brings into focus the fact that Mansfield Park is sustained less by the management of an old-fashioned agrarian economy than by the falling profits of West Indian sugar plantations, and hence by slave labour.[22] The occluded

---

[22] See the following exchange between Fanny and Edmund after Sir Thomas Bertram's return from Antigua: 'Did not you hear me ask [Sir Thomas] about the slave trade last night? . . . but there was such a dead silence! And while my cousins were sitting by without speaking a word, or seeming at all interested in the subject, I did not like—I thought it would appear as if I wanted to set myself off at their expense, by shewing a curiosity and pleasure in his information which he must wish his own daughters to feel' (*MP* 213). For the precise dating of this reference to issues of the (officially abolished) slave-trade in 1812, see Brian Southam, 'The Silence of the Bertrams', *Times Literary Supplement*, 17 Feb. 1995; repr. in Claudia L. Johnson (ed.), *Mansfield Park* (New York and London, 1998), 493–8; see also Michael Steffes, 'Slavery and *Mansfield Park*: The Historical and Biographical Context', *English Language Notes*, 34 (1996), 23–41. Like other Caribbean landowners of the period, Sir Thomas may have wished to set an enlightened example in the management of his slave-run estates in the wake of the abolition of the British slave-trade in 1807. For the complexities of Austen's relation to, and representation of, colonialism in

margins of the novel are occupied by this unthinkable form of colonial cultivation, the slave-run plantation visited by Sir Thomas and his older son. But the only background we are actually allowed to see is taken up with the cultivation and 'improvement' of the traditional English landscape—a landscape, however, that depends in turn on an earlier form of domestic appropriation, the enclosure of common land to form the extensive parks and pleasure grounds required by the landed gentry.[23] If form itself is ideology, it is

Mansfield Park, see, for instance, Edward W. Said, *Culture and Imperialism* (New York, 1993), 80–97. Moira Ferguson also considers the relation of gender to slavery in *Mansfield Park*, detailing Austen's abolitionist sympathies and her 'recommendations for a kinder, gentler plantocracy'; see 'Mansfield Park: Slavery, Colonialism and Gender', *Oxford Literary Review*, 13 (1991), 118–38, repr. as 'Mansfield Park: Plantocratic Paradigms', in *Colonialism and Gender Relations from Mary Wollstonecraft to Jamaica Kincaid: East Caribbean Connections* (New York, 1993), 65–89, and, for the larger context, see also Moira Ferguson, *Subject to Others: British Women Writers and Colonial Slavery, 1670–1834* (New York and London, 1992). For *Mansfield Park*'s combination of feminist and abolitionist issues, see Joseph Lew, ' "That Abominable Traffic": *Mansfield Park* and the Dynamics of Slavery', in Beth Fowkes Tobin (ed.), *History, Gender, and Eighteenth-Century Literature* (Athens, Ga. 1994), 271–300; repr. in Johnson (ed.), *Mansfield Park*, 498–510. Byatt gives surprisingly short shrift to such issues, which were undoubtedly in Austen's Christian and Abolitionist mind (see, for instance, *Imagining Characters*, 41). Lord Mansfield, coincidentally, was the judge who, by his ruling in 1772 that former slaves could not be forcibly returned from England to slavery in the Caribbean, provided a legal stepping-stone towards the abolition of the British slave-trade thirty years later.

[23] Humphrey Repton coined the term 'appropriation' specifically to describe 'extent of property' both owned and viewed by the landowner: 'The pleasure of appropriation is gratified in viewing a landscape which cannot be injured by the malice or bad taste of a neighbouring intruder: thus an ugly barn, a ploughed field, or any obtrusive object which disgraces the scenery of a park, looks as if it belonged to another, and therefore robs the mind of the pleasure derived from appropriation, or the unity and continuity of unmixed property'; see *An Enquiry into the Changes of Taste in Landscape Gardening* (1806; repr. Farnborough, Hants, 1969), 165–6, and compare this aesthetic justification for 'unmixed property' with the lover's phantasy of undisputed possession of the beloved. Cf. also John Barrell, *The Dark Side of the Landscape: The Rural Poor in English Painting 1730–1840* (Cambridge, 1980), for another striking exclusion from the park landscape—that of the rural poor. Henry Crawford's suggestions about how Edmund Bertram might improve his parsonage so that it better fits with the idea of a gentleman's residence provide a similar reminder that the history of enclosure also involved the removal of traces of other people's ownership from view: 'The meadows beyond what *will be* the garden . . . must be all laid together of course; very pretty meadows they are, finely sprinkled with timber. They belong to the living, I suppose. If not, you must purchase them' (*MP* 250–1).

tempting to conclude that the landscape of memory in *Mansfield Park* is the conservative form of an ideological attachment to the past which has forgotten its implication in the displacement, not just of one poor relation, but of entire populations.[24]

In the psychic economy of *Mansfield Park*, the best form of improvement is judicious conservation; memory embodies an element of disavowal—indeed, outright appropriation. Respect for tradition, embodied by Sir Thomas Bertram, goes hand in hand with the contradictions implicit in the idea of enlightened plantocracy. Change is registered as an attack on the landscape, or else as a destabilizing intrusion in the form of disruptive people and ideas. In the face of this assault on the values enshrined in an imaginary past, memory offers a saving fantasy of continuity.[25] But it also offers an avenue to the internal world of the novel, and to understanding the peculiar nature of Fanny's conservative attachment to place—what Edmund later calls 'all the holds upon things animate and inanimate, which so many years' growth have confirmed' (*MP* 344). In 'The Unconscious Phantasy of an Inner World', Riviere writes that 'the nearest a normal person, at any rate in the Western culture, comes to conscious realization of his own inner world is through the processes of memory' (*IW* 318–19). Fanny's rhapsody on memory, prompted by a recently created shrubbery, represents such a moment of near-conscious realization. The conversion of a rough hedgerow into a sheltered walk, in a brief recapitulation of the history of enclosure, occasions her reflections on the subtle improvements brought by time and growth. Austen makes her argue for the inseparability of

---

[24] For a contemporary debate over the past and present social and cultural uses of the country house and its park, see the symposium on Norbury Park, Vicki Berger and Isabel Vasseur (eds.), *Arcadia Revisted: The Place of Landscape*, (London, 1997); see also Simon Schama, *Landscape and Memory* (New York, 1995), esp. 153–74 for the British oak, and, for arcadia redesigned—'a product of the orderly mind rather than the playground of the unchained senses', 517–38.

[25] See W. R. Bion's suggestive paper on the link, 'Attacks on Linking' (1959), in *Second Thoughts*, 93–109, for an account of 'phantasized attacks on the breast as the prototype of attacks on objects that serve as a link and projective identification as the mechanism employed by the psyche to dispose of the fragments produced by its destructiveness' (93). For Bion, the destructive attack on a link is also directed at the phantasy of the parental couple and at verbal thought itself.

recollecting and forgetting, and for the inextricability of knowledge from what is 'past [i.e. beyond] finding out'. Forgetting carries
within it an unexpected potential for destruction—a tyrannical
amnesia, or *mal d'archive*, within the public and private spaces of
memory.[26] The present overgrows and obliterates the past; we
create our natural environment by ruthlessly re-creating it. In this
sense, memory is always prosthetic, always an improvement
on a prior state of things. In her conversation with A. S. Byatt,
Ignes Sodre links Fanny's rhapsody on memory to the theme of
constancy in the novel as a whole. But she suggests, shrewdly, that
Fanny only wants to remember the good experiences associated
with Mansfield; Portsmouth, her home of origin, becomes a
convenient repository for bad experiences such as feeling out
of place or unwanted—all split-off features of her actual life at
Mansfield.[27] For Byatt, as we have seen, the shrubbery is an image
of what grows organically, over time, in the reader's head (while
paradoxically obscuring the past as it does so). Constancy and
inconstancy are inextricably entwined in Austen's organicist
trope of memory.

Continuing in what she calls 'this sort of wondering strain',
Fanny enthuses about evergreens as a sign of nature's astonishing variety: 'one cannot fix one's eye on the commonest natural
production without finding food for a rambling fancy' (*MP* 223).
Everything she sees in nature nourishes a literary imagination.
Fanny's rambling mind colonizes her environment, constituting
a kind of mental 'enclosure'; where fields and hedgerows were,
there ornamental shrubberies shall be. Austen is pointing to the
cultural uses of an unproductive landscape for the production of
an educated sensibility such as Fanny comes to represent in the
novel. Here, for instance, she reproduces the aestheticized reflections of a late eighteenth-century sufferer from seasonal affective

[26] Cf. Jacques Derrida's exploration of *mal d'archive* in *Archive Fever: A Freudian Impression*, trans. Eric Prenowitz (Chicago, 1996).

[27] According to Sodre, '[Fanny's] reference to "forgetting, almost forgetting what was before" . . . is connected to the wish to forget her bad experiences. What she says about the wonderfulness of memory is also linked to the central theme of constancy: remaining attached to one's good experiences, and being faithful, and grateful, to the past' (*Imagining Characters*, 37).

disorder (known to modern fellow sufferers by the melancoly acronym, SAD). Rambling—a leisure pursuit recently adopted by the upper classes—involves the same unpurposive activity, the same potential for reflective melancholy. The enclosed landscape 'feeds' a rambling fancy rather than growing crops. Given Sir Thomas Bertram's absentee ownership of colonial estates abroad, the cash-crop that matters is in any case sugar rather than corn. Plantations of evergreens allow Fanny to think pensive thoughts, while overcoming and naturalizing the reality of change as seasonal continuity. Her internal landscape is this landscape of unchanging evergreen absence. Fanny is a heroine who never manages to be 'there' (wherever it is), however much she longs to be. Typically, she thinks about being there when she is somewhere else. In a way, she never moves beyond the shrubbery, just as her aunt seems never to leave the sofa. This is surprising in a novel that ostensibly focuses attention on the idea of gaining access to landscape (on foot or horse, or in the mind's eye) for the purpose of deriving aesthetic pleasure from it. I want to focus on a single, well-known episode from *Mansfield Park* (spead out over chapters 9 and 10 of Volume I) in order to explore in more detail the function of Austen's landscape of absence—the way external space is used to map the inner boundaries and divisions of the novel's characters, who take on the aspect of intrusive internal objects within the mind of Fanny herself.

The subject of improvement comes up most insistently in connection with Sotherton, the neighbouring estate belonging to Mr Rushworth (the suitable but none-too-bright young man to whom Maria, the older and more headstrong of the two Bertram sisters, is unenthusiastically engaged). Lady Bertram, who almost never goes out, opines complacently: 'One likes to get out into a shrubbery in fine weather' (*MP* 86). Her remark prompts Mr Rushworth to enlarge on his plans for drastic improvements to his park, in the hope of impressing his listeners and capturing his indifferent fiancée's attention:

'There have been two of three fine old trees cut down that grew too near the house, and it opens the prospect amazingly, which makes me think that Repton, or any body of that sort, would certainly have the avenue at Sotherton down; the avenue that leads from the west front to the top of the hill you know,' turning to Miss Bertram particularly as he spoke. But Miss Bertram thought it most becoming to reply:

'The avenue! Oh! I do not recollect it. I really know very little of Sotherton.' (*MP* 87)

In the politico-aesthetic wars of the picturesque, Repton claimed that his own system of improvement resembled the same happy medium between liberty and despotic restraint as the British constitution.[28] Mr Rushworth is hardly a revolutionary. But his plan to cut down an avenue of oak trees ('It is oak entirely', *MP* 111) in order to improve the view goes against both Burkean tradition and reverence for the patriotic oak associated with the British constitution. Although representative of the fashion for landscape make-over, Repton himself was also responsible for massive tree-planting programmes—not to mention the burgeoning of innumerable shrubberies. If we turn to Repton's *Enquiry into the Changes of Taste in Landscape Gardening* (1806), we find him praising the aesthetics of 'continuity' in the form of 'the delight expressed in a long avenue'.[29] Apropos of cutting down avenues,

[28] In *Sketches and Hints on Landscape Gardening* (1795), Repton compares 'The happy medium betwixt the wildness of nature and the stiffness of art' to the way in which 'the English constitution is the happy medium between the liberty of savages and the restraint of despotic government'; see Edward Hyams, *Capability Brown and Humphrey Repton* (London, 1971), 162; for the picturesque controversy during the 1790s, see ibid. 158–64, and Dorothy Stroud, *Humphrey Repton* (London, 1962), 82–92. The most helpful discussion of Repton's work in relation to Austen's own Reptonian landscape aesthetic is to be found in John Dixon Hunt's essay, 'Sense and Sensibility in the Landscape Designs of Humphrey Repton', in *Gardens and the Picturesque* (Cambridge, Mass., 1992), 139–68. For the political wars of the picturesque in relation to literature, see also Liu, *Wordsworth: The Sense of History*, 61–137, esp. 104–15. See also Edward Malins, *English Landscaping and Literature 1660–1840* (London, 1966), and Kay Diana Kris, *The Idea of the English Landscape Painter* (New Haven, 1997).

[29] Here is Repton on the aesthetic pleasures of 'continuity': 'This seems evidently to be a source of pleasure, for the delight expressed in a long avenue, and the disgust at an abrupt break between objects that look as if they ought to be united; as in the chasm betwixt two large woods, or the separation betwixt two pieces of water; and even a walk, which terminates without affording a continued line of communication, is always unsatisfactory'; see *An Enquiry into the Changes of Taste in Landscape Gardening*, 164.

he concludes: 'the change of fashion in Gardening destroys the work
of ages, when lofty avenues are cut down for no other reason
but because they were planted in straight rows, according to the
fashion of former times.'[30] Austen is laughing at Mr Rushworth
('an inferior young man, as ignorant in business as in books',
MP 214) for having misunderstood Repton so thoroughly. But his
misunderstanding leads to an attack which the novel implicitly
codes as the symbolic destruction of a vital link with the past: a
link of which Fanny's solitary consciousness becomes the principle bearer in the novel.

Both Austen and Fanny—Reptonians in their appreciation
of natural variety and in their respect for the fashion of former
times—appear to mourn the passing of the traditional landscape
represented by Sotherton. Fanny (who will find the chapel at
Sotherton insufficiently historical) wistfully expresses her wish
to see the avenue 'before it is cut down, to see the place as it is
now, in its old state, but I do not suppose I shall' (*MP* 87).[31] But
her immediate response is a form of literary memory. She turns
to Edmund, saying 'in a low voice, "Cut down an avenue! What
a pity! Does not it make you think of Cowper? 'Ye fallen avenues,
once more I mourn your fate unmerited.'"' (*MP* 87)[32] Fanny's
quotation comes from the first book of Cowper's protracted,
reflective nature-poem, *The Task* (1785). Cowper—who was also
the best-known anti-slavery poet of the late eighteenth century
—undertook *The Task* as a therapeutic exercise, urged on by a
lady who proposed a poem on a mock-epic subject of her own

[30] *An Enquiry into the Changes of Taste*, 24–8. 'Every sacrifice of large trees must
be made with caution', Repton notes (27 n.).

[31] Fanny complains to Edmund that 'This is not my idea of a chapel. There is
nothing awful here, nothing melancholy, nothing grand. Here are no aisles, no arches,
no inscriptions, no banners' (*MP* 114); she goes on to quote Sir Walter Scott's *The
Lay of the Last Minstrel*, giving her interest in the past a specifically literary turn.

[32] Elsewhere, Fanny responds to a starry night in terms of 'what poetry only can
attempt to describe'; on this occasion too, her feelings are couched in the literary
language of 18th-century enthusiasm: 'Here's repose! . . . Here's what may tranquilize
every care, and lift the heart to rapture!' (*MP* 139). As so often in the novel, Fanny's
turn from nature to literary language—equally associated with repose, tranquillity,
and uplift—serves as a retreat from the fatigue, division, and dissatisfaction that characterizes Austenian sociality.

choosing: the sofa. Hailed as the culmination of the progress of eighteenth-century leisure, the sofa provided Cowper with an unusual vantage-point for writing poetry, at once indoors and outdoors. 'Having much leisure', he explains disarmingly, he 'connected another subject with it; and pursued the train of thought to which his situation and turn of mind led him.'[33] Unlike Lady Bertram, he gets off the sofa for a literary ramble—a ramble, however, that takes place in his and the reader's head. Klein's 'On the Sense of Loneliness' refers to a claustrophobic patient whose flight into nature was not only prompted by 'anxiety of imprisonment' in the maternal body, or the feeling of being 'hemmed in by resentful internal objects', but by the underlying conviction that nature was a good object able to repair itself and withstand his destructive assaults.[34] The rambling, free-associative mode of *The Task* allows Cowper to link past and present selves, while reaffirming his connection with landscape as unbroken and reparative in the face of mental anguish and breakdown: 'scenes that sooth'ed | Or charm'd me young, no longer young, I find | Still soothing . . .' (*T* i. 141–3). This sounds surprisingly like Byatt's reflection on rereading *Mansfield Park*. Soothed by books, the re-reader asserts the continuity of past and present selves, defended against ideas of loss or change.

Cowper deploys the familiar topography of the eighteenth-century landscape poem to anchor his wandering thoughts—directing our eyes to a clump of elms here, a river there; here a village, there a horizon, where 'the sloping land recedes into the clouds' (*T* i. 171). Riviere's aesthetic topography of nearness and distance should alert us to the representation of an inner world. Sure enough, we move from a catalogue of sights to sounds ('heard in scenes where peace for ever reigns', *T* i. 208) to the unheard

---

[33] *The Poems of William Cowper*, ed. John D. Baird and Charles Ryskamp (3 vols., Oxford, 1980–95), ii. 113, cited hereafter as *T*. Subsequent references are to the book and line numbers of *The Task*.

[34] See *Envy and Gratitude*, *WMK* iii. 307–8. For recent essays on the psychoanalytic meaning of landscape and place, see R. D. Hinshelwood, 'The Countryside', *British Journal of Psychotherapy*, 10 (1993), 203–10, and Andrew Samuels, 'I am a Place: Depth Psychology and Environmentalism', ibid. 211–19.

sound—silence—that Cowper equates with poetry ('the poet's treasure, silence', *T* i. 235). Cowper invokes the special form of protection offered by the avenues of poetic tradition. Our ancestors, he writes, 'knew the value of a screen | From sultry suns', of 'shaded walks | And long-protracted bowers' (*T* i. 255–7). The rambling chiaroscuro of *The Task* (half-serious, half-playful) allows Cowper to refer semi-facetiously to an avenue of chestnut-trees, 'ranged in corresponding lines', in terms of 'The obsolete prolixity of shade' (*T* i. 263–5). *The Task*'s obsolete Miltonic prolixities— its 'corresponding lines'—remind us that the temporarily reprieved avenue is a figure for the refuge provided by poetry and tradition alike. Cowper's fallen avenues are a monument to survival—a natural ruin, open to the sky, suffused with the religious feeling Fanny had missed in Sotherton's chapel ('nothing awful here, nothing melancholy, nothing grand', *MP* 114):

> Ye fallen avenues! Once more I mourn
> Your fate unmerited, once more rejoice
> That yet a remnant of your race survives.
> How airy and how light the graceful arch,
> Yet awful as the consecrated roof
> Re-echoing pious anthems! While beneath
> The chequer'd earth seems restless as a flood
> Brush'd by the wind. So sportive is the light
> Shot through the boughs, it dances as they dance,
> Shadow and sunshine intermingling quick,
> And darkning and enlightning, as the leaves
> Play wanton, ev'ry moment, ev'ry spot.

> (*T* i. 338–49)

The fallen avenues represent the very space of reflection, 'darkning and enlightning' from moment to moment. The self-observing mind—at rest but not immobile, responsive to shifts of mood and the quick play of passing thoughts—preserves the vital link between sense perception and consciousness. This landscape of reverie (not the sofa) is the real subject of *The Task*. But Cowper goes out of his way to invest the fallen avenues with retrospective political meaning when he invokes 'Our arch of empire . . . A mutilated structure, soon to fall' (*T* i. 773–4). Mansfield is a similarly 'mutilated structure', rendered imperfect by an Empire predicated on the slavery from which Sir Thomas Bertram derives his wealth.

For once included in the family outing, Fanny arrives at Sotherton full of 'respect'—her term (*MP* 111)—for the history of a great country house, and on the look-out for the avenue of oak trees. She never reaches it, but her imaginary relation to the distant avenue shapes the abortive trajectory of the entire episode. Oppressed by their guided tour of a great house that represents the formality and restraint of the past, the young people 'as by one impulse, one wish for air and liberty, all walked out' (*MP* 118). In their different groupings, they find their way through an open door into the shady wilderness beyond the formal gardens and terraces ('they were all agreed in turning joyfully through it, and leaving the unmitigated glare of day behind', *MP* 119). The wilderness, like Julie's wilderness in *La Nouvelle Héloïse*, is an enlarged shrubbery whose limits have been disguised by ingenious planting (the effect 'was darkness and shade, and natural beauty', *MP* 119). On this border between garden and park, boundaries become permeable. The Sotherton wilderness forms a stage for Austen's unquiet comedy of matched and mismatched lovers in pursuit of each other; two's company but three's a jealous crowd. Each couple finds a way to get rid of the unwanted third, breaching the confines of the ha-ha and locked gates and escaping into the relative freedom of the park. Austen minutely calibrates her characters' relations to each other—their mingled but unequally distributed feelings of attraction, resentment, jealousy, disappointment, and depression (the last two terms are Austen's; the emotions belong to Fanny). Their claustrophobic desire to get out is the underside of Fanny's exaggerated respect for limits. Austen conveys the deathly inertia and fear which keeps the agoraphobe from exploring her environment, while all the while longing to reach the distant avenue.

'Knocked up' by the walk, Fanny is left on a bench by her two companions to recover ('to sit in the shade on a fine day, and look upon verdure, is the most perfect refreshment', *MP* 123). Like Byatt's middle-aged Austen on her sofa, she is relegated to observing—and envying—the life lived by others. By contrast, 'resting fatigues' her companion, the lively and restless Mary Crawford. She and Edmund Bertram walk off to measure the extent of the wilderness and explore their mutual attraction; Edmund has felt a new 'connection' to Mary Crawford when she takes his arm for the first time during their walk. Their expedition is protracted to an hour when they find their way into the park via an open side-gate. Meanwhile, another trio appears—Maria Bertram, Mr Rushworth, and Mary Crawford's sophisticated brother Henry, serving as adviser in the scheme of 'improving' Sotherton. They are eager to reach a distant knoll, in order to get a good view of the house and the surrounding park; but the iron gate is locked. While Mr Rushworth obediently goes for the key, Maria confides her dismay at the 'smiling prospect' before her (marriage to Mr Rushworth): 'Yes, certainly, the sun shines and the park looks very cheerful. But unluckily that iron gate, that ha-ha, give me a feeling of restraint and hardship. I cannot get out, as the starling said' (*MP* 127). Henry Crawford suggests taking a short cut (as he will do again), and the pair climb round the gate to a chorus of distress from Fanny: 'You will hurt yourself Miss Bertram . . . you will certainly hurt yourself against those spikes—you will tear your gown—you will be in danger of slipping into the ha-ha' (*MP* 127). Fanny knows where all this tends: one slip, and you're out of the novel for good: 'Let other pens dwell on guilt and misery' (*MP* 446—Austen's way of dealing with the adultery foretold here). As Maria and Henry stroll off into the park, the remaining characters enter and exit in pursuit of one another (Julia Bertram, chagrined that her sister has out-manœuvred her in the competition for the eligible but elusive Henry Crawford, Mr Rushworth mortified that his future wife has already dumped him for a more attractive man). When at last Fanny goes in search of Edmund and Mary, she finds that 'they had been across a portion of the park into the very avenue which Fanny had been hoping the whole morning to reach at last; and had been sitting down under the trees. This was their history. It was evident that they had been spending their time pleasantly' (*MP* 130).

The avenue that Cowper had associated with the chiaroscuro of reflection, and Fanny with reverence for the past, becomes a place where two people might take legitimate pleasure in each other's company. Linking the great house and the park, its past history and its smiling prospects, the avenue links Edmund and Mary Crawford in a hypothetical future that excludes Fanny. Austen allows us to know 'that the absence of the loved one is painful'; Fanny loves Edmund and is jealous of Mary Crawford. We register her feelings of abandonment and exclusion—'the pain of having been left a whole hour . . . the sort of curiosity she felt, to know what they had been conversing about all that time . . . her disappointment and depression' (*MP* 130). Throughout the novel, Fanny's most vivid connection to others in fact occurs via this suffering consciousness. Her feelings of pain and curiosity, disappointment and depression, anticipate the amateur theatricals at Mansfield, when she and Julia Bertram, both onlookers at the flirtations of others, become 'two solitary sufferers, or connected only by Fanny's consciousness' (*MP* 183). Fanny's connecting consciousness—a projection of Austen's—makes her a fictional looker-on at life, middle-aged before her time (confined to a sofa of her own). Her solution is to attach herself to what is not (or is no longer) there, deriving melancholy satisfaction from its contemplation.[35] For Fanny, it isn't a matter of replacing an object of desire by a symbol (the distant avenue).[36] Rather, the object has become identified with absence itself, and the hatred mobilized against it—as we can now see with hindsight—displaced on to

---

[35] Compare D. W. Winnicott's patient in 'Transitional Objects and Transitional Phenomena' (1953), for whom the rug that is not there is more real than the rug that is there, just as her previous analyst is more important to her than her present analyst (Winnicott): 'she formulated the sentence: "All I have got is what I have not got." There is a desperate attempt here to turn the negative into a last-ditch defence against the end of everything. The negative is the only positive'; see *Playing and Reality* (1971; repr. London, 1991), 22–4.

[36] Cf. Hanna Segal, 'Notes on Symbol Formation' (1957), in *The Work of Hanna Segal*, 51, summarizing Ernest Jones: 'when a desire has to be given up because of conflict and is suppressed, it may express itself in a symbolic way, and the object of the desire which had to be given up can be replaced by a symbol.' Segal argues for extending Jones's definition from this primitive symbolic process to the symbols used in self-expression, communication, discovery, and creation.

stupid Mr Rushworth's unthinking enthusiasm for Reptonian 'improvement', or on to the envied and resented Mary Crawford, who is systematically cut down to size during the course of the novel by both Fanny and Austen herself. The fallen avenues of the past become a magnet for this attachment to an absent object, always lost, but made permanently available in the surrogate form of literary memory. Maria Bertram's sense of confinement expresses itself in pathetic fallacy and the sentimental cliché of the caged starling in Sterne's *Sentimental Journey*. By contrast, Fanny's attachment to a lost object expresses itself in 'what poetry only can attempt to describe' (*MP* 139)—in elegy, diffused over the literary landscape of the entire novel; in having only got what she has not got. *Mansfield Park* uses the trope of landscape to gather up a complex skein of interpersonal, intra-psychic, and symbolic meanings, as well as political, ideological, and economic agendas that may not, in fact, have been consciously available to its author. But perhaps the meaning that emerges most clearly from Austen's use of the avenue as a link to the past is the simplest one: namely, Fanny's wish to preserve it. By installing Cowper's 'fallen avenues' in her internal world, Fanny does her best to conserve them, producing elegiac food for thought. Like the pained lover of Hoskins's poem, Fanny knows that the best kind of presence is absence after all. Conservation, you might say, keeps the fallen avenues permanently on line—just as rereading and remembering tread the same recursive path when they return to the sites of meaning embodied by literary tradition.

Another poem by Cowper, also about an avenue, draws these reflections on landscape, memory, and literary tradition into a different relation. *The Task*, as we have seen, uses the 'corresponding lines' of a classical colonnade as a metaphor for poetry. 'The Poplar-Field' is at once a graceful elegy for felled trees and a poet's epitaph:

> The Poplars are fell'd, farewell to the shade
> And the whispering sound of the cool colonnade,
> The winds play no longer, and sing in the leaves,
> Nor Ouse on his bosom their image receives.

Twelve years have elapsed since I first took a view
Of my favourite field and the bank where they grew,
And now in the grass behold they are laid,
And the tree is my seat that once lent me a shade.

The black-bird has fled to another retreat
Where the hazels afford him a screen from the heat,
And the scene where his melody charm'd me before,
Resounds with his sweet-flowing ditty no more.

My fugitive years are all hasting away,
And I must e'er long lie as lowly as they,
With a turf on my breast, and a stone at my head
E'er another such grove shall arise in its stead.

'Tis a sight to engage me if any thing can
To muse on the perishing pleasures of Man;
Though his life be a dream, his enjoyments, I see,
Have a Being less durable even than he.[37]

Cowper's rippling anapaests state the 'plain emotional fact' of absence ('The Poplars are fell'd . . . And now in the grass behold they are laid'). But they also contain a subtler, contrary play of possibility. Whose, really, is the subjectivity that records shade, movement, sound? Whose bosom preserves the absent 'image'? The equivalence of poplars and reflected image reintroduces the temporal dimension of reflection: 'Twelve years have elapsed . . .' The vantage point of memory is at once a 'seat' and a (psychic) 'retreat' ('The black-bird has fled to another retreat'). The *fort/da* of 'before' | 'no more'—the on-again, off-again effects of rhyme and rhythm—puts the stress on what is 'fugitive', what comes and goes but will never return. We remember how Freud's grandson tried to master his mother's absence with a game (throwing a cotton reel out of his cot and retrieving it), for ever playing out the departure and return of his lost object. But

---

[37] *The Poems of William Cowper*, ii. 25–6; first published in *The Gentleman's Magazine* for 1784. Cowper apparently wrote 'The Poplar-Field' (written to a favourite tune of Lady Austen) 'after having conducted Lady Austen to the site of a Poplar Grove, which he intended to show her, but found just cut down' (see *The Poems of William Cowper*, ii. 316).

although the sight of something gone ("Tis a sight to engage
me if any thing can . . .') brings painful thoughts of transience,
it also generates a characteristic activity of mind called 'musing'
('To muse on the perishing pleasures of Man'). Reflection allows
us to glimpse, for a moment, what it means not to lose sight
of something in the mind's eye, to hold something in mind; to
muse, even, on perishing pleasures. Or rather, Cowper's seeing
('I see')—his thinking—takes place in the absence of anything
to see. As Freud might have said, in the projective time of the
future past perfect, 'objects' (and even life itself) 'shall have been
lost which once brought real satisfaction'.[38]

In 'The Poplar-Field', the loss of a reflected image, or the silencing of a bird, become metaphors for the poet's own anticipated
loss of vision and voice. Life is a dream; can transitory enjoyments
endure? Cowper's reflections on death are deliberately sententious,
even formulaic ('I must e'er long lie as lowly as they'). Such
thoughts belong to classical convention, like his rising and falling anapaests. But the subtlety of his elegy eludes the thudding
finality of '. . . and a stone at my head'. A tree casts a reflection,
but it cannot 'reflect', still less muse. Only the poem, in this
sense, truly remembers. 'The Poplar-Field' is a poet's farewell
to poetry—a speaking epitaph, this time the writer's own. We
identify with its capacity to remember, as much as with the painful
absence it records. Rereading a book or poem, like revisiting an
imagined landscape, similarly depends on the to-and-fro movement of retreat and conservation, forgetting and memory: the
movement that we call reflection. In this sense, the book (or
poem, or landscape) functions as a link—as what Wilfred Bion
(in 'Attacks on Linking') calls the linking function of thought. I
want to end with a passage from Joan Riviere's essay on literature and the internal world. Riviere writes, strongly, movingly, and
directly, that death means not simply the end of life, but the disappearance of a complex identity predicated on the relation
between present and past:

[38] See 'Negation' (1923); SE xix. 238.

death is not only a matter of whether the breath leaves the body and the heart ceases to beat. That is one item of the experience of death, it is true; but is that all that death means to us? It is probably the most important factor in death because it is irrevocable, and thus all else that death means becomes irrevocable: namely, the cessation, the disappearance, so comparatively sudden, of a living existence, an entity, a person, a personality, a most complex and composite structure of attributes, tendencies, experiences, memories, idiosyncracies good and bad, as well as the body they belong to. It is all this which disappears; from one moment to the next it was here and it is gone. So when one fears one's own death, it is all that which one will lose, one's 'life'—in both senses—one's present breath of life, and one's 'past life' out of which one's identity is constituted. (*IW* 316)

The absence that we most fear is our own forgetting. Kleinian accounts of literary creation tend to emphasize the impulse to recover past times and lost objects, or to repair damaged ones.[39] But literary memory—mourning the trees—is not just a form of reparation, or a way to preserve the 'past life' on which identity is predicated. By the same token, Riviere's eloquent account of the finality of life's disappearance ('it was here and it was gone') goes beyond the *fort/da* of object loss. She writes not only that present life includes the sense of having a past to lose, but that the capacity for reflecting on death is inseparable from being fully alive.

---

[39] See Janine Chasseguet-Smirgel, 'Thoughts on the Concept of Reparation and the Hierarchy of Creative Acts', *International Review of Psycho-Analysis*, 11 (1984), 399–406, for a distinction between reparation of objects and reparation of the subject via creative acts; I am grateful to Rosika Parker for drawing my attention to this essay.

PART TWO

Reading Trauma

THREE

White Skin, Black Masks
Reading with Different Eyes

AROUND 1 September 1802 Wordsworth composed a sonnet about a woman who was his fellow passenger on the crossing from Calais to Dover; he was returning from his first, momentous visit to France since the Revolution. His sonnet was published in the radical *Morning Post* in February 1803 under the title 'The Banished Negroes':

> We had a fellow-passenger that came
> From Calais with us, gaudy in array,
> A negro woman, like a lady gay,
>   Yet silent as a woman fearing blame;
> Dejected, downcast, meek, and more than tame:
>   She sate, from notice turning not away,
>   But on our proffer'd kindness still did lay
> A weight of languid speech, or at the same
>   Was silent, motionless in eyes and face.
> She was a negro woman, out of France
>   Rejected, like all others of that race:
> Not one of whom may now find footing there.
> What is the meaning of this ordinance?
> Dishonour'd Despots, tell us if ye dare.[1]

---

[1] *Morning Post*, 11 Feb. 1803. Later included among 'Poems Dedicated to National Independence and Liberty', the sonnet underwent extensive revisions. In 1807, the final lines were revised to temper their defiance: 'This the poor Out-cast did to us declare, | Nor murmur'd at the unfeeling Ordinance' (ll. 13–14); see William Wordsworth, *Poems, in Two Volumes, and Other Poems, 1800–1807*, ed. Jared Curtis (Ithaca, NY, 1983), 161–2 and *app. crit.* For Wordsworth's brief post-Treaty of Amiens visit to

Three months before Wordsworth's encounter with this dejected woman of colour, in May 1802, Toussaint L'Ouverture had been tricked, arrested, and sent to Paris after losing the struggle against Napoleon's re-establishment of the French empire in the Caribbean. The reimposition of slavery followed, after fierce local resistance, in Santo Domingo, as well as Martinique and Guadeloupe (where slavery had been reinstituted in all but name after its abolition in 1795). But what *was* 'the meaning of this ordinance?' For blacks, it meant expulsion as the result of a government decree of July 1802 which forbade them entry, exiling all those living in France without government approval. The edict also included a clause banning interracial marriage.[2] This racist ordinance, along with the restoration of slavery and Toussaint's arrest, put an end to any lingering hope that the French Revolution would bring about the simultaneous fall of slavery and empire.[3] 'Dishonour'd Despots' ruled OK.

Wordsworth's fellow passenger is characterized by the languid depression and stasis that typifies the female outcasts and solitaries of his protest poetry. But she is also an emblem of racial trauma—'Dejected', 'Rejected'—and ejected. The spirit of Toussaint, symbol of 'man's unconquerable mind', has been feminized, meekened, and deported. Wordsworth's companion sonnet of the same moment (also published in the *Morning Post*) imagines Toussaint, soon to die of his degrading imprisonment in the Jura, in exalted terms

France in order to visit Annette Vallon and his daughter, see Stephen Gill, *William Wordsworth: A Life* (Oxford, 1989), 207–9. I would like to acknowledge my gratitude to Cora Kaplan for drawing my attention to the revisions to Wordsworth's sonnet and for sharing her thoughts on its racial, political, and pictorial context .

[2] See Judith W. Page, *Wordsworth and the Cultivation of Women* (Berkeley, 1994), 67–76; Page refers in passing to 'the colonialist mentality shared by much abolitionist writing' (72), and provides an extended reading of the sonnet and its revisions in relation to Wordsworth's personal as well as political situation. See also *Recueil général, annoté, des lois, décrets, ordonnances, etc. 1789–1830* (16 vols., Paris, 1838), ix. 361 for the decree itself. For an account of French encounters with blacks and colonial policy during this period, see also Shelby T. McCloy, *The Negro in France* (New York, 1973), and William B. Cohen, *The French Encounter with Africans: White Response to Blacks 1530–1880* (Bloomington, Ind., 1980), esp. chs. 4 and 5.

[3] Wordsworth had hoped that 'this most rotten branch of human shame . . . Would fall together with its parent tree' (see *The Prelude*, x. 224–6).

as leaving a legacy that would work for blacks in the future.[4] By contrast, this anonymous woman occupies the margins of history. In his later revisions to the sonnet, Wordsworth subjected her to a campaign of what Frantz Fanon calls 'lactification'—whitening— while at the same time, paradoxically, orientalizing her.[5] By 1827 her 'gaudy' dress has become 'brilliant', and by 1845 she is 'spotless' and 'white-robed'. Perhaps Wordsworth was recollecting a celebrated icon of feminine *négritude*, Marie-Guilhelmine Benoist's gravely dignified, bare-breasted *Portrait d'une négresse* (originally exhibited in the Paris Salon in 1800).[6] But in 1827 Wordsworth also rewrote the closing lines of his sonnet to suggest a residual capacity for revolt at odds with her apparent meekness:

[4] 'Thou hast left behind | Powers that will work for thee . . . Thy friends are exultations, agonies, | And love, and Man's unconquerable mind' ('To Toussaint L'Ouverture', ll. 9–14).

[5] Fanon uses the term 'lactification' apropos of the black Antillean woman's destructive internalization of the desire for whiteness: 'What Mayotte wants is a kind of lactification. For, in a word, the race must be whitened; every woman in Martinique knows this, says it, repeats it'. See *Black Skin, White Masks* (1952), trans. Charles Lam Markmann (London, 1986), hereafter cited as *BSWM*, 47; the reference is to Mayotte Capécia's *Je suis Martiniquaise* (1948). For a contestation of Fanon's account in relation to the economic and social conditions of black Antillean women (Capécia works as a laundress), see Lola Young, 'Missing Persons: Fantasising Black Women in *Black Skin, White Masks*', in Alan Read (ed.), *The Fact of Blackness: Frantz Fanon and Visual Representation* (London, 1996), 89–94.

[6] It is not known whether Wordsworth actually saw Benoist's painting in the 1820s, when his sonnet underwent its first significant revisions. Benoist's magnificent portrait, in the manner of David, had been painted in the period between the emancipation of the slaves of the French Antilles in the mid-1790s and the subsequent restoration of slavery in 1802; her black woman is a *citoyenne* and her bare breast is emblematic of Liberty herself, but, although lustrous, she is not dressed as a woman of fashion; compare Anne-Louis Girodet's contemporary *Portrait of Jean-Baptiste Belley* (1797), in full European dress. See Hugh Honour, *The Image of the Black in Western Art*, iv. *From the American Revolution to World War I* (2 vols., Cambridge, Mass., 1989), ii. 7–8 (fig. 2) and i. 104–6 (fig. 55). Benoist's portrait remained in her own hands for two decades until it was acquired by the crown for the museum of contemporary French art in the Luxembourg in 1818, and then transferred to the Louvre after her death in 1826; it was reproduced in an engraving in 1829. Wordsworth might have seen it either in the Louvre or as a print. One contemporary reviewer—presumably recalling the bloody history of Santo Domingo's black uprising against the whites—referred satirically to the sitter's pride 'Après une pareille horreur!', while observing of Benoist's aesthetics of *négritude*, 'C'est une main blanche et jolie | Qui nous a fait cette *noirceur*' (see ibid. ii. 12).

Meanwhile those eyes retained their tropic fire,
Which, burning independent of the mind,
Joined with the lustre of her rich attire
To mock the outcast—O ye Heavens, be kind!
And feel, thou Earth, for this afflicted Race![7]

The sonnet's ocular siting of the spirit of independence in an imagined interiority ('her eyes . . . burning independent of the mind') joins with the class connotations of her dress 'To mock the Outcast' (ironizing her real or apparent submission). Toussaint's unconquerable mind has been relocated in the ambiguous elsewhere of the tropical eye, out of mind, but not quite out of sight.

Wordsworth's sonnet can be read as projecting on to a black woman a white male writer's post-Revolutionary malaise—loss of hope, feminization, powerlessness. His successive revisions register the shifting iconography and meanings of blackness during the post-Revolutionary period; blackness as freedom gives way to blackness as mockery of betrayed political ideals. Exoticism, displaced from skin to lustrous clothes, is now to be glimpsed in the darkness of an eye that signifies racial otherness. The outcast of the 1820s is less than tame, yet it is Wordsworth (not her) who keeps the fires of revolt burning in the distant tropics. What price a defiance relegated to the unconscious, or located in Freud's notorious 'dark continent' of femininity? And what would it take, by contrast, to envisage a form of black female insurgence located in the mind of the colonial subject, as well as in the poet's eye—in other words, one that posed a challenge to the colonial gaze that holds her firmly captive? These are questions asked by Fanon, for whom the black male Antillean is similarly tamed and mocked by the pathological internalization of whiteness, or by what he calls the 'epidermalization' of blackness, its projection on to the skin.[8] When blackness is reflected off whiteness (as Fanon famously argues), whiteness becomes the measure of black subjectivity. In *Black Skin, White Masks* (1952), Fanon's

---

[7] See Wordsworth, *Poems, in Two Volumes*, 162 app. crit.

[8] Fanon writes of the colonial's so-called 'inferiority complex' as 'the outcome of a double process:—primarily economic;—subsequently, the internalization—or, better, the epidermalization—of this inferiority' (*BSWM* 13).

analysis of the psychic effects of colonial domination include their corrosive effects on himself. 'The fact of blackness' (the title he gives to his explosively autobiographical fifth chapter) only became traumatically visible to him on his arrival in metropolitan France. But Fanon's masculinist focus contains a notorious blind spot; as for the woman of colour, he writes, in a controversial back-handed disclaimer, 'I know nothing about her.'[9] Or rather, Fanon attributes to black and mulatto women the desire both to be white and to have a light-skinned man. This identification with whiteness is what he intends by the derogatory term 'lactification'.[10] Doubly patho-logized by the white look and by the woman of colour, Fanon's black Antillean loses his masculinity along with his mind.

I want to leave aside the debate over Fanon's (mis)appropria-tion of the Lacanian dialectics of desire and misrecognition in his account of the colonial other.[11] Instead, I will be asking whether Fanon's account of racial trauma might best be served, not by the more familiar term 'identification', but by the term 'projection', both in its psychoanalytic sense of casting out unwanted parts of the self, and with the connotation of projection on to a surface such as skin.[12] Madness, according to Lacan (in a formulation

[9] Ibid. 180. By contrast, Fanon does explore white women's fantasies of rape by a black man, drawing on the work of Helene Deutsch and Marie Bonaparte (ibid. 178–9).

[10] 'I shall attempt to grasp the living reactions of the woman of color to the European. First of all, there are two such women: the Negress and the mulatto. The first has only one possibility and one concern: to turn white. The second wants not only to turn white but also to avoid slipping back. What indeed could be more illogical than a mulatto woman's acceptance of a Negro husband?' (ibid. 54).

[11] For an account of Fanon's relation to issues of identity and identification, see Homi K. Bhabha, 'Interrogating Identity: Frantz Fanon and the Postcolonial Prerogative', in *The Location of Culture* (London and New York, 1994), 40–65; for the 'primal scenes' of *Black Skin, White Masks*, see Bhabha, 'Interrogating Identity', 75–84. For mis-recognition and identity in relation to Fanon's (mis)reading of Lacan, see also Stuart Hall, 'The After-Life of Frantz Fanon', in Read (ed.), *The Fact of Blackness*, 13–37.

[12] For an acute discussion of Fanon in terms of identification and identificatory processes, see Diana Fuss, 'Interior Colonies: Frantz Fanon and the Politics of Identification,' in *Identification Papers* (New York and London, 1995), 141–72. For a different account of Fanon that derives from Freud's account of the bodily ego as the projection of a surface, see Kaja Silverman, *The Threshold of the Visible World* (New York and London, 1996), 26–31. For an especially relevant discussion of the psy-choanalysis of race in terms of object relations, see M. Fakhry Davids, 'Frantz Fanon: The Struggle for Inner Freedom', *Free Associations*, 6 (1996), 205–34.

approvingly cited by Fanon in his unpublished medical thesis), shadows freedom as its companion.[13] I will be considering two novels involving racial trauma in which melancholia and madness shadow black women's struggle for freedom and recognition. Both novels engage with the argument of *Black Skin, White Masks* by enlisting psychoanalytic or proto-psychoanalytic discourses in order to understand the psychic effects of slavery, and both focus on the immediate or lasting after-effects of the French Revolution for French colonial subjects. But they occupy very different historical and political positions, and they envisage radically different kinds of agency for black women. And their authors happen to be white. The first novel, Claire de Duras's *Ourika* (composed in 1821, published in 1823) anticipates by more than a century Fanon's critique of the internalization of whiteness by the black colonial subject, giving a specifically racial aetiology to its heroine's melancholia.[14] Duras's central figure is a black Senegalese woman, as imagined by a white woman who had lived through the French Revolution as both exile and emigrée. The second novel, André Schwarz-Bart's *A Woman Named Solitude* (1972; in French, *La Mulâtresse Solitude*—a title that emphasizes the heroine's *métisse* status) was written by a Jewish writer in the wake of the Holocaust.[15] Juxtaposing madness with the struggle for freedom, it retells the story of a mulatto slave woman involved in the doomed uprising against the reimposition of slavery on Guadeloupe in 1802, when women fought alongside men in the struggle against the

[13] 'Madness, far from being an "insult" to freedom, is his most faithful companion, following him like its shadow' (*La Causalité essentialle de la folie*, cited by Fanon in his medical thesis); see Françoise Vergès, 'Chains of Madness, Chains of Colonialism', in Read (ed.), *The Fact of Blackness*, 50 and n. For the psychoanalytic discourses on which Fanon drew, see Vergès, 'Chains of Madness', 47–55, and 'To Cure and to Free: The Fanonian Project of "Decolonized Psychiatry" ', in Lewis R. Gordon, T. Denean Sharpley-Whiting, and Renée T. White (eds.), *Fanon: A Critical Reader* (Oxford, 1996), 85–99.

[14] Claire de Duras, *Ourika*, trans. John Fowles, introd. Joan DeJean and Margaret Waller (New York, 1994), cited hereafter as *O*; subsequent page references in the text are to this edition and (in French), to Claire de Duras, *Ourika*, introd. Joan DeJean and Margaret Waller (New York, 1994). I find that I am not the first to have noticed this parallel; see David O'Connell, '*Ourika*: Black Face, White Mask', *French Review*, 47 (1974), 47–56.

[15] André Schwarz-Bart, *A Woman Named Solitude*, trans. Ralph Manheim, introd. Arnold Rampersad (San Franscisco, 1985), cited hereafter as *WNS*; subsequent references in the text are to this edition.

reoccupying Napoleonic (and formerly Republican) black and white troops. The dialogue between Duras's melancholic Ourika and Schwarz-Bart's *mulâtresse* unpacks the historical and political implications of Wordsworth's sonnet, providing an implicit commentary on Fanon's account of the Antillean woman. But these novels do more than view the French Revolution through the lens of slavery; they speak to the limits and possibilities of the transracial imaginary at specific historical moments.

Claire de Duras experienced the French Revolutionary period from her own position as a liberal aristocrat. Her father, a Girondist, had initially supported the Revolution, but was executed in 1793. Her Creole mother came from the wealthy slavocracy of Martinique, where mother and daughter fled during the Terror to recover their fortune. While living in exile in London, Duras married a royalist, resuming the life of a literary intellectual in France when her husband became a court official under the Restoration. In the early 1820s, she told the story of Ourika to her progressive literary salon.[16] Her heroine is based on a black child brought from Senegal by its enlightened Governor, the Chevalier de Boufflers, and presented to a friend, the Princess de Beauvau (the girl died at 16 of a mysterious illness). Duras's Ourika, rescued from slavery as a 2 year old after her mother's death, is similarly raised as the surrogate daughter of a cultivated French princess, under whose protection she survives the Revolution. But the novel's buried premiss is the reinstitution of slavery in 1802 and the spectre of miscegenation that haunted the Napoleonic racist imaginary and subsequent nineteenth-century fantasies of racial mixing.[17] Although Ourika participates in the culture of

[16] See Françoise Massardier-Kenney, 'Duras, Racism, and Class', in Doris Y. Kadish and Françoise Massardier-Kenney (eds.), *Translating Slavery: Gender and Race in French Women's Writing, 1783–1823* (Kent, Oh., 1994), 185–93.

[17] See Fanon for a representative quotation from the modern, eugenic version of this premiss: 'Under no conditions did [the white man] wish any intimacy between the races, for it is a truism that "crossings between widely different races can lower the physical and mental level . . . Until we have a more definite knowledge of the effect of race-crossings we shall certainly do best to avoid crossings between widely different races"' (*BSWM* 120); Fanon is quoting from a paper by Jon Alfred Mjoen, 'Harmonic and Disharmonic Race-Crossings', given at the Second International Congress of Eugenics in 1921 (see *BSWM* 120 n.). For the cultural history of race theory,

her adoptive class, she is banned from marriage and denied the possibility of reproductive life. Ostensibly, she succumbs to the isolation of being a black among aristocratic whites. But her melancholia stages an ambiguous revolt, and when she takes the veil at the end of the novel her seeming submission could also be read as containing a potential for resistance. Miming blackness, she uses a traditional symbol (that of Fanon's Algerian women) to pack a potentially revolutionary weapon.[18] But her melancholia also raises questions about history and its repetitions. The doctor to whom Ourika relates her story before she dies declares: 'It's the past we must cure.' The legacy of colonialism in the wake of the French Revolution—Duras implies—is the uncured malady from which she suffers.

A Woman Named Solitude, written 150 years later, was envisaged as one of a series of collaborative novels by André Schwarz-Bart and his wife, the black Guadeloupean writer Simone Schwarz-Bart; the series aimed to span the history of Guadeloupe from the colonial period to the France of the 1950s. *A Woman Named Solitude* followed the coauthored *A Plate of Pork with Green Bananas* (*Un plat de porc aux bananes vertes*, 1967), dedicated to Aimé Césaire and Elie Wiesel, as well as Schwarz-Bart's controversial Pris Goncourt-winning novel, *The Last of the Just* (*Le Dernier des justes*, 1959)—a bitterly ironic, deeply affecting chronicle of the sufferings of European Jewry from medieval times to the gas chambers.[19] The

---

miscegenation, eugenics, and attempts to reappropriate 'hybridity' for contemporary post-colonial theory and cultural criticism, see Robert J. C. Young, *Colonial Desire: Hybridity in Theory, Culture and Race* (London and New York, 1995), esp. 22–8; for the fantasy of miscegenation, see ibid. 142–58.

[18] For the ambiguities of veiling and the wearing of Western dress by Muslim women in Algeria, see Fuss, *Identification Papers*, 149–53.

[19] For Schwarz-Bart's continuing preoccupation with the Shoah, and his view of *A Plate of Pork with Green Bananas* as relating the Jewish Holocaust to slavery and the Middle Passage, see Ronnie Scharfman, 'Exiled from the Shoah: André and Simone Schwarz-Bart's *Un plat de porc aux bananes vertes*', in Lawrence D. Kritzman (ed.), *Auschwitz and After: Race, Culture, and 'the Jewish Question' in France* (New York and London, 1995), 250–63. For a joint consideration of André Schwarz-Bart's and Simone Schwarz-Bart's Caribbean writings, see Fanta Toureh, *L'Imaginaire dans l'œuvre de Simone Schwarz-Bart* (Paris, 1986). For the controversy surrounding *The Last of the Just*, see Francine Kaufmann, *Pour relire Le Dernier des justes* (Paris, 1986), 13–28.

story of Ernie Levy, unsung hero of the Nazi genocide, personifies the historical fate of a modern, unbelieving, Jew.[20] *A Woman Named Solitude* is also a historical novel. In its lyrical opening movement, the story of a young aristocratic woman, Bayangumay, recapitulates the rhythms of village life by the Gambia river, with its water-based agriculture and intricate belief-systems. History intrudes on this lost paradise in the form of the African slave-trade (indigenous and colonial) and the nightmare of the Middle Passage. The novel's central figure is Bayangumay's racially mixed daughter, the 'mulâtresse Solitude' whose capture and execution after the slave uprising of 1802 is recorded in histories of Guadeloupe.[21] Where Ourika falls ill of the Romantic malady of her time and place, Solitude grows up to be a zombie (the Antillean term used to describe her depersonalization under slavery). Her racial division is symbolized by mismatched eyes, one black, one green. Abandoned by her black mother on account of her mixed blood, cast off by the white Guadeloupean slavocracy that alternately pampers and neglects her, Solitude lives her *métissage* as psychic splitting. But, by the end of the novel, she has become an agent in black Guadeloupe's history of revolt.[22] When the novel compares the last stand of the slaves of Guadeloupe in 1802 to the Warsaw Ghetto uprising of 1943, it makes both uprisings inaugurating moments in a common struggle for freedom that leaves its

[20] Two later Guadeloupean novels by Simone Schwarz-Bart, *The Bridge of Beyond* (*Pluie et vent sur Télumée Miracle* (1972)) and *Between Two Worlds* (*Ti-Jean l'horizon* (1979)), draw on the rich fabric of Guadeloupian life and oral traditions as well as mythic links to Africa. See Marie-Denise Shelton, 'Women Writers of the French-Speaking Caribbean: An Overview', in Selwyn R. Cudjoe (ed.), *Caribbean Women Writers* (Wellesley, Mass., 1990), 354–6.

[21] See Oruno Lara, *La Guadeloupe dans l'histoire* (Paris, 1921), 138. For a detailed account of the events of 1802, see Jacques Adélaïde-Merlande, *Delgrès, ou, la Guadeloupe en 1802* (Paris, 1986). For the larger history of black women under Caribbean slavery to which Solitude's story belongs, see Arlette Gautier, *Les Sœurs de Solitude: la condition féminine dans l'esclave aux Antilles du xviiième au xixième siècle* (Paris, 1985), esp. 220–57. For an overview of the Caribbean during the Revolutionary period, see Jan Rogozinski, *A Brief History of the Caribbean* (New York and Oxford, 1992), 140–73.

[22] See *BSWM* 217–18, for the Hegelian aspect of this struggle for recognition, and Hall in Read (ed.), *The Fact of Blackness*, 28–9.

mark on the landscape as the trace of an otherwise inaccessible historical trauma.[23]

In the argument over Fanon's vexed relation to psychoanalysis (his progressive Lacanification by contemporary theorists), we shouldn't forget his statement that 'only a psychoanalytic interpretation of the black problem can lay bare [its] anomalies of affect'.[24] 'The Fact of Blackness' is notable for taking the doctor as his own patient; Fanon's phenomenological case-histories draw on both fiction and autobiography.[25] Despite his critique of Octave Mannoni's thesis about the dependency complex of the black colonial subject (the so-called 'Prospero complex'), Fanon insists on the affective anomalies actually produced by colonialism in himself and others, while holding out the possibility of a 'cure' represented by the struggle for political and social change.[26]

---

[23] I am indebted to Bella Brodzki, 'Nomadism and the Textualization of Memory in André Schwarz-Bart's *La Mulâtresse Solitude*', *Yale French Studies*, 83 (1993), 213–30, for her account of Schwarz-Bart's attempt to textualize the double histories of slavery and the Warsaw Ghetto uprising; Brodzki points especially to the fact that *A Woman Named Solitude* has proved difficult to accommodate within existing literary paradigms (writing by Caribbean women on the one hand, Holocaust studies on the other), emphasizing its challenge to cultural stereotyping and its allegorical representation of colonial dispossession and *dépaysement*.

[24] 'What is important in phenomenology, is less the study of a large number of instances than the intuitive and deep understanding of a few individual cases' (*BSWM* 10). Apropos of Lacan, Fanon cites Germaine Geux's *La Névrose d'abandon* (1950) on the privileging of the idea of psychic structure: 'embracing unconscious psychic life, as we are able to know it in part, especially in the form of repression and inhibition, insofar as these elements take an active part in the organization peculiar to each psychic individuality' (ibid. 80).

[25] 'What matters for us is not to collect facts and behaviour, but to find their meaning. Here we can refer to Jaspers, when he wrote "Comprehension in depth of a single instance will often enable us, phenomenologically, to apply this understanding in general to innumerable cases" ' (*BSWM* 168 and n.). For Fanon's relation to contemporary psychoanalysis and existential phenomenology, see also Lewis R. Gordon, 'The Black and the Body Politic: Fanon's Existential Phenomenological Critique of Psychoanalysis', in Gordon *et al.* (eds.), *Fanon: A Critical Reader*, 74–84.

[26] Fanon observes: 'As a psychoanalyst, I should help my patient to become *conscious* of his unconscious and abandon his attempts at a hallucinatory whitening, but also to act in the direction of a change in the social structure' (*BSWM* 100). Fanon argues against the well-known thesis of Octave Mannoni's *Psychologie de la colonisation* (1950)—'The So-Called Dependency Complex of Colonized Peoples'—in ch. 4 of *Black Skin, White Masks* (83–108).

History, for him, is never simply the referent of the unconscious. Rather, he points to the existence of collective cultural and historical trauma in the face of colonialism, foregrounding the issue of representation. The importance of *Black Skin, White Masks* lies in locating the 'racial epidermal schema' in the multiple displacements of psychic reality that are enacted in dreams and projected on to the skin.[27] *Ourika* and *A Woman Named Solitude* involve a similar impingement of collective racial trauma on the individual's psychic skin.[28] Where Duras provides an anticipatorily Fanonian account of the black female subject's internal mirroring of the gaze of French metropolitan colonialism, Schwarz-Bart makes the slave return a divisive (even derisive) look on the colonialist. Freud argues that the breaching of the protective shield activates the defensive use of projection, the mechanism which plays such a major role in psychic life.[29] This defensive casting out (the basis for the elaborated Kleinian concept of projective identification) allows for a rereading of Fanon's racial epidermal schema in a way that crosses the boundaries of psyche and history, individual pathology and external event. But it may also suggest another, more benign form of projective identification, one that lends itself to communication, understanding, and even empathy—perhaps to thought itself. To put one's thoughts into someone else is not just to refind the (colonial) self reflected in the elsewhere of another's eye. The trans-racial imaginary enables a more radical displacement; we not only read with different

[27] Even when Fanon reads the terrifying black dream-images of the colonial unconscious as references to the actual use of black Senegalese soldiers and policemen to terrorize French colonial subjects, the penis is not just a rifle (see ibid. 106).

[28] In a well-known passage from *Beyond the Pleasure Principle* (1920), Freud refers figuratively to trauma as a breach in the organism's protective shield (its psychic skin): 'We describe as "traumatic" any excitations from outside which are powerful enough to break through the protective shield. It seems to me that the concept of trauma necessarily implies a connection of this kind with a breach in an otherwise efficacious barrier against stimuli' (*SE* xviii. 29).

[29] Freud suggests that there is a tendency to treat internal excitations 'as though they were acting, not from the inside, but from the outside, so that it may be possible to bring the shield against stimuli into operation as a means of defence against them. This is the origin of *projection*, which is destined to play such a large part in the causation of pathological processes' (*SE* xviii. 29).

eyes, but read one historical trauma in and through another, glimpsing the connection between two diasporas (African and Jewish) that have shaped modern consciousness on both sides of the (Black) Atlantic.[30]

This, This is Solitude!

Etre 'l'autre', ou pire encore, n'avoir sa place nulle part, c'est se sentir dans une solitude effroyable et totalement impuissant en face d'elle. On ne saurait assez tenir compte de l'intensité de souffrance qui accompagne de tels états d'abandon . . . (Germaine Geux)[31]

Fanon draws on Geux's *La Névrose d'abandon* to express the anguish of abandonment experienced by the racial 'other'.[32] Duras anticipates both of them when she uses a line from Byron's *Childe Harold* as her epigraph to *Ourika*: 'This is to be alone, this, this is solitude!' (*Childe Harold*, ii. 234). In the absence of other beings 'with kindred consciousness endued', the Byronic solitary is doomed to misunderstanding. Stripped of its transgressiveness, Byronic solitude becomes a diffuse form of exilic melancholy. Apropos of her reluctance to publish, Duras confessed that 'mes livres aiment la solitude', collapsing heroine, novel, and author.[33]

[30] See Paul Gilroy, *The Black Atlantic: Modernity and Double Consciousness* (Cambridge, Mass., 1993), 205–23 for an exploration of the linkage of Jewish and African diasporas within modernity. Gilroy's project—'to set the Holocaust of European Jews in a provocative relationship with the modern history of racial slavery and terror in the western hemisphere' (217)—is strikingly embodied by a contemporary Caribbean novelist such as Caryl Phillips, whose *The Nature of Blood* (1997) links the story of European Jewry in the early modern period to the plot of Othello, and a contemporary Holocaust narrative to the emergence of the modern Jewish state with its meeting of European and African ethnicities.

[31] Germaine Geux, *La Névrose d'abandon* (Paris, 1950), 36.

[32] For Fanon's extensive quotations and citations of Geux, see *BSWM* 73–80. Geux is articulating the 'abandonment-neurosis' of those rejected in early childhood rather than those who have experienced a specifically racial trauma.

[33] See G. Pailhès, *La Duchesse de Duras et Chateaubriand d'après des documents inédits* (Paris, 1910), 290; cited by Kari Weil in her illuminating and psychoanalytically informed study of Chateaubriand's *René* and Duras's *Ourika*, 'Romantic Exile and the Melancholia of Identification', *Differences*, 7 (1995), 111–26.

Ourika compares her wasted life to that of the flower in Gray's *Elegy*, 'born to blush unseen | And waste its sweetness on the desert air' (O 41)—in the French original, an allusion to a foreign flower, 'la fleur du poète anglais, qui perdait son parfum dans le désert' (O 40–1; Gray's unseen flower is not only spared sway over the rod of empire, but deprived of the opportunity to be a revolutionary). In her use of foreign poetic fragments to evoke Ourika's isolation as a black woman among whites, Duras adds yet another layer of translation to her cultural displacement.[34] As Fanon puts it apropos of the black Antillean's relation to literary language, 'In France one says, "He talks like a book." In Martinique, [one says] "He talks like a white man." '[35] Ourika talks like a book *and* like a white woman; this is the sign of her colonization. But, in the end, her racial consciousness eludes translation. Duras herself wrote of literary translation, 'What is beautiful in a work is precisely what is least translatable . . . A translation is like a disguise through which one attempts to recognize someone . . .'[36] John Fowles, the novel's modern translator, gives an unexpected spin to this scene of recognition when he traces the mysterious, black-clad Sarah in *The French Lieutenant's Woman* back to an unwitting recollection of Ourika ('an image of a woman standing with her back to me. She was in black, and her stance had a disturbing mixture of both rejection and accusation . . . a woman who had been unfairly exiled from society'). But, he goes on, the realization of 'who that woman really was' shockingly revealed his own veiled colour prejudice: 'The woman in my mind

---

[34] For Duras's interest in translation and its relation to instabilities of identity and difference, see Françoise Messardier-Kenney in Kadish and Messardier-Kenney (eds.), *Translating Slavery*, 188. For the melancholia of translation as 'the trauma of [the work of art] being cut off from itself', a trauma that can equally affect a text or a life, see Nicolas Abraham, *Rhythms: On the Work, Translation, and Psychoanalysis*, trans. Benjamin Thigpen and Nicholas T. Rand (Stanford, Calif., 1995), 151.

[35] BSWM 21. Cf. Fanon's insistence on the cultural mastery acquired through use of the tool of metropolitan French in the Antilles: 'To speak a language is to take on a world, a culture' (ibid. 38); so much so that 'a black man who quotes Montesquieu had better be watched' (ibid. 35).

[36] See Pailhès, *La Duchesse de Duras et Chateaubriand d'après des documents inédits*, 280; a letter of 1824, cited by Françoise Messardier-Kenney in *Translating Slavery*, 188.

who would not turn had black clothes but a white face' (*O* xxx). Fowles calls Duras's novel 'the first serious attempt by a white novelist to enter a black mind'. In this connection, we might recall that the denouement of *The French Lieutenant's Woman* turns on the sexual penetration of a woman's body by a man named Charles (the name of the man Ourika loves). Fanon's emphasis on the sexualization of the black subject in relation to the white colonial gaze serves to underscore Fowles's language of fictional forced entry. Perhaps any act of cultural translation involves an element of penetrative appropriation; racial difference itself can be thought of as involving a linguistic register.[37] The question to be asked of Duras's novel, however, is whether the limits of its author's liberalism become apparent when its black-veiled Ourika succumbs to Duras's own post-Revolutionary melancholia; or whether the mimicry that subjects the black colonial subject to the disciplining gaze of colonial surveillance can also serve to displace it.[38]

Duras tells a proto-Fanonian story of the projection of 'blackness' on to skin colour by a society obsessed with its own whiteness. The melancholia that transforms Ourika's blackness into a psychic condition also refuses the pseudo-normality enjoined on her by her society. This would entail acceptance of her 'natural'—read 'social'—destiny as a black woman (that is, her reproductive exclusion from white society). Fanon writes of a violent 'hemorrhage that spattered [his] whole body with black

---

[37] For Fanon's own complex relation to translation as a French-speaking Antillean working in Europe and Algeria, and the importance he attached to speech in relation to subjectivity, see Fuss, *Identification Papers*, 161–4. For a critique of Fowles's own translation-practice in *Ourika* as a mistranslation of Duras's 'voice' (and for a critique of his novel as a male-centred appropriation of Ourika's story), see Doris Y. Kadish, 'Rewriting Women's Stories: *Ourika* and the *French Lieutenant's Woman*', *South Atlantic Review*, 62 (1997), 74–87.

[38] For the shifting theory and politics of masquerade and mimicry in colonial as well as feminist discourse, see ibid. 142–54. For camouflage, mimicry, and the double articulation of difference, see Homi K. Bhabha, 'Of Mimicry and Man: The Ambivalence of Colonial Discourse', in *The Location of Culture*, 85–92; for an innovative account of mimetic strategies of performance and displacement, see also Michael T. Taussig, *Mimesis and Alterity: A Particular History of the Senses* (New York and London, 1993).

blood' when he confronted the French obsession with colour for the first time, seeing himself through its eyes as an object of phobogenic desire and fear. His bodily coherence disintegrates, returning to him in the guise of an inchoate melancholic object accompanied by a litany of hatred: 'My body was given back to me sprawled out, distorted, recolored, clad in mourning in that white winter day. The Negro is an animal, the Negro is bad, the Negro is mean, the Negro is ugly . . .'[39] At the start of *Ourika*, a young doctor narrates how he was called to attend a sick nun. Amidst the vaulted arches and illegible tombstones of a half-destroyed religious building, he sees a figure veiled in black. Expecting to find 'a new victim of the convent system' (recently restored by Napoleon, but still bearing the scars of its recent dismantling), he prepares to sympathize with a tale of injustice. But when she turns round, 'I had a strange shock. I was looking at a negress' (*O* 4). This moment of shock anticipates other moments in the novel when incompatible thoughts and feelings are brought into sudden juxtaposition with each other: whiteness and blackness, sexuality and racial prejudice, reproduction and mis-cegenation; or—as here—sympathy and estrangement. The effect is not so much a reversal of expectation, but rather the unexpected breaching of a protective layer of unknowing. Typically, such shocks occur when a figure with privileged knowledge reveals the existence of the racist 'real' foreclosed by Ourika's internalization of white aristocratic culture.

In this opening scene, Ourika is a study in white on an all-black ground: 'The sole things that gave light to her face were her extraordinary large and luminous eyes and her dazzlingly white teeth . . . She showed every sign of having suffered from prolonged melancholia' (*O* 4). What are we to make of this luminous interior whiteness? During a series of interviews with the young doctor, Ourika calls her history one of extravagance, unreason, and unhappiness; hers, she tells him, is a self-imposed pathology. Understood differently, her health has been destroyed by the

---

[39] *BSWM* 112–13. Cf. Fakhry Davids, 'Frantz Fanon', 228–9 for the case of a young black child who similarly lodges his bad feelings in his skin colour.

history of French colonialism. Ourika experiences her blackness
as a violent and traumatic imposition played out, not at the peri-
phery, but in metropolitan France, just as Fanon turns black when
he sees himself through the eyes of French cinema-goers.[40] Her
racialization takes place via similar scenes of public 'screening'. As
a child, she sits in oriental costume at the feet of a woman whom
everybody feels they resemble when in her company. The princess
educates her black Galatea as a daughter of the Enlightenment,
telling her that she is angelic and skin-colour irrelevant: 'I didn't
regret being black, I was told I was an angel. There was nothing
to warn me that the color of my skin might be a disadvantage'
(O 9). But Ourika's *négritude* is destined to play the role of
black supplement to white colonial society. The slave-child on
whom Duras based her story had been acquired as an exotic gift
(among other gifts from Africa such as parakeets, sultan hens,
and ostriches).[41] Duras shows how orientalism serves to enrich
Western culture's view of itself by means of an ethnographic
allegory in which the adolescent Ourika plays the part of Africa:

Mme de B. often praised what she considered my natural grace and she
had had me taught to dance to perfection. To show this talent of mine
to the world she gave a ball—ostensibly for her grandsons, but really to
display me, much to my advantage, in a quadrille symbolizing the four
corners of the globe. I was to represent Africa. Travellers were asked for
advice, books of costumes were ransacked, and learned tomes on African
music consulted. At last a *comba*—the national dance of my country
[Senegal]—was chosen. My partner covered his face in a mask of black
crepe, a disguise I did not need. (O 10)

Trained as a 'natural' dancer, Ourika is unmasked as an instinct-
ive actress. Her dance 'consisted of stately steps broken by various
poses, describing love, grief, triumph, and despair. I was totally
ignorant of such violent emotions, but some instinct taught me

---

[40] 'I cannot go to a film without seeing myself. I wait for me. In the interval, just
before the film starts, I wait for me. The people in the theater are watching me,
examining me, waiting for me. A Negro groom is going to appear. My heart makes
my head swim' (BSWM 140); for the negro as a phobogenic object of anxiety and
desire, see ibid. 151.

[41] See Massardier-Kenney in *Translating Slavery*, 189.

to mimic their effects. I short, I triumphed' (O 11).[42] Her dance—
the triumph of mimicry over essence—is really an allegory of
Western civilization's need to represent itself, to itself, through
such spectacles of colonial encounter and subjugation.[43]

Applauded for acting unstudied 'African' effects and affects,
Ourika holds up a flattering image designed to consolidate the
class and racial privilege of *la nation* in the post-Revolutionary
period.[44] Reared to reflect its imperial riches, she also serves as
the bearer of its nostalgia for instinctual life. Duras uses the image
of scales falling from Ourika's eyes to convey the effect of her
access to traumatic racial and sexual knowledge. As she works
on a miniature behind a lacquer screen, Ourika overhears 'a
certain marquise, a bleakly practical lady with an incisive mind,
and frank to the point of dryness' (O 11) taking the princess to
task about Ourika's future: 'She's talented, unusual, has ease of
manner. But what next? To come to the point—what do you
intend doing with her?' (O 12). The princess replies sadly, 'I love
her as if she were my own daughter. I'd do anything to make her
happy. And yet—the more seriously I think about it, the further
away a solution seems. I see the poor girl alone, always alone

[42] In *Identification Papers*, Fuss writes of the colonized subject as 'commanded to
imitate the coloniser's version of their essential difference' (146); Fuss follows Bhabha
in pointing to the ways in which mimicry—understood 'not as a tactic of dissent
but as a condition of domination'—reinscribes the elusive but effective techniques
of *trompe-l'œil*, irony, mimicry, and repetition by which colonial authority is exer-
cised; see Bhabha, *The Location of Culture*, 85.

[43] Cf. Michael Taussig's account of the dancing British tar on Darwin's *Beagle*
voyage as a representation of civilization's need for 'a savage mirror' and its staging
of a ' "space between," a space permeated by the colonial tension of mimesis and
alterity, in which it is far from easy to say who is the imitator and who is the
imitated, which is copy and which is original' (*Mimesis and Alterity*, 78).

[44] 'Like those servants who are allowed once every year to dance in the drawing
room . . .' (*BSWM* 219). There is a strange symmetry between Ourika's initiation to
her role via the dance, at puberty, and the case-history cited at length by Fanon to
illustrate the fear of imaginary negroes in a white girl which arose from listening
as a young adolescent to her ex-Colonial Service father playing records of African
music. Her hallucinations centre on circles of African dancers; an angel—at the white
doctor's suggestion—comes to her rescue in these repeated oral and visual hallucinations: 'She wanted to go away with her angel, somewhere where she would really
be at home, with her mother, her brothers, and her sisters' (ibid. 207).

in the world' (O 12). As if she has always known the emotions of
which she is supposedly ignorant, Ourika instantly understands
the true meaning of her blackness: 'Lightning does not strike more
swiftly. I comprehended all. I was black. Dependent, despised,
without fortune, without resource, without a single other being
of my kind to help me through life. All I had been until then was
a toy, an amusement for my mistress; and soon I was to be cast
out of a world that could never admit me' (O 12–13). Illumination
'strikes' like interior lightning. 'What kind of man would marry
a negress?', asks the marquise; surely, only a man of inferior
birth could be bribed to father mulatto children. The princess responds that Ourika 'still knows nothing' (presumably, nothing about
sexuality); perhaps she will rise above her fate. Wishful thinking,
replies the marquise: 'Ourika has flouted her natural destiny.
She has entered society without its permission. It will have its
revenge' (O 14). When the princess protests Ourika's innocence,
the marquise counters by accusing her of destroying Ourika's
happiness. In this sharply worded quarrel between nescience
and miscegenation, enlightened sentimentality and racist realism,
Duras allows us to see that the princess has unwittingly formed
Ourika to occupy the contradictory subject-position of the black
who defines the limits of her all-white world.

When Ourika opens her eyes to the paradox of her invisibil-
ity as a black woman, her thoughts 'fastened on [her] like furies'
('I saw myself . . . destined to be the bride of some venal "fellow"
who might condescend to get half-breed children on me', O 14–15).
Thoughts of blackness spawn themselves with the repetitive,
serial forms of traumatic representation:

Above all, it was the isolation. Had I not heard it from Mme de B.'s own
mouth—'alone, always alone in the world'? Again and again I repeated
that phrase: alone, always alone . . . Endless permutations of the same
thoughts obsessed every hour of my day. They reproduced themselves
in a thousand different shapes, and my imagination endowed them with
the darkest colors. (O 15)

Skin trauma reproduces itself in *Ourika* with 'the darkest colors'
of the mulatto babies that swarm in the miscegenist imaginary,

making its heroine's mind a breeding-ground for racial self-hatred. In *Black Skin, White Masks*, Fanon draws on Germaine Geux for his psychoanalytic account of the Martinican writer, Jean Veneuse. Writing of the 'painful and obsessive feelings of exclusion, of having no place anywhere' that result from a specifically pre-Oedipal childhood trauma, Geux introduces the psychoanalytic notion of the Other that inflects Fanon's use of the term:

'I am The Other' is an expression that I have heard time and again in the language of the abandonment-neurotic. To be 'The Other' is to feel that one is always in a shaky position, to be always on guard, ready to be rejected and . . . unconsciously doing everything needed to bring about exactly this catastrophe.

It would be impossible to overestimate the intensity of the suffering that accompanies such desertion states . . .[45]

Fanon appropriates Geux's account of the abandonment-neurotic for the black (male) colonial subject, but he has nothing (good) to say about black women. By contrast, Duras not only recapitulates the history of the slave-child's traumatic removal from her black mother in infancy, but makes Ourika's sexual and reproductive potential the central feature of her racialization.

Ourika, the unstudied actress, becomes a monkey in her own eyes—or rather, in the eyes through which she sees herself, those of the white men to whom she can only be a perverse object of desire:

My face revolted me. I no longer dared to look in a mirror. My black hands seemed like a monkey's paws. I exaggerated my ugliness to myself, and this skin color of mine seemed to me like the brand of shame. It exiled me from everyone else of my natural kind. It condemned me to be alone, always alone in the world. For the price of a dowry, a fellow might consent to have mulatto children! My whole being rose in a rage against that idea . . .

I no longer belonged anywhere. I was cut off from the entire human race. (*O* 15–16)

---

[45] Ibid. 76; cf. Geux, *La Névrose d'abandon*, 35–6, whose so-called 'abandonment-neurotic' is paralysed by the frustrations and defeats of the past, cultivating a zone of disillusioned resentment alongside his sense of hopelessness (ibid. 27–8).

Duras makes Ourika's rage at her 'brand of shame' (her skin colour)
converge with the new political consciousness made available to
people of colour by the outbreak of the French Revolution: 'the
Revolution brought a change in my views of life . . . I sensed
that at the end of this great chaos I might find my true place.
When personal destiny was turned upside down, all social caste
overthrown, all prejudices had disappeared, a state of affairs
might one day come to pass where I would feel myself less exiled'
(O 19). But in the midst of talk of emancipation, her new-found
identification with the slaves of the Antilles is thrown into dis-
array by the 1791 Santo Domingo massacres, when blacks joined
in the revolutionary struggle on their own account with an out-
pouring of violence against white slave-owners:

> About this time talk started of emancipating the Negroes. Of course
> this question passionately interested me. I still cherished the illusion that
> at least somewhere else in the world there were others like myself . . .
> But alas, I soon learned my lesson. The Santo Domingo massacres gave
> me cause for fresh and heartrending sadness. Till then I had regretted
> belonging to a race of outcasts. Now I had the shame of belonging to
> a race of barbarous murderers. (O 21)

Like the nightmare of miscegenation that shadows the sexualization of the black woman, the spectre of violence emerges to
haunt Girondist sympathy with black struggles for freedom and
citizenship of the new French Republic.[46] When Ourika feels not
only 'sadness' but 'shame' at belonging to a race of murderers as
well as a race of outcasts, she has become the bearer of Duras's
conflicted Girondin sentiments. As Fanon observes, Liberty and
Justice turn out to mean white liberty and white justice.[47] The
limits of Duras's liberalism become visible at this crucial political and historical juncture.

---

[46] See Robin Blackburn, *The Overthrow of Colonial Slavery 1776–1848* (London
and New York, 1988), 161–211, for an account of events leading up to the Santo
Domingo uprising and for the French Revolution in the Antilles more generally.

[47] 'From time to time [the negro] has fought for Liberty and Justice, but these
were always white liberty and white justice; that is, values secreted by his masters'
(*BSWM* 221).

Bloodshed in the colonies allows Duras to displace the history of colonialism on to the history of the Terror: 'all the world was miserable, and I no longer felt alone . . . It was as if misfortune had strengthened all the bonds between us. Then, at least, I did not feel myself an outsider' (O 23–4). Author and character can unite in deploring revolutionary violence. At this point, symptomatically, the novel reverts to a plot of racial condescension that turns on Ourika's self-destructive passion for a white man, her childhood companion, Charles (the princess's grandson).[48] A true son of the Enlightenment, Charles claims that all suffering 'had to have some rational foundation' (O 27). But, Ourika wonders, is her suffering rational, or is it madness? 'Who can say what is or isn't rational? Is reason the same for everyone? Do we all feel the same desires?' (O 27–8). Reason and desire, she comprehends, are experienced differently according to one's racial, gendered, and ideological position.[49] As Fanon puts it, 'my unreason was countered with reason, my reason with "real reason." Every hand was a losing hand for me.'[50] Obsessed by 'the face of [an] imaginary monster' (the monster of colour prejudice), Ourika tries to render herself invisible according to the terrible ultimatum ventriloquized by Fanon, 'turn white or disappear'.[51] She removes the mirrors from her bedroom, wears gloves and dresses that hide her neck and arms, and covers her face with a large hat and a veil when she goes out ('Like a child, I shut my eyes, and supposed myself invisible', O 28).[52] Haunted by the 'sneering face'

[48] Cf. Fanon's account of the 'lactified' woman of colour, based on Mayotte Capécia's Je suis Martiniquaise (1948) in ch. 2 of Black Skin, White Masks; see also Lola Young in Read (ed.), The Fact of Blackness, 89–94.

[49] Ventriloquizing his own intellectual and emotional vicissitudes in the face of white racism, Fanon recalls: 'I had rationalized the world and the world had rejected me on the basis of color prejudice. Since no agreement was possible on the level of reason, I threw myself back toward unreason. It was up to the white man to be more irrational than I. Out of the necessities of my struggle I had chosen the method of regression, but the fact remained that it was an unfamiliar weapon; here I am at home; I am made of the irrational; I wade in the irrational. Up to the neck in the irrational. And how my voice vibrates!' (BSWM 123).

[50] Ibid. 132.   [51] Ibid. 100; Fanon's italics.

[52] Cf. Fanon, who writes in a pungent footnote: 'Quite literally I can say without any risk of error that the Antillean who goes to France in order to convince

of her society, she recognizes it as '[her] own reflection' (*O* 29), the specular image of projected and re-introjected racial (self-) hatred. The only 'angel' allowed to figure in this racial epidermal schema is the 16-year-old orphan heiress destined to be Charles's wife. Instead of being cut by the overseer's lash, Ourika has to endure laceration by Charles's words about his young bride: ' "I want a trust between us exactly like yours and mine." "*Exactly like yours and mine!*" The phrase cut deep' (*O* 31). This moment of textual mimesis reveals the complementarity of the monstrous (suffering, orphaned) Ourika and angelic (sneering, orphaned) heiress. Both are products of the binarism of racist representation, face to face in a distorting mirror where the colonized other serves as a magnet for ambivalence and monstrosity.

Duras's novel shows us how the collective trauma of slavery can be transposed on to an individual trauma of isolation, displacing the disavowed violence of the slave's uprooting from Africa on to the violence of Ourika's own reflections: 'Why wasn't it ended on that slaver from which she had been snatched—or at her mother's breast? A handful of African sand would have been enough to cover my small body . . . Nobody needed me. I was isolated from all. This terrible thought gripped me with more violence than ever before' (*O* 33). Where once she harboured rage, envy, and revenge, now Duras makes her nourish a sentimental fantasy about slavery: 'What did it matter that I might now have been the black slave of some rich planter? Scorched by the sun, I should be laboring on someone else's land. But I would have a poor hut of my own to go to at day's end; a partner in my life, children of my own race who would call me their mother . . .' (*O* 39). The slave's poor hut—the blind spot of Duras's trans-racial

himself that he is white will find his real face there' (ibid. 153 n.). Fanon's longest discussion of the mirror occurs in the famous footnote about Lacan (ibid. 161–4 n.). In Fanon's (disputed) reading of Lacan, the mirror-phase gives rise to a pathological imago (already necessarily alienated and misrecognized in Lacan's own account) with the entrance of the black man on the scene: 'the real Other for the white man is and will continue to be the black man' (ibid. 161 n.). For the black Antillean, 'perception always occurs on the level of the imaginary. It is in white terms that one perceives one's fellows' (ibid. 163 n.). For Fanon's ambivalent dialogue with Lacan and its Hegelian and Sartrean refractions, see Stuart Hall in Read (ed.), *The Fact of Blackness*, 26–9.

imaginary—is emptied of slavery's systemic violence, which takes up residence in the interior of the colonial subject. It only remains for the incisive marquise to reveal the true cause of Ourika's mysterious illness as her secret passion for Charles ('if you weren't madly in love with him, you could come perfectly well to terms with being black', *O* 42), transforming the real of racial exclusion into 'the sour by-products of a forbidden lust' (*O* 43)—just sour grapes. Fanon, at least, understands that the fantasy of marrying a white man might have as its aim 'recognition, incorporation into a group that had seemed hermetic . . . no longer the woman who wanted to be white, she was white. She was joining the white world.'[53] But Ourika's only means of 'passing' is to join a religious order, embracing the conventional ideology of sacrifice demanded of an unmarriagable (in her case, black) woman in her aristocratic society. The priest to whom she confesses her unhappy passion reinforces the angelic logic of her society's ostensible colour-blindness: 'For [God] there is neither black nor white. All hearts are equal in his eyes' (*O* 45). The novel closes with the doctor's post-mortem: *'my science proved sadly unavailing. She died at the end of October, with the last of the autumn leaves'* (*O* 47; Durras's italics). This dying fall, suffused with seasonal melancholy for the failed Revolutionary project of racial equality, contains no glimpse of a transformed future; as for Fanon, the morbid legacy of slavery constitutes an obstacle to imagining freedom.[54] But Ourika's masquerade of blackness can be read as pointing to a different diagnosis—unmasking colonial representation through the very tropes of resemblance and specularity by which (as Homi Bhabha has argued) it attempts to maintain its power.[55] Just

---

[53] *BSWM* 58.

[54] Cf. Françoise Vergès: 'Fanonian theory construes memory as a series of lifeless monuments, a morbid legacy, a melancholic nostalgia for a past long gone. There is no place for dreams, for inventing a future. Memories are shackles to progress and movement' (in Read (ed.), *The Fact of Blackness*, 62–3).

[55] Cf. Homi Bhabha: 'Mimicry conceals no presence or identity behind its mask . . . The *menace* of mimicry is its *double* vision which in disclosing the ambivalence of colonial discourse also disrupts its authority'; for Bhabha, 'the gaze of otherness . . . shares the acuity of the genealogical gaze which . . . liberates marginal elements and shatters the unity of man's being . . . the look of surveillance returns as the displacing gaze of the disciplined' (*The Location of Culture*, 88–9).

as Ourika's mimicry conceals no 'African' essence—how can one tell the mimic from the mask?—Duras' persistent, performative monkeying disturbs the reflection of the black other projected by (and in) the colonial eye during the post-Revolutionary period.

Seeing with Different Eyes

> I say that he who looks into my eyes for anything but a perpetual question will have to lose his sight; neither re-cognition nor hate. And if I cry out, it will not be a black cry.
>
> (Frantz Fanon)[56]

At the end of *Black Skin, White Masks*, Fanon asserts that the black must cease to be the slave of his historical past, attempting to detach revolution from the inherited ills of the black Antillean psyche. The ambiguous and often ironic discourse of his own mimetic anti-colonialism sidesteps the simple reversals of projection in much the same way (refusing, for instance, to return the demand for love as a look of hatred).[57] Could the unconscious resist the specular legacy of colonial oppression? Does madness open a door to a different form of racial consciousness and revolutionary agency? And what form might this outcry take, if not a specifically black cry? In Schwarz-Bart's *A Woman Named Solitude*, the heroine's mismatched eyes signify the confused racial identities generated when Africa and Europe collide in a violent sexual encounter. Solitude is a mulatto child of the *pariade*, the ritualized mass rape of black slave women which took place in mid-Atlantic a month before the slave-ships reached port. Her beautiful eyes—'eyes divided between two worlds' (*WNS* 51)—mock the colonial onlooker, refusing to return a recognizable

---

[56] Fanon is responding with oblique irony to a quotation from Sartre's *Orphée Noir*: 'What then did you expect when you unbound the gag that had muted those black mouths? That they would chant your praises? Did you think that . . . you would find adoration in their eyes?' (*BSWM* 29).

[57] See Bhabha, *The Location of Culture*, 100, for the trope of 'sly civility' in relation to the language of paranoia; see also Françoise Vergès on 'the projective past' that breaks with repetition (in Read (ed.), *The Fact of Blackness*, 640).

reflection of slave society. At times they function as angry, split-off organs of sense-perception or as an enraged form of seeing that threatens the colonial onlooker.[58] But they also become the lens for a peculiar form of authorial irony—a mode of free indirect discourse expressive both of cultural diaspora and of what Édouard Glissant calls a 'poetics of relation'. As well as being a symptom of the psychic split which slavery induces in slaves and masters alike, ocular difference—*métissage*—is the sign of an aesthetic that allows for being (as Édouard Glissant puts it) both 'there and elsewhere', and represents 'the meeting and synthesis of two differences . . . its elements diffracted and its consequences unforeseeable'.[59] Schwarz-Bart's cultural binocularity allows him (perhaps controversially) to represent the events of revolutionary Guadeloupe with one eye on the history of Jewish suffering and resistance in twentieth-century Europe, establishing what he himself refers to as 'the delicate joint . . . between slavery and the concentration camp theme'.[60]

Solitude's mother, Bayangumay, is born into an ancient confluence of African waters, 'in a calm and intricate estuary landscape,

---

[58] For the 'bizarre object' and its relation to psychotic and schizophrenic perception, see W. R. Bion 'Differentiation of the Psychotic from the Non-Psychotic Personalities' (1957), *Second Thoughts* (repr. London, 1984), 43–64.

[59] For the Caribbean viewed as 'a place of encounter and connivance', see Édouard Glissant, *Poetics of Relation*, trans. Betsy Wing (Ann Arbor, 1997), 33. Glissant continues: 'What took place in the Caribbean, which could be summed up in the word *creolization*, . . . [i]s not merely an encounter, a shock . . . [or] a *métissage*, but a new and original dimension allowing each person to be there and elsewhere, rooted and open . . .'; in particular, Antillean creolization—'limitless *métissage*'—carries 'the adventure of multilingualism' and a poetics involving the dialects of oral and written language (ibid. 34–5). Creolization characterizes the language of Simone Schwarz-Bart's Antillean novels, in marked contrast to her husband's adoption of the ironic mode of an oral historian; as Bella Brodzki points out, *A Woman Named Solitude* makes no attempt to approximate to 'le style antillais' ('Npmadism and the Textualization of Memory' 227–8). See also Françoise Lionnet, 'The Politics and Aesthetics of *Métissage*', in *Autobiographical Voices: Race, Gender, Self-Portraiture* (Ithaca, NY, and London, 1989), 1–29.

[60] Cited by Ronnie Scharfman, *Auschwitz and After*, 256; a translation of an article by Schwarz-Bart in *Le Figaro littéraire* (6 Jan. 1967). In his introduction to *A Woman Named Solitude*, Arnold Rampasad touches on its contemporary reception in 1973, when British and American reviewers questioned the appropriateness of linking the Warsaw Ghetto Uprising with Delgrès's last stand (pp. xviii–xix).

where the clear water of a river, the green water of an ocean, and
the black water of a delta channel mingled' (*WNS* 3). Promised
at her birth to an old man for whom she is the reincarnation of
her grandmother, Bayangumay also occupies a world of generational mingling, lyrical songs, and ritually resolved conflict. Not
far away is the big city on the river, once named Sigi ('Sit Down'),
now known as Sigi-Thyor ('Sit down and weep') on account of
the African slave-trade. She wakes from the timeless dream of
Diola village life to the trauma of forced migration and exile
into slavery. Bayangumay survives the dehumanization of the
Middle Passage, but tries to swallow her own tongue and has to
be tethered until her confinement. 'The métisse Solitude', we're
told by the anonymous voice of the chronicler, 'was born into
slavery about 1772 on the French island of Gaudeloupe: du Parc
plantation, commune of Carbet de Capesterre' (*WNS* 49). Named
Rosalie after a recently dead slave, she is almost white. But
'What troubled the young mother most of all was the eyes, one
dark and one light-green, as though belonging to two different
persons' (*WNS* 50; one dark for her mother's West African delta,
one for her ocean begetting). As a potentially beautiful—hence
valuable—*métisse*, this exotic hybrid is destined to be brought up
at the Big House on the plantation estate. But she refuses to nurse
at any breast beside her mother's, and suffers so excruciatingly at
the separation ('as though . . . the umbilical cord had not really
been cut', *WNS* 52) that she is returned to her mother's hut. In
spite of her mother's ambivalence and rejection, the baby crawls
to her at night and clasps her by one of her legs; by her fourth
year, 'the child was becoming weaned from her mother's body,
for now it was only the tip of her toe that she hugged and kissed'
(*WNS* 52). Her mother is the part-object for which she will ever
after yearn. Rosalie—whom the overseer finds one day admiring
her reflection in the brook after having plastered her face with
black mud—is fascinated by Man (creole for *maman*) Bobette,
Bayangumay's slave name. In her search for *négritude*, she is drawn
to her mother's African past and her still beautiful but marked,
mutilated, and prematurely aged body. What, she wonders, is the
secret of her blackness and her well-hidden defiance?

Observing her mother and an old man with a wooden leg (amputated as a punishment for a failed escape attempt), Rosalie notices how they look on at the hideous tortures of slavery without betraying any sign of insurrection. Only their eyes dart about like 'two little land crabs darting this way and that, searching, biting the air roundabout':

It was very hard to look at the world with such eyes. When you examined it coldly in this way, the claws of your eyes turned back into your head and tore it to pieces . . . Man Bobette and the peg leg always had those eyes under their inflamed eyelids, and no one on earth suspected it. Sometimes you could make out the tip of a claw in Bobette's eyes. But those of the peg leg were so well veiled, so perfectly smooth that he had not been whipped since he could remember. (WNS 59–60)

At night, however, the two plot together with 'eyes of flame, sulphur, and ashes' (WNS 61), like the furious wild woman who dies defying the atrocities of the masters as her molasses-covered skin is consumed by ants. They speak of a country that is not beyond the sea but located on the body itself, as the old man indicates, 'put[ting] down his fingernail on the black skin of his forearm in a gesture [Rosalie] had seen dozens of times in the course of her short life. It was the *color sign*, which for the whites, blacks, and mulattoes of the du Parc plantation summed up all things here below' (WNS 64–5). A detour by way of 'The Unconscious' (1915) makes it possible to link the signs of this secret resistance to the epidermal scheme of slavery and the metaphors of sight deployed both here and elsewhere in Schwarz-Bart's novel. Freud writes, apropos of the schizophrenic's speech, that references to 'bodily organs or innervations' often have a prominent place. As an example, he cites a female schizophrenic patient apparently driven mad by her lover's lies:

A patient of Tausk's, a girl who was brought to the clinic after a quarrel with her lover, complained that *her eyes were not right, they were twisted*. This she herself explained by bringing forward a series of reproaches against her lover in coherent language. 'She could not understand him at all, he looked different every time; he was a hypocrite, an eye-twister

[*Augenverdreher*, a deceiver], he had twisted her eyes; they were not her eyes any more; now she saw the world with different eyes.[61]

Freud glosses Tausk's clinical example of schizophrenic word-formation as follows: 'the patient's relation to a bodily organ (the eye) has arrogated to itself the representation of the whole content [of her thoughts] . . . it has become *"organ-speech."* '[62] Like the girl deceived by her hypocritical lover, the slave who sees the world with different eyes—accurately perceiving the (white) madness and (white) lies of slavery—goes mad because she sees things that 'tore [your head] to pieces' (*WNS* 59).

Tausk's patient goes on to complain of being suddenly jerked into position, as if she is a puppet or a doll. Her lover, she says, 'had *put her in a false position*'—further evidence for Freud of the way in which '*words* are subjected to the same process as that which makes the dream-images out of latent dream-thoughts' (i.e. primary psychical processes).[63] Schizophrenic seeing fragments not only the ego, but perception itself; there is (Freud writes) only the law of the talion ('an eye for an eye')—the law which in reality governs the world of the slave, where reprisals are taken against the body or skin of the runaway.[64] Interestingly, Freud goes on to argue that schizophrenics' cathexis of word-presentation represents a tenuous attempt to recover a lost object: 'they set off on a path that leads to the object *via* the verbal part of it, but then find themselves obliged to be content with words instead of things.'[65] In *A Woman Named Solitude*, Rosalie's lost object is figured as the lyrical language associated with her mother ('even as a child,' muses Bayangumay's aged Diola husband, 'she was a flute which her ancestors played all day long', *WNS* 27). When Man Bobette runs away to the mountains for a life of *marronnage*, leaving her mulatto daughter behind, Rosalie develops an 'unfortunate stammer, which had come over her soon after her mother's departure' and which

---

[61] *SE* xiv. 197–8.   [62] *SE* xiv. 198.   [63] *SE* xiv. 198–9.

[64] For an account of schizoid modes of being, processes, and language relevant to the slave's predicament as represented by Schwarz-Bart, see J. H. Rey, 'Schizoid Phenomena in the Borderline' (1979), in Elizabeth Bott Spillius (ed.), *Melanie Klein Today* (2 vols., London, 1988), i. 203–29.

[65] *SE* xiv. 204.

the overseer hears as 'her way of running away like her mother' (*WNS* 73–4). Much later, on the run herself, she rarely speaks: 'Long ago she had learned to distrust the words that came out of her mouth: they were mirrors that fell at her feet, shattering her reflection' (*WNS* 124). The shattering of language shatters self-representation. Freud's schizophrenic is unable to differentiate between word and thing, metaphorical and literal registers. Laid bare by staring eyes, Schwarz-Bart's Solitude can't tell if she has dreamed she is a yellow dog running naked on all fours through the city, or if she is a dog who dreams she is a human being named Solitude ('was she Solitude who had dreamt she was a yellow dog, or was she a dog dreaming it was a human woman named Solitude?', *WNS* 129).[66] Unlike the psychotic, who dreams while awake and therefore is never able to sleep, Schwarz-Bart's slave is compelled to dream the real of her enslavement; is she animal or human?[67]

Pampered and petted in the overseer's house, where she is given to his daughter as a little slave-girl, Rosalie acquiesces in the forms of the racist imaginary. Both little girls enjoy the pleasures of luxurious pain in a parody of the mistress/slave relation enacted by a playful scene of mock whipping (shocked, the overseer glimpses that masters and slaves are 'both riveted to a chain that bound them more closely than love', *WNS* 76). Soon Rosalie is 'quite the drawing-room shepherdess', holding her arms at her sides 'like an articulated wax doll' (*WNS* 77). But, we're told, 'there was a chilling absence in her eyes,' and behind them, 'deep in her doll-like head, all sorts of new thoughts darted about like crabs' (*WNS* 77). Remembering her mother's voice murmuring ' "Land of white men, land of madness" ', she lowers her eyelids while 'the crabs darted their claws into her head' (*WNS* 77).

[66] Cf. Ernie Levy's life as a dog when he is on the run in Free France during the penultimate movement of *The Last of the Just*; reduced to a dog by the rhetoric of anti-Semitism ('No dogs or Jews'), Ernie dreams of himself as a dog and impersonates a canine creature in his imagination.

[67] Cf. W. R. Bion on a failure of what he calls 'alpha function' (the conversion of raw sense data and emotions into the material of conscious and dream-thought): 'the patient who cannot dream cannot go to sleep and cannot wake up'; see *Learning from Experience* (1962; repr. London, 1984), 7.

Sometimes she lets the crabs fly at Man Bobette, or at the big house, fantasizing insurrection or immolation. Glimpsing the luxurious sadomasochism concealed by her little mistress's wax-pale, sad features, 'she murmured to herself with secret rage, "Land of white women, land of lies"' (*WNS* 81). But when she hears news of her mother from a returned runaway, living high on the slopes of La Soufrère with a new black baby, she gives up hope of joining her. Instead, she begins to worry about '*changing*'; before long, Rosalie is poisoning the chickens, thinks she's turning into a dog, begins to bark in her dreams, and gets consigned to an outhouse. At about 11, according to the oral tradition noted by the narrator, she turns into a zombie ('Zombies were simply humans whose souls had deserted them; they were still alive, but the soul was gone', *WNS* 89). Sold on as a field slave, she is quickly resold by her new masters: 'They thought they had bought a body with a soul attached, but when they heard her laugh they spread their ten fingers and unloaded her at another slave market' (*WNS* 89). Repeatedly changing hands and rebranded with the initials of her different owners, Rosalie one day 'put her own mark on her shoulders, in a manner of speaking' (*WNS* 89) when she renames herself in response to a casual sexual solicitation as she works naked in the fields: 'By your leave, master: My name is Solitude' (*WNS* 90).

Solitude, who refuses to speak the language of colonialism, lives its preposterous dream as her nightmare. A philosophic, sentimentally inclined chevalier, struck by 'two transparent eyes of different colors in a face of silk and ashes, the sybilline face of a dead child' (*WNS* 94), purchases her on impulse at a slave auction. The chevalier (a deliciously satirized figure) takes part in debates about the intrinsic virtues of '*man*', renames his slave ship *La Nouvelle Héloïse* (Voltaire himself is rumoured to have invested in it), and dreams of an ideal slave-trade. Educating his hand-picked domestic slaves according to 'the precepts of his master Jean-Jacques' (*WNS* 93), he makes them the chorus-line in a colonial version of the Enlightenment salon: 'They spoke like philosophers, sang like angels, and played all the fashionable instruments, including the French horn' (*WNS* 93). Solitude plays her part like a mechanical dancing doll, got up in an exotic Creole costume known as *la pimpante*, but she remains strangely absent; the drawing-room slaves 'seemed to think she was "different," essentially different, and some said she had no soul' (*WNS* 95). Her old 'ailment' returns and she starts to scream at the jokes she hears in the smoking-room. In a recurrent nightmare, 'she saw herself changed into a sugar statue, which the Frenchmen of France were slowly eating far far away at the other end of the world' (*WNS* 96). Solitude's dream reflects the reality of colonial economic relations; her cultural consumption in the Antillean salon is inseparable from the metropolitan consumption of sugar on the other side of the Atlantic. Transferred to the kitchen, 'for several years she led the peaceful life of a zombie' (*WNS* 96). But with the abolition of slavery in 1795, the chevalier throws in his lot with the royalists and the English, leaving his slaves to fend for themselves. In a sentimental parody of Pinel's liberation of the insane from their chains in the hospital of Bicêtre during the Revolution, he murmurs to Solitude 'with infinite sadness, "Who will deliver you from your chains?" "What chains, Seigneur?" ', she replies (Solitude, after all, has never assumed the chains of colonial metaphor).

Schwarz-Bart makes Solitude a barometer of Revolutionary upheaval. Dressed in the colours of the *tricoleur*, drifting in the turbulent wake of the Revolution, she gives up her mad laugh for floods of tears through which smiles filter. Soon she witnesses successive waves of guillotining—first whites, then blacks—before the reinstitution of forced black labour under the surveillance of the National Guard. She is rejected as 'yellow shit' by the black rebels who roam the countryside, but manages to make her way across the river Goyave to one of the last bastions of the runaway slaves of Gaudeloupe—an enclave of *marronnage* whose charismatic pan-Africanist leader preaches that all blacks have the same father and the same mother, and appropriates the magic of the masters by judicious use of a sacred book called *The Reveries of the Solitary Walker*. Just before the camp is overrun by the former Republican forces, 'a small yellow woman, tattered and half naked' (*WNS* 113) appears on the banks of the river. It is Solitude, still stammering. Her ironic smile, we're told, 'seemed to address itself to an ancient presence, a shade, infinitely near and infinitely inaccessible' (*WNS* 114): the shade of Bayangumay. Her new friends, 'saltwater' or first-generation slaves from Africa, call her 'Little leaf', 'Little yellow leaf'—'The poor yellow leaf; you can see she must have been beautiful . . .' (*WNS* 114, 117). Here Solitude dreams nostalgically of refinding Africa and her mother's *négritude*. When she runs amok, killing an incredulous white soldier in full military regalia with her bloody machete (shouting 'Kill me, kill me, I say . . .' as she goes), her comrades recognize in this unwitting embrace of Fanonian violence proof that she is black ('for', they tell her, 'she had always had a beautiful heart, a black woman's heart', *WNS* 137). After the retributive destruction of the camp by black Republican soldiers, she leads a dwindling band of survivors ever further up the mountain. Here, 'grown yellow again' (*WNS* 145), she encounters a reclusive, flute-playing, organic-farming African (a tribal slave from birth), who lovingly fathers her child. Maimouni, in his wisdom, 'could not wish [the baby] an African heart, which would be useless in a foreign country, and still less could he resign himself to a white, black, or mulatto heart beating to the obscure rhythms of Guadeloupe' (*WNS* 153). What future can be imagined for this child whose heart beats to rhythms as yet unknown?

In the final movement of *A Woman Named Solitude*, the heavily pregnant Solitude joins the 300-strong rebel army of black and mulatto men, women, and children gathered to resist the reimposition of slavery under the insurrectionary leader Delgrès, the hero of black Guadeloupian history. The novel culminates in Schwarz-Bart's account of the uprising of May 1802, when women took part in the fighting, shouting, 'Lan mô, lan mô, viva lan mô'—creole for 'La mort, la mort, vive la mort'.[68] The rest, as they say, is history: Delgrès's mining of the Danglemont mansion on the slopes of Matouba (at terrible loss of life to his own forces), the savage reprisals against thousands of black and

---

[68] For the role of women in the uprising of 1802, see Gautier, *Les Sœurs de Solitude*, 251–2. For runaways and rebels, see also Rogozinski, *A Brief History of the Caribbean*, 152–73, and for Delgrès's last stand at Matouba, see Adélaîde-Merlande, *Delgrès, ou, La Guadeloupe en 1802*, pp. 135–49.

mulatto rebels, and the subsequent execution of Solitude herself. The novel's epigraph, Oruno Lara's terse account of Solitude's execution in his *Histoire de Guadeloupe* (1921), insists on the ironic form of her 'delivery' from slavery: 'The mulatto woman Solitude was with child at the time of her arrest; she was executed on November 20, 1802, immediately after the delivery ['*sa délivrance*'] of her child' (*WNS*, p. xxvii). Her execution takes place in a flower-strewn holiday atmosphere. As she goes to her death, she laughs her legendary, song-like laugh and speaks her last, lyrical words, in excellent metropolitan French: 'It seems one must never say, *Fountain, I shall not drink your water*' (*WNS* 174). Solitude drains her cup in the lyrical language, not of her imaginary mother-tongue, but of Schwarz-Bart's metropolitan French, as if to inflect this moment of boyancy with authorial presence.[69] His European perspective surfaces, without irony, in the novel's sombre epilogue. The anonymous narrator revisits the scene of Delgrès's last stand at Matouba in the guise of a tourist, stumbling on 'a remnant of knee-high wall and a mound of earth intermingled with bone splinters'. He goes on: 'Conscious of a faint taste of ashes, the visitor will take a few steps at random, tracing wider and wider circles around the site of the mansion. His foot will collide with one of the building stones . . . dispersed by the explosion and then over the years buried, dug up, covered over, and dug up again . . .' (*WNS* 178). This chance collision with the fragments and ashes of a dispersed history, emblematic of the dialectic of remembering and forgetting, seems to mark the emergence of what Pierre Nora, in the introduction to his history of French collective memory, calls '*lieux de mémoire*'—places of memory, or collective memorials to the past.[70]

---

[69] In connection with this drinking in of a 'maternal' legacy, cf. J. H. Rey's account of the patient who dreams he can't drink from a feeding bottle, failing 'to transform the experience of the movement of water from the exterior to the interior of his body into a good experience in the form of a representation and a memory . . . The teat . . . represents a maternal breast and a mother whose presence and whose bodily contact is absolutely necessary . . .' (Bott Spillius, *Melanie Klein Today*, (ed.), 213).

[70] See Pierre Nora, 'General Introduction: Between Memory and History', *Realms of Memory: Rethinking the French Past*, under the direction of Pierre Nora, trans. Arthur Goldman (2 vols., New York, 1996–7), i. 1–20. Cf. Bella Brodzki, who makes

For Nora, modern preoccupation with *lieux de mémoire* is associated with 'a turning point in which a sense of rupture with the
past is inextricably bound up with a sense that a rift has occurred
in memory. But that rift has stirred memory sufficiently to raise
the question of its embodiment: there are sites, *lieux de mémoire*,
in which a residual sense of continuity remains.'[71] Nora identifies the first of such recent ruptures with the past as the French
Revolution. It's tempting to regard Schwarz-Bart's epilogue as
raising the same question of embodiment in the form of a literary topos that deconstructs Nora's opposition between history—
bound to continuity, trace, distance, mediation—and torn memory.
This is a form of memory that only seems to stumble on the
concrete (like the deranged language of the slave), yet remains
intensely metaphorical. While the forms of memory associated with
such sites of residual continuity pose the greatest difficulty to historical understanding—what but the traumas of the Holocaust
and of slavery confront us with memory in their most pathological
and inescapable forms?—Schwarz-Bart's novel implicitly reminds
us that we are not dealing with an archival depository, but with
a text. Nora defines *lieux de mémoire* as the last, vestigial stand
of historical consciousness, 'the ultimate embodiments of a
commemorative consciousness that survives in a history which,
having renounced memory, calls out for it'; history, in his terms,
is for ever besieging the bastions of memory, distorting, transforming, reshaping, and petrifying it. In language that is often
strikingly poetic and metaphorical (not to say apocalyptic), he writes
of *lieux de mémoire* as involving a two-stage process, 'moments of
history plucked out of the flow of history, then returned to it'.[72]
The invention of classical mnemonics was associated (we know)

---

suggestive use of Nora's account of the transmission and effacement of memory
in relation to Schwarz-Bart's 'Epilogue' ('Nomadism and the Textualization of
Memory', 220 n., 224), without, however, questioning the distinction between
'history' and (historical) 'memory' or considering the link with trauma.

[71] Nora, *Realms of Memory*, i. 1. Coincidentally, Arnold Rampersad's introduction
refers to Solitude's 'irreparably torn psyche' (p. xi), as if she herself were an embodiment of just such a violent inauguration of memory.

[72] Ibid. i. 6, 7.

with the visualization of a site of a mass disaster by the sole survivor.[73] Such moments of survival and return are reminiscent of contemporary accounts of trauma, where the event impinges with a violence that can no longer be integrated into experience, where our relation to the past similarly consists of the illumination of discontinuity in the present, and where memory returns not only 'to inhibit forgetting' but 'to fix a state of things' and 'to materialize' (in the sense of literalizing) 'the immaterial' so that the survivor is compelled to revisit the site of the disaster again and again.

Hence the paradoxical attachment of traumatized or alienated memory both to specific topoi or sites and to an excess of signification; an excess, however, that may make it possible 'to resurrect old meanings and generate new ones along with new and unforeseeable connections' (Nora again).[74] The *lieu de mémoire* is a hybrid place (or even, generically speaking, a memoir—the product of personal reflection). At the end of *A Woman Named Solitude*, Schwarz-Bart, in his role as tourist-narrator, revisits in imagination the site of a more recent historical trauma. 'If', he writes, 'the visitor'

---

[73] See Natalie Zemon Davis and Randolph Starn, in their introduction to a special issue of *Representations* devoted to memory and counter-memory, *Representations*, 26 (1989), 1–6: 'We have learned from Frances Yates how the ancient "art of memory" involved associating some text or idea to be remembered to the image of a place . . . Simonides of Ceos supposedly invented the classical *ars memoriae* by visualizing the places occupied by the victims of a disaster of which he was the only survivor' (2–3); the same issue of *Representations* included an earlier translation of Nora's introduction by Marc Roudebush and Young's essay on Rapoport's Warsaw Ghetto Monument (see n. 75). Referring to memory as 'a substitute, surrogate, or consolation for something [i.e. history] that is missing', Davis and Starn point to the role of the historian in 'reclaiming the stories of more or less forgotten people who had been losers, victims, or only ordinary folk' (ibid. 1, 3)—a project to which Schwarz-Bart also contributes as a historian of the European and Antillean past.

[74] Nora, *Realms of Memory*, i. 15; for Nora, 'What we call memory is in fact a gigantic and breathtaking effort to store the material vestiges of what we cannot possibly remember, thereby amassing an unfathomable collection of things that we might someday need to recall' (ibid. i. 8)—in short, an archive. At the same time, Nora argues, in the wake of Freud and Proust, 'Memory became a private affair'; the combined effects of psychologization and atomization 'imposes a duty to remember on each individual' (ibid. i. 11).

is in the mood to salute a memory, his imagination will people the environing space, and human figures will rise up around him, just as the phantoms that wander about the humiliated ruins of the Warsaw ghetto are said to rise up before the eyes of other travellers. (*WNS* 178–9)

Nathan Rapoport's heroic Warsaw Ghetto Monument, unveiled in 1948 on the fifth anniversary of the six-week Warsaw Ghetto Uprising, commemorated the first and most sustained armed Jewish revolt in the history of Nazi-occupied Europe.[75] Constructed on rubble cleared painstakingly, stone by stone, it occupied the site of the bunker where the leader of the rebellion, Mordechai Anielewicz, died in May 1943 (the same year Schwarz-Bart himself had joined the resistance at the age of 15 after the deportation of his family to the death camps).[76] In his 'biography' of the Rapoport monument, James Young observes: 'Memory is not merely passed down from generation to generation in the Warsaw Ghetto Monument, but is necessarily recast in the minds of each new generation'.[77] Succeeding generations, he notes, have adopted the Warsaw Ghetto Monument as a *place de résistance* for more recent dissident movements. *A Woman Named Solitude* can be read as just such an attempt to recast memory in the wake of an ealier uprising, a different Holocaust. From the perspective of a later insurgent moment, one disaster remembers another.

[75] See James E. Young, 'The Biography of a Memorial Icon: Nathan Rapoport's Warsaw Ghetto Monument', *Holocaust Memorials and Meaning* (New Haven, 1993), 155–84; originally published in *Representations*, 26 (1989), 69–106. Prior to June 1942, 100,000 Jews had died in the Warsaw ghetto. Between July and Sept. 1942, over 300,000 more Jews were deported from the Warsaw ghetto to Treblinka where they were gassed. The accelerated scale of the liquidation brought the Jewish Fighting Organization into being as a coalition committed to militant resistance and self-defence (see ibid. 160–3; for the many accounts of the uprising since the war, see ibid. 361–2 n. For the significance and rhetoric attached to the Warsaw Ghetto Uprising in retrospect, see, for instance, Israel Gutman, *Resistance: The Warsaw Ghetto Uprising* (Boston and New York, 1994): 'No act of Jewish resistance during the Holocaust fired the imagination quite as much as the Warsaw Ghetto Uprising of April 1943. It was an event of epic proportions, pitting a few poorly armed, starving Jews against the might of Nazi power. The ghetto Uprising was the first urban rebellion of consequence in any of the Nazi-occupied countries and was a significant point in Jewish history' (p. xi).

[76] For a brief account of Schwarz-Bart's wartime adolescence, see Kaufman, *Pour relire Le Dernier des justes*, 15–17.

[77] *Holocaust Memorials and Meaning*, 175.

For Schwarz-Bart, the fragmentary remains at the Danglemont plantation on the slopes of Matouba mark the site of two historical ruptures, distinct yet related diasporas that shape the interrelated forms of memory and modernity. Solitude's 'Eyes divided between two worlds' aptly describes Schwarz-Bart's double vision, seeing the history of the Antilles in terms of his own recent catastrophe. When memory is torn, the comforting fiction of historical continuity turns into the nightmare of history's repetition-with-a-difference. One night during her sojourn in the woods, in a moment of impossible intertextual memory, Solitude hears the voices of the dead crying out 'with the plaintive voices of the children, friends, brothers and sisters fallen by the banks of the Goyave. And the living were at a loss, wondering how to answer, how to be silent . . .' (WNS 142). The banks of the river Goyave recall the banks of the Gambian river where Solitude's mother grows up, near a city named 'Sit-down-and-weep' on account of the encroaching slave-trade. By the waters of Babylon . . . As the voices of collective lamentation and mourning echo across the Atlantic, mingling the voices of dead slaves with the ancient history of Jewish enslavement and the voices of Schwarz-Bart's immediate past, one might well ask: whose exiled mind has entered whose? This outcry is not (only, or any more) a black cry. With hindsight, we can re-read Nora's *lieux de mémoire* as a figure of speech for the excess of signification—memory, as it were, in the wrong place—that tends to accompany the literary representation of historical trauma, making it possible to generate new meanings and unforeseeable connections from the accidents of memory, even as we register the ambiguous and inevitably belated movement of the trans-racial imaginary.

FOUR

Border Crossings
Traumatic Reading and Holocaust Memory

> Investigate the caesura; not the analyst; not the analysand;
> not the unconscious; not the conscious; not sanity; not insan-
> ity. But the caesura, the link, the synapse, the (counter-trans)-
> ference, the transitive-intransitive mood. (W. R. Bion)[1]

I N a recent essay on the relation between trauma theory
and literary studies, Geoffrey Hartman suggests that reading
itself can sometimes seem less like an intersubjective dialogue
than an address to, or encounter with, the dead:

We habitually view literary interpretation as a binary process, one
that takes place between object-like texts and subject-like readers.
We try to call this process a dialogue, or claim, using a conventional
prosopopoeia, that texts 'speak' to us. But the animating metaphor in
this is all too obvious. It betrays the fact that while we feel that books
are alive, we cannot find a good model, a way to picture that. The
more we try to animate books, the more they reveal their resemblance
to the dead—who are made to address us in epitaphs or whom we address
in thought or dream. Every time we read we are in danger of waking
the dead, whose return can be ghoulish as well as comforting. It is, in

---

[1] W. R. Bion, 'Caesura', *Two Papers: The Grid and Caesura* (London, 1989), 56. Bion's
essay is especially concerned with the idea of 'movement from one state of mind
to another', or 'the translation in the direction of what we do not know into something which we do know or which we can communicate, and also from what we
do know and can communicate to what we do not know and are not aware of because
it is unconscious' (ibid. 53–4).

any case, always the reader who is alive and the book that is dead, and must be resurrected by the reader.[2]

In this construction of the fantasized relation between living reader and dead book, Hartman summons up the ghost of a Romantic epitaphic poetics (*Siste viator!*).[3] But when we think of ourselves as the resurrecters or dreamers of the unspeaking dead, with the book playing the part of revenant, what animates these uneasy tropes? And whose is the death in the book, anyway? Perhaps we imagine the textual object as dead because we've made it a lodging place for what Joan Riviere, redefining fear of death as the death drive, calls 'the capacity for death in oneself'.[4] André Green, more recently, suggests that we can only read a book, in the sense of engaging in an interpretive conversation with it, 'if something *has already happened* between the text and the analyst. *The analysis of the text is an analysis after the fact.*'[5] In this sense, reading resembles the *après coup* of trauma, where the 'something' that has already happened also acquires meaning after the fact, in the same double movement that problematizes both temporality and the event when it comes to narrating trauma.[6]

[2] Geoffrey H. Hartman, 'On Traumatic Knowledge and Literary Studies', *New Literary History*, 26 (1995), 548. For important recent contributions to the literary and psychoanalytic reading of trauma which continue to provoke debate, see Cathy Caruth, *Unclaimed Experience: Trauma, Narrative, and History* (Baltimore and London, 1996), and Cathy Caruth (ed.), *Trauma: Explorations in Memory* (Baltimore and London, 1995); see also, for a specific focus on Holocaust trauma, Shoshana Felman and Dori Laub, *Testimony: Crises of Witnessing in Literature, Psychoanalysis, and History* (New York and London, 1992).

[3] Cf. also Cathy Caruth, 'An Interview with Geoffrey Hartman', *Studies in Romanticism*, 35 (1996), 631–52, for the relation between trauma and Hartman's extensive writings on Romantic poetry, especially *The Prelude*.

[4] Joan Riviere, 'The Unconscious Phantasy of an Inner World Reflected in Examples from Literature', *IW* 314.

[5] See André Green, 'The Double and the Absent', in *On Private Madness* (Madison, Conn., 1986), 312.

[6] Cf. Jean Laplanche on trauma: 'If it is true to say that *it always takes two traumas to make a trauma*, or two distinct events to produce repression, then it is also true to say that primary repression, or trauma, is not something that can be pinpointed thanks to observation, even if the observer is a psychoanalyst. Analytic observers are fated to being either too early or too late . . .' (*New Foundations for Psychoanalysis*, trans. David Macey (Oxford, 1989), 88).

Literary-critical accounts of trauma theory such as Hartman's typically define the traumatic encounter as a missed meeting. Trauma theory, as a theory of knowledge, derives from psychoanalysis its scepticism about whether the past can ever be fully experienced or known—let alone completely retrieved or communicated; hence its insistence on the limits of understanding, representation, memory, and transmission. The traumatic event, Hartman writes, 'seems to have bypassed perception and consciousness, and falls directly into the psyche'; it resists being known, refusing to be integrated into ordinary, ongoing experience.[7] As long ago as Sándor Ferenczi, psychoanalysts were observing in their patients the radical splitting between emotion, thought, and representation that psychical trauma leaves in its wake.[8] Memory—far from providing a reliable form of historical witness or testimony—takes 'the form of a perpetual troping of [the event] in the bypassed or severely split (dissociated) psyche' (Hartman again, conflating the mechanisms of primal repression and splitting).[9] Because of its peculiar temporal structure, trauma reverses conventional relations between cause and effect as they are understood in narrative and history. Hence the belatedness or 'afterwardsness' (Jean Laplanche's well-known neologism for *Nachträglichkeit*) that distinguishes the traumatic neuroses. Laplanche's 'afterwardsness' returns trauma theory, via Ferenczi, to its earliest Freudian scene, the scene of seduction.[10] A more generalized (less specifically sexual) model of trauma, by contrast, might appeal to the idea of 'an original inner catastrophe'—an experience which cannot be experienced at the time, but none the less leaves traces of devastation in the psyche, like a shattered

---

[7] Hartman, 'On Traumatic Knowledge', 537.

[8] See Sándor Ferenczi on 'Trauma and Splitting of the Personality' (*Clinical Diary*, 14 Aug. 1932): 'after a shock the emotions become severed from representations and thought processes and hidden away deep in the unconscious, indeed in the corporeal unconscious'. See *The Clinical Diary of Sándor Ferenczi*, ed. Judith Dupont, trans. Michael Balint and Nicola Zarday Jackson (Cambridge, Mass., and London, 1998), 203.

[9] 'On Traumatic Knowledge', 537.

[10] For Laplanche's reading of Ferenczi's paper, 'Confusion of Tongues between Adults and the Child' (1933), see *New Foundations for Psychoanalysis*, especially 121–31.

or ruined landscape to which the survivor returns again and again, or which returns in the form of recurrent dreams, unsolicited memories, and disturbances in mental functioning. As Freud points out, compulsive repetition (whether in dreams or in the transference) is the hallmark of trauma.[11] Hartman's traumatic knowledge thus resembles a terrible nescience, while the structure of memory is equated with the structure of tropes, viewed as the product of a 'severe' (i.e. painful and dissociative) splitting, in a move that pathologizes figuration itself.

For Hartman, the vexed relations between experience and understanding, knowledge and figuration, are the peculiar province of literary language, and, above all, the literary construction of memory—by definition, the representation of an impossible, fragmented non-memory. This idea that the negativity or absence inherent in both experience and figurative language constitutes a catastrophic hole in the real (*un trou réel*, or Lacan's punning *troumatique*) has by now achieved a certain critical orthodoxy.[12] But a pan-traumatic account of the literary arguably risks attributing the same status to figurative language in general as to the testimony and memoirs of—for instance—Holocaust survivors. Indeed, given the current critical standing of trauma theory, it has become possible to think of all subjectivity as shaped by an originary trauma, whether via our traumatic, castrated entry into the symbolic (Lacan); through the traumatic mode of our sexualization (Laplanche); or by way of the early anxieties about separation and object loss emphasized by Freud himself—if not through what Freud, in a memorable phrase (questioning Rank's theory of birth trauma) called 'the impressive caesura' of birth.[13] Why not, then, think of traumatized subjectivity in terms of the missed meanings and figural mortifications of the deconstructive reading encounter? I want, however, to resist too

---

[11] See *Beyond the Pleasure Principle* (1920), SE xviii. 32–6.

[12] See Hartman, 'On Traumatic Knowledge', 539; cf. also Caruth, 'An Interview with Geoffrey Hartman', 641, for what is missing or mute.

[13] See *Inhibitions, Symptoms, and Anxiety* (1926), SE xx. 138: 'There is much more continuity between intra-uterine life and earliest infancy than the impressive caesura of birth would have us believe.'

easy a conflation of trauma and textuality, or trauma and reading, and instead to limit myself tactically to the specific form of
traumatic reading involved in literary memorials and autobiographical accounts of the Holocaust. It's often asserted that we
are at risk of a species of 'secondary' or 'muted' trauma when
we read, listen to, or view the testimony of Holocaust survivors.
Holocaust memoirs can undoubtedly function as traumatic objects
in themselves, whether or not they are also objects of analytic,
textual, or even historical inquiry; they both demand and evoke
intense emotional responses in their readers (Green's prior textual
'event').[14] The reflective moment interposed by way of literary
forms of representation or critical interpretation risks breaking
down under the impact of affects and experiences which tap into
our deepest anxieties about annihilation. In the wake of such reading, we may experience—so the argument goes—what amounts
to a simulacrum of the survivor's own anxiety, anaesthesia,
fragmentation, or despair.[15] But the temptation to view trauma as
having a kind of chain-letter effect, as in psychologistic accounts
of the passing on of trauma (monkey see, monkey do), assumes
a mimetic or contagious model of trauma.[16] Although trauma may
indeed have a transferential afterlife, it is not in mimesis, but in
repetition, that its delayed effects make themselves felt.

When Laplanche writes that as soon as you put words like
'dream' or 'trauma' on the page, they become traumatic ('Before

[14] Cf. Dominick LaCapra, 'History, Language, and Reading: Waiting for Crillon',
American Historical Review, 100 (1995), 799–828, apropos of historical and dialogical
inquiry: 'exchange with the object of inquiry (which is always mediated by exchange
with other inquirers) is necessary, notably with respect to intensely "cathected" or
traumatizing objects, such as the Holocaust, or texts that themselves raise problems
of continuing concern and demand a response from the reader not restricted to purely
empirical-analytic inquiry or contextualization' (825).

[15] See, for instance, Caruth, 'An Interview with Geoffrey Hartman', 643–5, and
the aesthetic questions raised by Geoffrey Hartman in 'Holocaust Testimony, Art,
and Trauma', *The Longest Shadow: In the Aftermath of the Holocaust* (Bloomington, Ind.,
1996), 151–72.

[16] Mark Seltzer notices how popular versions of trauma theory (the victimizer
who perpetrates his own childhood trauma on the victim) assume a form of
mimetic reproduction: 'This amounts to a mimetic coalescence of self and other: a
mimetic identification intensified to the point of reproduction'. See *Serial Killer: Death
and Life in America's Wound Culture* (New York and London, 1998), 257.

you have read the first lines, you auto-traumatize with these terms
. . . and then you try to bind it'), he points to the double movement that takes place in the course of the literary encounter.[17]
In an important sense, any reading involves a rewriting of the text
as well as a prior textual encounter. Laplanche goes on to suggest that 'the way is wide open for studies of the effect, rather
than the production, of the work'.[18] I will be arguing that the reading of traumatic literary 'objects' such as Holocaust memoirs
necessarily involves both Laplanche's 'auto-traumatization' and
the attempt to rebind affect to representation—here, by means
of what Hartman calls 'an interpretive conversation'.[19] In what
follows, I will be attempting to respond to the literary dimensions
of a specific representation of Holocaust memory—one among
many—while implicitly acknowledging its fragmenting effects on
the reader (if only via the form taken by my own critical account).
At the same time I will be tracing the enigmatic processes of
affective binding in a text that is continually being unmade and
remade in the double time of trauma narrative.[20]

The Trauma of Object Loss

My initial point of departure for thinking about trauma is Freud's
Inhibitions, Symptoms, and Anxiety (1926). Here, Freud's divided
response to Rank's theory of birth trauma represents an exemplary
attempt to restrict the meaning of trauma to the exceptional rather
than the universal (struggling with the universalizing tendencies

[17] *Jean Laplanche: Seduction, Translation and the Drives*, ed. John Fletcher and
Martin Stanton (London, 1992), 32: 'And maybe you reproduce something of the
trauma in your own incentive to research or paint . . . I think that in any creative
adventure, there is something like that. You push forward things that traumatize
you' (ibid. 32).

[18] Ibid. 35.   [19] 'On Traumatic Knowledge', 541.

[20] For binding and unbinding in literature and psychoanalysis, see also André
Green, 'The Unbinding Process', in *On Private Madness*, 331–59; Green argues that 'The
analyst . . . becomes the *analyzed of the text*. It is within himself-as-text that he must
find an answer to [the] questioning' provoked by the awakening of idea and affect
in the reader (ibid. 338).

of psychoanalysis itself), while acknowledging that trauma always takes its meaning from a prior psychic catastrophe—not castration, but object loss. Traumatic anxiety signals the recurrence of a past danger situation. Birth trauma functions in Freud's text as symbol —rather than as explanation—for the trauma of separation and object loss; the fear of annihilation reflects the so-called 'fact' of the human infant's prematurity and dependence. A benign trauma, birth is not for Freud the founding moment of a traumatized subjectivity (babies, he points out, don't actually know that birth can be life threatening). Only by virtue of its metaphoricity does 'the impressive caesura of birth' illuminate the disaster zone of psychic trauma, the damaging loss of a maternal object or pro- tecting parental figure. In Freud's account, this annihilatory dis- aster zone is already occupied by a potentially annihilating force in ourselves—the death drive, which posits a primitive destruct- iveness and tendency towards the repetition of unpleasure. In doing so, it further complicates relations between internal and external. No longer envisaged as a 'shock' from the outside only, this new, intra-subjective trauma puts pressure on the distinction between world and subject, body and psyche; it represents, in Laplanche's phrase, 'A kind of *internal-external* instance'.[21] Trauma itself is a borderline theoretical concept.[22]

The figure of a breached frontier looks back nostalgically to the 'little fragment of living substance' in *Beyond the Pleasure Principle*

---

[21] See Jean Laplanche, *Life and Death in Psychoanalysis*, trans. Jeffrey Mehlman (Baltimore and London, 1976), 42: 'From the model of physical trauma we have moved to psychical trauma, not through any vague or unthematized analogy from one domain to another, but through a precise transition: the movement from the external to the internal. What defines psychical trauma is not any general quality of the psyche, but the fact that the psychical trauma comes from within.'

[22] In an aside, Mark Seltzer offers an excellent formulation of this borderline status by which trauma is defined by the breaking-in of the boundaries between inside and outside: 'One might say of the trauma what Freud said of the instincts: the trauma "appears to us as a borderland concept between the mental and physical"' (*Serial Killers*, 259). He goes on: 'The concept of trauma is, on this view, foundational to psychoanalysis even as it undermines its foundations and the specificity of its domain' (ibid. 260). Seltzer's concern is to track the breakdown between psychical and somatic, inner and outer, as it bears on the breakdown between psychic and social registers, or what he terms 'the pathological public sphere'.

(1920). Freud writes that 'we describe as "traumatic" any excitations from outside which are powerful enough to break through the protective shield'.[23] But even here he dissociates himself from 'the old, naive theory of shock' as opposed to 'the later and psychologically more ambitious theory which attributes aetiological importance not to the effects of mechanical violence but to fright and the threat to life'.[24] Freud invokes trauma because it provides evidence for something 'beyond' (or rather, *before*—more primitive than) the pleasure principle. The recurrent dreams of those suffering from traumatic neuroses, which return again and again to the original danger situation, are driven not by wish-fulfilment (as in Freud's earlier theory of dreams), but by the compulsion to repeat. This is how the death drive manifests itself. Melanie Klein will transform Freudian fear of object loss into fear of losing the internal object, and fear of death into fear of the annihilation of the ego from within, on account of the destructive workings of the death instinct.[25] In her post-Second World War paper, 'On the Theory of Anxiety and Guilt' (1948), she disagrees with Freud's statement that no fear of death (and therefore no representation of it) exists in the unconscious, arguing vigorously that the fear of annihilation can be observed in very young children.[26] Anxiety, for Klein, is primordial, since destructiveness is primordial too. Projection deflects the death instinct outward; in other words, splitting masters persecutory anxiety in the face of the fear of both internal and external bad objects.[27] Given the

---

[23] *SE* xviii. 27, 29.   [24] *SE* xviii. 31.

[25] For a brief, late restatement of Klein's views, based on important earlier papers, see 'On the Development of Mental Functioning' (1958), *Envy and Gratitude*, *WMK* iii. 236–46.

[26] See ibid. 25–42. See also Joan Riviere's account of Klein's position in her 1936 essay, 'On the Genesis of Psychical Conflict in Earliest Infancy', in which she writes, apropos of Freud's denial of anxiety of death in the infant: 'I am not suggesting that there is any such "kind of knowledge" in the child; but I think there is reason to suppose that a child experiences *feelings* of the kind, just as any adult can *feel* "like death", and in a state of great anxiety often does' (*IW* 279). For an excellent account of Klein's concept of anxiety and its relation both to war and to aesthetics, see Lyndsey Stonebridge, 'Anxiety in Klein: The Missing Witch's Letter', in John Phillips and Lyndsey Stonebridge (eds.), *Reading Melanie Klein* (London and New York, 1998), 190–202.

[27] See 'On the Theory of Anxiety and Guilt', *Envy and Gratitude*, *WMK* iii. 31–2.

reintrojection of objects previously rendered dangerous by this outward deflection of destructive impulses, is it really possible to distinguish between 'inner' and 'outer' at all? Klein's figure of crossing transforms Freud's figure of the breached border into that of a border-crossing.

These vicissitudes in trauma theory bear on reading, to the extent that one can think of the 'traumatic' literary object as the bearer of split-off affects and drives that include our own. In Klein's terms, these negated aspects of the internal world—'rejected because they arouse anxiety and give pain'—are a powerful source of both artistic and intellectual production.[28] Hartman's essay refers in passing to trauma theory's focus on disturbances in mental functioning. By this Hartman means that trauma theory, when it occupies the realm of literary studies, 'instead of seeking premature knowledge, . . . stays longer in the negative and allows disturbances of language and mind the quality of time we give to literature'.[29] The unthought, unremembered, and unrepresentable, yet repetitive nature of such disturbances enjoins traumatic reading to 'stay longer' (to tarry) in a negative realm that is implicitly associated with death and the death drive. Negativity (what has been split off, rendered missing, mute, or invisible) is the peculiar domain of traumatic aesthetics.[30] Klein goes on to suggest that a more integrated ego, one which has moved beyond the stage

[28] For the aesthetic implications of this aspect of Kleinian theory, see 'The Development of Mental Functioning': 'The more the ego can integrate its destructive impulses and synthesize the different aspects of its objects, the richer it becomes; for the split-off parts of the self and of impulses which are rejected because they arouse anxiety and give pain also contain valuable aspects of the personality and of the phantasy life which is impoverished by splitting them off. Though the rejected aspects of the self and of internalized objects contribute to instability, they are also at the source of inspiration in artistic productions and in various intellectual activities' (ibid. WMK iii. 245).

[29] 'On Traumatic Knowledge', 547; Hartman is referring to G. W. F. Hegel's phrase, 'tarrying with the negative' (i.e. death and devastation), from the 'Preface' to Phenomenology of Spirit.

[30] For the importance of negation and negativity, and a particularly subtle and telling analysis of their role in Kleinian theory, as well as the aesthetics of (black) holes, see especially Jacqueline Rose, 'Negativity in the Work of Melanie Klein', in Why War?—Psychoanalysis, Politics, and the Return to Melanie Klein (Oxford, 1993), 137–90; see also Stonebridge, in Reading Melanie Klein, 190–202.

of splitting to the possibility of entertaining psychic pain (the movement from the so-called paranoid-schizoid position to the depressive position), may also experience 'an over-riding urge to preserve, repair, or revive the loved objects: the tendency to make reparation' (a reparative tendency as omnipotent as that of splitting).³¹ Viewed from this perspective, Hartman's scenario of the reader animating the dead book in fantasy starts to look more like an attempt at reparation of the loved object than simply a matter of reanimation or resurrection. Implicit in the post-Kleinian development is the idea of a constant fluctuation between the two states (persecutory anxiety on one hand, depressive anxiety on the other). I want to suggest that Holocaust writing in particular, given the intensity of the anxieties involved for both writer and reader, typically operates on this borderline where one state of mind crosses over to another (and indeed, where one's state of mind may be transferred to another). Referring to the way in which part of the survivor continues to address the dead, Hartman remarks on the 'chiasmic relation between the survivor and his past self as camp inmate', the crossover between life and death, and the coexistence of ordinary, ongoing experience alongside the timeless and frontierless universe of the camp.³² This paradigmatic loitering on the border relates not only to the question of address (the apostrophe to the dead), but to narrative. The temporal scheme of Holocaust memoirs is a double one; telling in the narrative present holds the fragments of an unkown past.

The metaphor of border-crossing frames my reading of the 'memoirs' of a child survivor, Binjamin Wilkomirski's *Fragments: Memories of a Wartime Childhood* (1995).³³ *Fragments* ostensibly sets out to record the unbearable recovered memories, feelings, and experiences of the *univers concentrationnaire* from a child's

---

³¹ See 'On the Theory of Anxiety and Guilt', *Envy and Gratitude*, WMK iii. 35–6.
³² Caruth, 'An Interview with Geoffrey Hartman', 649–50.
³³ Binjamin Wilkomirski, *Fragments: Memories of a Wartime Childhood*, trans. Carol Brown Janeway (New York, 1996) cited hereafter as *F*; subsequent page references in the text are to this edition. For an older child's memories of the war and the camps, see Thomas Geve, *Guns and Barbed Wire: A Child Survives the Holocaust* (Chicago, 1987). See also Deborah Dwork, *Children with a Star: Jewish Youth in Nazi Europe* (New Haven, 1991), esp. 209–49.

perspective, recovered, as it were, for the future. Paradoxically, however, it recovers or reproduces many of the recognizable literary tropes and topoi of Holocaust writing and trauma theory; the child's-eye view is inevitably mediated by other writings on the Holocaust, by generic aspects of Holocaust testimony, not to mention by the complications surrounding the historical status of the traumatic event itself. Both memory and identity are constructs over a void or *vide*. This reproductive troping suggests that even (or especially) when it comes to trauma, the only available form of memory is literary construction, reconstruction, and the troping of absence; and that traumatic narrative is bound to be belated, both its telling and its meaning retrospective, since the experience remains uncomprehended and incomprehensible at the time. I will be focusing on specific sites of meaning in Wilkomirski's *Memories of a Wartime Childhood* that provide nodal points for both narrative and interpretive organization in the face of trauma: the fragmentation of memory; the missed meeting; birth after Auschwitz; the killing machine; and finally, the scene of weeping, in which the bare bones of trauma simultaneously find a containing envelope, a coherent narrative form, and a witness or responsive listener.[34]

Shards of Memory

The novelist Henri Raczymow has written of 'A memory devoid of memory, without content, beyond exile, beyond the forgotten,' a memory 'shot through with holes, with missing links: the names of the dead.' This is a past *not* handed on, a past filled only with

---

[34] See Dori Laub, 'Bearing Witness or the Vicissitudes of Listening,' in *Testimony: Crises of Witnessing in Literature, Psychoanalysis, and History*, 57–74, for the role of the listener in the testimonial process of constructing video archives of Holocaust survivors. For an illuminating categorization of traumatic memory in a psychotherapeutic context which includes the relation of 'unintegrated fragments' to 'overpowering narrative', see also Dori Laub and Nanette C. Auerhahn, 'Knowing and Not Knowing —Massive Psychic Trauma: Forms of Traumatic Memory', *IJP-A* 74 (1993), 287–302; Laub and Auerhahn conclude that 'reconstruction of the event, construction of a narrative and abstraction of a theme are all necessary if the fragment—the symptom —is to lose its power and be properly integrated into memory (ibid. 300).

gaps and fragments. 'Writing', he says, 'was and still is the only way I could deal with the past, the whole past, the only way I could tell myself about the past—even if it is, by definition, a recreated past. It is a question of filling in gaps, of putting scraps together.' But such writing doesn't so much try to fill the gaps, as 'restore a non-memory, which by definition cannot be filled in or recovered'.[35] Raczymov is referring to a catastrophe of memory that involves the failed transmission of the past from one generation to the next, specifically as it affected those born in the aftermath of the Holocaust. But what he says of his own immediately post-war generation could also be applied to the child survivor, with his lost past. Wilkomirski's memoirs are a history of fragmented memory and missing links, similarly beyond both memory and forgetting. Apparently a small child when he entered the world of the camps, he narrates a primitive psychic disaster associated with the very earliest years of his life. Repeated trauma is literalized in his story as the savage blows directed at his head by camp guards, and as the unpredictably violent smashing-in of other children's skulls. Ferenczi, apropos of the ways in which 'Psycho-analysis, like every psychology, in its attempts to dig to the depths must strike somewhere on the rock of the organic', refers to memory-traces as 'scars, so to speak, of traumatic impressions, *i.e.* as products of the destructive instinct', employed, however, not for destruction, but 'for the preservation of life'.[36] Elsewhere he writes of 'Systems

---

[35] See 'Memory Shot Through with Holes' (1986), trans. Alan Astro, *Yale French Studies*, 85 (1994), 100–4. For Raczymow, the 'pre-past' or prehistory of the Holocaust is knowable only as a secondary trauma, the paradoxical '*nothingness*' of his Jewish identity. In 'War Memories: On Autobiographical Reading', Susan Rubin Suleiman writes movingly of her own relation to the memoirs of Jewish child survivors; see Lawrence D. Kritzman (ed.), *Auschwitz and After: Race, Culture, and 'the Jewish Question' in France* (New York and London, 1995), 47–62. See also Saul Friedlander (himself a child survivor and author of an autobiography), in 'Trauma and Transference', in *Memory, History, and the Extermination of the Jews of Europe* (Bloomington, Ind., and Indianapolis, 1993), 117–37, for a historian's reflections on the relation between individual and collective memory and Holocaust memory that takes into account related issues of transference, defence, and 'working through'.

[36] 'The Problem of Acceptance of Unpleasant Ideas' (1926), in John Rickman (ed.), *Further Contributions to the Theory and Technique of Psycho-Analysis* (1926; repr. New York, 1980), 377.

of memory scars form[ing] new tissue with its own functions',
placed in the service of self-preservation as '*alloplastically directed
thought work*' (adhering to the organic metaphor provided by
trauma).[37] Memory, then, is both the wound and the scar that
preserves it, like the ridge that Wilkomirski can still feel on the
back of his own head. This preservative scar-tissue—at once a
bodily and a psychic inscription of memory—forms the basis of
his painfully reconstructed identity.[38]

Noting that 'The immediate effect of a trauma which cannot
be dealt with at once is fragmentation', Ferenczi goes on to
wonder whether psychic fragmentation is 'merely a mechanical
consequence of the shock' or, already, a form of defence.[39] He
speculates that 'the giving up of . . . unified perception, at least puts
an end to the simultaneous suffering of pain. The single fragments
suffer for themselves.'[40] Painful splitting, in other words, makes
agglomerated suffering bearable, but at the cost of disintegration.
In trauma, Ferenczi suggests, these split-off fragments may be
reunified by an automatic caretaking function within the psyche,
an 'unconscious internal force' which functions as in sleep-
walking and makes the fragments manageable in the aftermath.[41]
Wilkomirski's *Fragments* defines memory at the outset as at once
disorderly and isolated, yet—because it defies the logic of extermination represented by the Holocaust—as simultaneously working
on behalf of life, resisting oblivion ('The plan was for us to die,
not survive', F 4). Laplanche's internal-external 'reminiscences',
however, behave as if they were 'an internal object continually
attacking the ego' ('a "spine in the flesh" or, we might say, a

---

[37] 'What is Trauma?', *The Clinical Diary of Sándor Ferenczi*, 182.

[38] In André Schwarz-Bart's *The Last of the Just* (1959), Ernie Levy's boyhood
suicide attempt in the face of anti-Semitic persecution leaves him permanently
scarred in just this way.

[39] 'Trauma and Striving for Health', in Michael Balint (ed.), *Final Contributions
to the Problems and Methods of Psycho-Analysis* (1955; repr. London, 1994), 231. Where
Ferenczi emphasizes fragmentation, Janet emphasizes the engraving of traumatic
memory; see Bessel A. van de Kolk and Onno van der Hart, 'The Intrusive Past:
The Flexibility of Memory and the Engraving of Trauma', in Caruth (ed.), *Trauma:
Explorations in Memory*, 158–82.

[40] *Final Contributions*, 230.   [41] Ibid. 231.

veritable spine in the *protective wall of the ego*').[42] In much the same way, Wilkomirski's memories function as persecutory, sharp-edged objects lodged in the protective skin of identity:

My earliest memories are a rubble field of isolated images and events. Shards of memory with hard knife-sharp edges, which still cut flesh if touched today. Mostly a chaotic jumble, with very little chronological fit; shards that keep surfacing against the orderly grain of grown-up life and escaping the laws of logic. (*F* 4)

Memory, then, is both the wound and the cutting instrument, a chaotic anti-narrative (unbinding) agency that disrupts the laws of chronology. Irreparably split and broken, it mounts a continual, destructive attack from within, yet the fragments 'keep surfacing' (and hence, perhaps, are subject to retaliatory attack).[43] All this makes it difficult to speak, metaphorically or in narrative terms, of piecing the fragments together. Rather, the archaeology of memory comes to resemble Bion's (originally Freud's) analogy of the analyst and 'the archaeologist who discovers in his field-work the evidences, not so much of a primitive civilization, as of a primitive catastrophe' whose extent can be only measured by the degree to which the evidence has been scattered.[44] Later, Wilkomirski writes of 'Shards of recollection, holding my brothers fast inside, like flakes of feldspar in a great rockslope of childhood memory' (*F* 26). Memory preserves the record of a developmental catastrophe in terms of this landslide of devastation. As Ferenczi writes, in the wake of such devastation 'A new ego cannot be formed directly from the previous ego, but from *fragments*, more or less elementary products of its disintegration.'[45]

---

[42] *Life and Death in Psychoanalysis*, 42.

[43] For a comparable account of this double process, cf. Klein's note on the mechanism of deflection (the redirection of the death instinct from the self to the object): 'Part of the death instinct is projected into the object, the object thereby becoming a persecutor; while that part of the death instinct which is retained in the ego causes aggression to be turned against that persecutory object'; see 'On The Development of Mental Functioning', *Envy and Gratitude*, WMK iii. 238 n.

[44] 'On Arrogance' (1957), *Second Thoughts* (1967; repr. London, 1984), 88.

[45] 'What is Trauma?', *Clinical Diary of Sándor Ferenczi*, 181.

Wilkomirski describes his childhood memories as a primitive form of photography. Affective and sensory images are 'planted . . . in exact snapshots'—first of all visual, then auditory, and only much later involving language: 'Just pictures, almost no thoughts attached' (*F* 4, 5). Freud refers similarly to 'Affective states . . . incorporated in the mind as precipitates of primaeval traumatic experiences', and 'revived like mnemic symbols' when danger threatens. 'Anxiety', he writes, is 'reproduced . . . in accordance with an already existing mnemic image.'[46] These affective states, or mnemic symbols and images, are like primitive thoughts and feelings in search of a language. The opening sentence of *Fragments* refers to the lack of a natal or parental tongue: 'I have no mother tongue, nor a father tongue either' (*F* 3). Metaphorically, since he can't speak, his mouth remains empty. The story Wilkomirski tells is (literally) that of the speechless *infans* whose first memories predate language. The Yiddish that Binjamin associates with his eldest brother, Mordechai, is 'overlaid with the Babel-babble of an assortment of children's barracks in the Nazis' death camps in Poland', 'gibberish which lost its usefulness with the end of the war' (*F* 3). In this polyglot confusion of tongues, inner confusion inevitably reigns. Henceforth, he writes, the languages he learned 'were only imitations of other people's speech', acquired as one might acquire a dictionary, swallowed piecemeal (this is what Abraham and Torok, in *The Shell and the Kernel*, call anti-metaphor, language literally incorporated).[47] The patched-up, rejected non-identity of the child-survivor—uncertain about his age, and even his name—seemingly overlays the heteroglossic Babel-babble

[46] *Inhibitions, Symptoms, and Anxiety*, SE xx. 93. The implication—that anxiety is not so much produced as reproduced—accords with Freud's emphasis on the pre-existence of a proto-typical traumatic situation.

[47] Nicolas Abraham and Maria Torok, 'Mourning *or* Melancholia: Introjection *versus* Incorporation' (1972), in *The Shell and the Kernel: Renewals of Psychoanalysis*, ed. and trans. Nicholas T. Rand (Chicago, 1994), 125–38. Abraham and Torok associate the initial stages of linguistic 'introjection' (the term coined by Ferenczi) not only with the difference 'between metaphoric and photographic images, between the acquisition of a language as opposed to buying a dictionary', but also with replacing 'the early satisfactions of the mouth, as yet filled with the maternal object' by 'the novel satisfactions of a mouth now empty of that object but filled with words pertaining to the subject' (127).

of the children's barracks in which he spent his linguistically and emotionally formative years. Wilkomirski's reconstruction of his past acknowledges the necessity for a myth of origin and a *telos*: 'If you don't remember where you came from, you will never really be able to know where you're going' (*F* 4). But his Latvian origins are a hypothetical reconstruction, and his early childhood is traversed by journeys whose destination he didn't know, then or later. The very word 'transport' (taken literally) will later trigger despair in the linguistically traumatized child-survivor: 'Almost nobody ever came back who'd been on a "transport"' (*F* 120)—a transport, in the terrible camp phrase, 'written down' (that is, officially consigned for shipment to the death-camps). This was to have been the logical *telos* of his journey, making narrative coherence and closure incompatible with the fact of his survival.[48]

At the start of *Fragments*, Wilkomirski creates a montage-like effect of photographic pictures from his early childhood—a magical wintry scene in Riga, containing the memory of being bundled up on a sled and surrounded by skaters; or a toddler's eyewitness impression of his father's violent, slow-motion, silent-movie death when the Latvian militia arrest and kill him: 'all I see is the line of his jaw and his hat falling backward off his head. No sound comes out of his mouth, but a big stream of something black shoots out of his neck as the transport squashes him with a big crack against the house' (*F* 6–7). Superimposed on these frozen, oversimplified, black-and-white 'screen memories'—for such they inevitably seem—we read of his confused recollections of flight along with his older brothers and a woman (presumably

---

[48] In a nightmare episode that recasts the motif of the interrupted journey as the end of the world, Binjamin—apparently loaded up on a 'transport'—survives a railway accident in a state of traumatized devastation that corresponds closely to Freud's account of railway-shock in *Beyond the Pleasure Principle*, where traumatic neurosis is said to depend on the survivor's unpreparedness for the experience (see *SE* xviii. 12); Freud takes up the railway accident again in *Moses and Monotheism* (1939) as an instance of belatedness in trauma neurosis (*SE* xxiii. 67). Commenting on the way in which latency is inherent in the experience of trauma, Cathy Caruth focuses on the issues of journeys and departures, including Freud's own, in 'Unclaimed Experience: Trauma and the Possibility of History', *Unclaimed Experience*, 10–24.

his mother), and an interrupted journey that seems predestined to end in the camps. Binjamin resumes this interrupted journey after the war, but by then he is on his own; thenceforth he has only a succession of adopted or temporary mothers and caretakers. These vivid pictures, caught by the blinded eye of cinematic memory, are overlaid by later memories—a more sustained and coherent narrative, or secondary revision—from the time when Binjamin leaves his Krakow children's orphanage for yet another unknown European destination, after the postwar resurgence of Polish anti-Semitism. Once across the Swiss border, he is abandoned yet again, by the woman who smuggles him into the west as her son. He becomes an official non-person, left behind in a railway station waiting room (as he was earlier separated from his mother and brothers), waiting for someone who never comes to meet him. At the end of the book, Wilkomirski reminds us how, as a child, he received a new name, place and date of birth, along with other children of the Holocaust whose false names and papers erased the traces of their Jewish or Eastern European origins so that they would not be deported. His fragmentary memories are his missing papers, the only guarantee of identity. But are they any more reliable than the identity issued to him after the war? The red-edged label round his neck which allows him to cross the border camouflaged among a group of French refugee children is symbolically blank. Properly speaking, he has no identity, and what memories he has are irremediably tied to the enclosed and limitless world of the camps.

The Missed Encounter

Hartman's paradigm for traumatic knowledge is the dream of the burning child, from *The Interpretation of Dreams* (1900).[49] For Freud, the dream can be explained as the father's wish to stay asleep so that his son can be thought of as alive for a little longer ('an *organic* tendency to keep sleeping'); why otherwise does he deny

---

[49] See *The Interpretation of Dreams* (1900), ch. 7 (*SE* v. 509–10).

waking reality?[50] In Lacan's well-known rereading, the traumatic-ally missed encounter with the real occurs in the space between perception and consciousness, as the father dreams the dead son's whispered reproach (*'Father, don't you see I'm burning?'*) while the overturned candle has already set his corpse alight in the next room.[51] More recently, Cathy Caruth's 'Traumatic Awakenings', an essay that speaks eloquently to the ethical dimensions of memory, reframes both Freudian and Lacanian accounts as 'the trauma of the necessity and impossibility of responding to another's death'.[52] In *Fragments*, Wilkomirski's version of the missed encounter speaks not only to the oneiric space between perception and consciousness, or to the intrusion of the (Lacanian) 'real', but to a missed encounter that involves his mother—in particular, his unpreparedness for her loss. Binjamin, you might say, is always missing something (just as the victim is unprepared for the trauma). As an adolescent, seeing film-footage of the liberation of the camps by the Allies, he feels that 'somehow I missed my

---

[50] 'On Traumatic Knowledge', 553–5; Hartman offers what he calls 'not a faith-ful exposition but a free interpretation of Lacan's commentary on the dream of the burning child' (563 n.).

[51] See Jacques Lacan, 'Tuché and Automaton', in *The Four Fundamental Concepts of Psycho-Analysis*, trans. Alan Sheridan (New York, 1978), 53–64. For Lacan, the missed encounter is paradigmatic of psychoanalysis itself ('what we have in the discovery of psycho-analysis is . . . an appointment to which we are always called with a real that eludes us', ibid. 53); the encounter itself 'forever missed, has occurred between dream and awakening, between the person who is still asleep . . . and the person who has dreamt merely in order not to wake up' (ibid. 58–9). In an interview Laplanche expresses his reservations about the claim that the reality that intrudes into the dream-structure is that of the death drive: 'Just because death is present in the man-ifest content of the dream as in many others, it doesn't mean that the death drive is manifesting itself at that place. For me the death drive is mainly the destructuration tendencies in the psychic apparatus; especially repression is an example of the death drive, that is putting a representation apart from its affect and de-binding it. I don't see a striking example of de-binding or un-binding in that dream' (*Jean Laplanche: Seduction, Translation, Drives*, ed. John Fletcher and Martin Stanton, 28).

[52] See 'Traumatic Awakenings: Freud, Lacan, and the Ethics of Memory', in *Unclaimed Experience*, 91–112: '*Awakening*, in Lacan's reading of the dream, *is itself the site of a trauma*, the trauma of the necessity and impossibility of responding to another's death' (ibid. 100); Caruth's notes provide an exceptionally full discussion of the extensive literature on Lacan, traumatic dreams, nightmares, and awaken-ings (ibid. 139–46).

own liberation'—'Why wasn't I there, too? Did something really happen there and I knew nothing about it?' (F 151–2). Much earlier, Wilkomirski relates, when he and his older brothers are hidden in the countryside with a tyrannical Polish farmer's wife, Binjamin (the youngest) sleeps through the round-up because he's been punished by being locked in the cellar for refusing to take cover when fighting suddenly engulfs the farm. Eventually he manages to climb out of a window, but he emerges—as he will do again—to find himself alone on the abandoned farm. Days later, he's found by the German mop-up operation in the wake of the Russian retreat, and taken to Majdan Lublin (Majdanek). He never sees his brothers again. The question Binjamin asks in the Swiss railway waiting room—'Why am I always the one who's left behind?'(F 18)—is the question he couldn't actually have asked as a small child, but retrospectively ventriloquizes in the aftermath of the war, as the children's barracks gradually empty and the camp system disintegrates around him: 'Why have I been left on my own? Have I missed something again, or slept through something? . . . Why am I always the only one who doesn't understand?' (F 107). Binjamin's belatedness (his hav-ing been left behind) is in one sense the sign of his survival. But this idea of something missed or unexperienced, whether an encounter or a loss, is also the founding trope of *Fragments*—in the sense that a baby misses its mother, without understanding what is being missed. In *Inhibitions, Symptoms and Anxiety* (making a crucial distinction between 'the traumatic situation of birth' and 'the traumatic situation of missing the mother'), Freud points to the difference between object-lessness and object-loss ('At birth no object existed and so no object could be missed').[53] The lost object of *Fragments* is the mother who can never be properly missed because her meaning has been lost too early.

The figure of Binjamin's mother soon recedes into the past as the anonymous 'woman' who once held him on her lap or bedded him down in a basket of rags. Much later, in a Swiss orphanage, memory stages Binjamin's final meeting with his mother, when

---

[53] *Inhibitions, Symptoms, and Anxiety* (SE xx. 170).

he is unexpectedly enveloped by the smell of newly baked bread. Or rather, what he remembers is 'the day when I learned what the smell of bread was' (F 46), since he scarcely knew what a mother was. The memory triggered by the delicious smell of bread functions, on one level, as a metaphor for the gift of survival offered him first by one woman, then by another. One day, in the children's barracks, a grey-uniformed woman guard had come to collect him: 'Today you can see your mother, but—only dahle' (F 46), she tells him. By now Binjamin no longer knows what 'mother' means, or even if he has one. The incomprehensible word 'mother' is accompanied by another strange, untranslatable word, *dahle,* pronounced 'with a very long, broad *aah*' ('What did "dahle" mean? I still have no idea today', F 46). The children in the barracks argue about whether there are mothers or not, some saying 'everyone has a mother', others insisting 'that there were no mothers anymore, that it had only been that way once, back then, a long time ago, in another world . . . But since then there hadn't been any mothers, and the other world had disappeared long ago, forever. They said: "There's no more world outside the fence!"' (F 47). When they fight over it, Binjamin understands that a mother 'must be something immensely important, something that was worth fighting for, the way you fought over food' (F 47). In the daily struggle for survival, food and mothers are interchangeable. Having a mother means emotional and psychic survival; but there are no mothers anymore, and not enough food either. Chronic hunger becomes the trace of the absent mother (*'Mother, can't you see I'm starving?'*).

Dragged on an interminable walk to the barracks for sick and dying women, Binjamin finds himself standing in the darkness before 'the shape of a body under a gray cover' (could one call this shape a representation of death in the unconscious?). 'Was this my mother, my dahle?' he wonders. During their phantasmal encounter, no words are exchanged between him and 'a face that looked back at [him] with huge eyes'. But before he leaves, the melancholy 'shape' gropes under the straw with one hand and beckons him closer; he notices that her face was 'was shiny and wet, and I saw that it was crying' (F 50). Then she gives him an 'object'—'what she had brought out from under the straw.' The touch of her feverish hand is their only physical contact ('her hand felt hot and damp'). On the way back to the children's barracks, Binjamin curiously explores 'the unknown object' with his free hand ('It had jagged edges and corners, and felt coarse and hard'). 'What is this?' he asks the uniformed woman. ' "That's bread," she said, and "You have to soften it in water, then you can eat it." Then she went away' (F 50). Black milk . . . Chewing on his crust, dunking it in his ration of water over and over again until the water is used up and the crust shrinks to a tiny ball, Binjamin is left with 'the indescribably delicious smell of bread on my fingers as I held them to my nose again and again' (F 51). His mother's last gift to him has been the precious daily bread ration. In the starvation economy of the camps, this means another day's survival. Offered bread for the first time in the Swiss orphanage, Binjamin screams with incomprehensible fury: 'I only take bread from my mother.' The Swiss nurse calmly gives him another piece of bread, spreads jam on it, and says, 'This is my present to you' (F 52).

Binjamin's crust of bread—the trace of a lost object—is the traumatic madeleine of Wilkomirski's *Recherche du temps perdu*, his only means of recovering a past that he could not have experienced at the time.[54] But the memory points to a phantasy. The aftermath of the missed encounter is a nostalgic and illusory incorporation which eradicates the idea of emptiness. Abraham and Torok call this 'one mouth work in place of another'—a phantasy 'directed at the very metaphor of introjection', or bread instead of words.[55] The phantasy of incorporation implements literally

---

[54] Cf. Hanna Segal, whose classic paper, 'A Psychoanalytic Approach to Aesthetics', uses Marcel Proust as her example of the reparative activity of creative memory: 'Through the many volumes of his work the past is being recaptured; all his lost, destroyed, and loved objects are being brought back to life'. See *The Work of Hanna Segal: A Kleinian Approach to Clinical Practice* (Northvale, NJ, and London, 1981), 189. Segal, however, emphasizes the relation of mourning to creativity in ways that may not be fully available to the trauma-survivor, leading to peculiar difficulties when it comes to the literary and artistic representations of trauma by survivors themselves.

[55] 'Because our mouth is unable to say certain words and unable to formulate certain sentences, we fantasize . . . that we are actually taking into our mouth the

something that only has figurative meaning: 'in order not to "swallow" a loss, we fantasize swallowing (or having swallowed) that which has been lost, as if it were some kind of thing.'[56] Ingesting the lost love-object precludes mourning. What is missing from Binjamin's premature encounter with death is the meaning of the mother he can't yet (or ever) mourn; incorporation implies a gap within the psyche which is also registered at the level of language ('something that is missing just where introjection should have occurred').[57] Haunting the mute exchange between mother and child is the missing affect that attaches itself, not to the frightened and silent child, but to the weeping mother ('I saw that it'—'the face'—'was crying'). Crying, as both we and Binjamin long before learned, is forbidden in the camps; it means weakness and death: '. . . nobody was allowed to be sad in the camps. Whoever was sad, even for a minute, was weak. Whoever was weak, died' (*F* 19). Binjamin is only able to cry with sheer sadness when he arrives in Switzerland, and finds no one to meet him. On this occasion, his tears remind him of crying long ago in the Polish farmhouse, and being comforted by his oldest brother, Mordecai (Motti). But when he remembers his mother, he feels nothing but fury. The hungry baby, Freud reminds us, hallucinates the presence of the mother; but when the hallucination fails, pain enters along with the unbearable realities of absence and unassuaged hunger. Negotiating the difference between the bad breast (the furious, internal attacks of hunger), and an absent mother (the idea of a missing breast) makes it possible for the infant to entertain the thought of a mother-not-there—to think and to feel; to put language in his mouth. But in the world of the camps, as the woman guard casually informs Binjamin when he asks to see his mother again, 'it's not possible any more' (*F* 51). The smell of bread is the trace of that

unnamable, the object itself. As the empty mouth calls out in vain to be filled with introjective speech, it reverts to being the food-craving mouth it was prior to the acquisition of speech. . . . The desperate ploy of filling the mouth with illusory nourishment has the equally illusory effect of eradicating the idea of a void to be filled with words' (*The Shell and the Kernel*, 128–9).

[56] Ibid. 126.   [57] Ibid. 127.

impossibility in a world of systematically organized dissociation, where a piece of bread stands for the lost object and a nonsense word ('dahle'—*daahle*) belongs to the same incomprehensible lexicon as the word 'mother'.

Birth after Auschwitz

In *Inhibitions, Symptoms, and Anxiety*, Freud rejects the idea that 'whenever there is an outbreak of anxiety something like a reproduction of the situation of birth goes on in the mind'.[58] But the ambiguous status of birth trauma as the prototype of a primeval traumatic experience (the anxiety produced by separation and object loss) points to a similar ambiguity in Wilkomirski's *Fragments*. When the Latvian militia come to arrest his father, Binjamin—still a toddler then—has a visceral memory of 'the feeling of deathly terror in my chest and throat, the heavy tramp of boots, a fist that yanks me out of my hiding place under the covers at the bottom of the bed and drops me onto the floorboards in the middle of an otherwise unfurnished little room' (*F* 5). This image of abrupt discovery and ejection—the prototypical figure for the small child's ruptured security—is the first of many in which Binjamin is concealed or bedded down, covered by cloth or rags, only to be catapulted into a world of emptiness, violence, and death. When he visits the nursery in his Swiss orphanage, years later, a terrifyingly aversive 'picture' comes back to him. As a small child in the camps, Binjamin had been hidden in a room where women prisoners work at sorting mountains of rags and clothes—the discarded effects of dead camp inmates. But his concealment in the clothes mountain comes to an end in a maelstrom of noise and blows, shouts and screams, as other small children who (unknown to him) have also been hidden in the clothes store are hunted from their burrows by the camp guards. Looking out from his hiding place, he sees two small wriggling bundles fly out of the window 'and in the silence, from

[58] *SE* xx. 94.

outside, twice over the unmistakable sound of breaking skulls' (*F* 102). When the women come back to fetch him that night (as often, he seems to be the only survivor), he has to make his getaway past the frozen, shattered bodies of the two dead children. The bundles flying out of the window become his own flying figure as he leaps in slow motion over the frozen bodies with their swollen stomachs, crushed faces, and smashed skulls ('a mass of yellow, sticky-shiny stuff had flowed out . . . right across the path I had to follow. My stomach heaved with horror and disgust', *F* 104). Still gripped by icy terror—'the numbing, crippling, freezing sensation that crept up from my feet, up past my knees, into my thighs and up against my innards' (*F* 105)—Binjamin's entire body becomes a frozen memory, arrested in time and space. The horrifying 'picture' is a mnemic image inscribed in the bodily unconscious, localized in his innards and 'freezing me there for all eternity' (*F* 104).[59]

The emptying-out of feeling ('nothing left in me, no sympathy, no pity, not even anger', *F* 105) as Binjamin is ejected from cosy concealment to premature exposure makes him wonder about the extent of his own childhood brutalization. Reduced to a traumatized apparatus for perception, the camp inmate witnesses his own transformation into the abject of Nazi ideology.[60] In Wilkomirski's revision of the metaphor of birth trauma, we see the un-birth of a Jewish child. One day towards the end of the war, when the organization of the camps is beginning to break down, Binjamin is playing in the mud by himself, close to a pile of female corpses who have not yet been collected by the daily

[59] See Roberta Culbertson, 'Embodied Memory, Transcendence, and Telling: Recounting Trauma, Re-establishing the Self', *New Literary History*, 26 (1995), 169–95, for an exploration of forms of trauma recoverable only in the body and silenced by the demands of narrative; her essay raises related and disturbing issues of 'recovered memory' in the context of sexual abuse.

[60] Cf. the representation of Jews as rodents which Art Spiegelman, in *Maus*, engages as a double-edged alienation effect; Geoffrey Hartman, in 'Darkness Visible', wonders if this comic-book estrangement 'questions whether a fully human knowledge about the Holocaust is possible' (*The Longest Shadow*, 54). For an extended inquiry into Spiegelman's depiction of Jews in relation to popular culture and animal stereotypes, see also Dominick LaCapra, ''Twas the Night before Christmas: Art Spiegelman's *Maus*', in *History and Memory after Auschwitz* (Ithaca, NY, and London, 1998), 139–79.

cart. He ponders his own origins ('where do babies come from?'): 'Some of the older children have told me that little children grow in women's bellies before they're born, and I wonder: everyone keeps saying I'm so small, that must mean that I grew in a belly too. I think about my mother' (*F* 85). As he remembers his last encounter with the woman who was said to be his mother, he notices something moving among the mountain of corpses: 'She's on her back, her body hanging down a little . . . her belly seems all swelled up. Is my mother lying like that now? Something *is* moving! It's the belly' (*F* 85). He is horrified yet fascinated:

Now I can see the whole belly. There's a big wound on one side, with something moving in it. I get to my feet, so that I can see better. I poke my head forward, and at this very moment the wound springs open, the wall of the stomach lifts back, and a huge, blood-smeared, shining rat darts down the mound of corpses . . .
I saw it, I saw it! The dead women are giving birth to rats! (*F* 86)

The child's cry of despair, accusation, and outrage ('Mother, mama, my mama, what have you done?') emerges from this traumatic wound to seeing. In Wilkomirski's narrative, the rhythms of simultaneity and mimesis ('I poke my head forward . . . the wound springs open') suggest the chiasmic figure of reversal by which humans are made to see themselves as rats and vermin, fit only for extermination.

The power of this dehumanizing projection makes Binjamin undo the rags on his legs to feel his skin: 'Is it skin, or do I actually have grey fur? Am I a rat or a human? I'm a child—but am I a human child or a rat child, or can you be both at once?' (*F* 87). Confronted by the hallucinatory evidence of his own dehumanization, Binjamin voids his identity, along with the entire contents of his body: 'Everything inside me comes loose and seems to flow away; I flow away along with my blood and vomit in the bright, muddy runnels of water . . . Nothing connects to anything else anymore. Nothing is in its right place. Nothing has any value. . . . I'm just an eye, taking what it sees, giving nothing back' (*F* 87). Reduced to the merest apparatus for traumatized seeing, Wilkomirski's Binjamin becomes all eye. Claude Lanzmann, referring to the cinematic eye of *Shoah*, calls this 'the only way not to turn away from a reality which is literally blinding'.[61] The fragility of the boundaries between inner and outer, the terror and disgust that accompanies the outing of the inside, makes this birth scene traumatic in ways not envisaged by either Rank, or even by Freud. As a first-time father attending the birth of his own child, the adult Wilkomirski hears the same ringing and cracking noise in his chest. But Binjamin's memory surely contains an additional level of (presumably unconscious) phantasy. The clue here lies in his self-identification with the rats that bite the children at night, leaving painful, infected wounds. For the camp child, consumed by the gnawing pangs of hunger, a particular anxiety must have arisen. In her lucid account of Klein's views, 'On the Genesis of Psychical Conflict in Earliest Infancy' (1936), Joan Riviere connects 'the pain and anxiety caused by hunger' with the sense of 'devouring agencies' within the self:

> Not only do the hunger-pangs feel like foreign agents within one, like biting, gnawing, wasting forces inside one, against which one is helpless; but the intense wishes to seize and devour (the breast) which accompany such hunger at its inception will be identified with these inner devouring agencies or pains. . . . Thus the destructive condition (starvation) becomes equated with the destructive impulses: *'My wishes inside me are devouring and destroying me.'*[62]

Riviere allows us to see this phantasy of the inside invaded by hunger-pangs as the common origin (the 'inception') of both hunger and destructive impulses directed against the self. Hunger gives birth to a devouring phantasy. Binjamin's un-birth trauma— the negation of birth—can be read as the trace of a 'traumatic situation' involving the starving child's double apprehension of its nearness to death and its 'danger from the forces of the death

---

[61] See 'The Obscenity of Understanding: An Evening with Claude Lanzmann', in Caruth (ed.), *Trauma: Explorations in Memory*, 204. Cf. also Dominick LaCapra's questioning of Lanzmann's filmic relation to the representation of trauma in 'Lanzmann's *Shoah*: "Here There Is No Why" ', in *History and Memory after Auschwitz*, 95–138.

[62] *IW* 283; Riviere's emphasis.

instinct operating within it'.[63] The starvation economy of the camp system gives birth to the gnawing pangs of hunger and death within the child survivor; where does the child end and the rat begin?

The Death Machine

In his later writing, Freud postulates the existence of a 'mute and silent' instinct that opposes life and tends towards dissolution. The earliest anxiety situation, he hypothesizes, is 'the fear of being eaten by the totem animal (the father)'.[64] Klein fleshes out this instinctual terror—the death drive in its most archaic form—as the destructive harshness of the superego, present from birth, attacking both life and the ego's functioning. 'The fear of being devoured by the father', she writes, 'derives from the projection of the infant's impulses to devour his objects.'[65] Wilkomirski relates just such a phantasy of being eaten in the form of a traumatically recurring nightmare which he dates to Binjamin's first arrival at the Swiss children's home, and which repeats itself, 'mercilessly in the years that followed, image by image, detail by detail, night by night, like an unstoppable copying machine' (F 38). This infernal copying machine—the death drive in the age of mechanical reproduction—is readily identified with the killing machine of the Nazi death camps (in other words, with the intrusion of

[63] Riviere writes that the resulting 'helplessness against destructive forces within constitutes the greatest psychical danger-situation known to the human organism, and . . . the deepest source of anxiety in human beings' (IW 278); the child *feels* 'like death'—the Kleinian equivalent of Freud's 'traumatic situation' or Jones's 'pre-ideational primal anxiety' (IW 278–9).

[64] See 'The Economic Problem of Maschochism' (1924), SE xix. 165; in 'Splitting of the Ego in the Process of Defence', apropos of regression to the oral phase under the threat of castration, Freud alludes similarly to 'a primitive fragment of Greek mythology which tells how Kronos, the old Father God, swallowed his children and sought to swallow his youngest son Zeus like the rest . . .' (SE xxiii. 278). Klein, in 'On the Theory of Anxiety and Guilt', views this primal anxiety-situation as 'an undisguised expression of the fear of total annihilation of the self' (Envy and Gratitude, WMK iii. 30).

[65] 'On the Theory of Anxiety and Guilt', ibid. 30.

the real and with history; with the role of technology); but the nightmare is also shaped by the demonic aesthetics of Holocaust representation.[66] Binjamin dreams of being 'the only child on earth', the last one alive in a desolate and deserted landscape— 'No other human being, no tree, no grass, no water—nothing. Just a great desert of stone and sand' (*F* 38). In the middle of this depopulated world is a cone-shaped mountain, 'capped with a black, metallic, glinting, ominous helmet':

At the foot of the mountain was a hut with a sort of canopy in front. Under the canopy were a lot of coal cars on rails. Some of the cars were full of dead people; their arms and legs stuck out over the edges. A narrow rail track ran straight up to the peak and in under the helmet, into a gaping jawbone with filthy brown teeth. The cars cycled uphill, disappearing into the jaw under the helmet, then cycled back down again, empty.

All over the plain around the mountain, hordes of biting insects suddenly came crawling out of the ground . . . I knew I was their last meal on earth. Where could I go to save myself? (*F* 39)

The only place to flee is the coal cars, but 'They travelled as unstoppably and regularly as clockwork up the mountain and tipped their contents into the awful gullet under the helmet. . . . I awoke with a sense of despair' (*F* 39). Binjamin's phantasy of being eaten up by a merciless power, an utterly corrupt and deathly superego, recapitulates Klein's unremittingly dark insistence on the cruelty of a superego that is formed on the archaic basis of the infant's devouring oral impulses.[67]

---

[66] Laub and Auerhahn comment on the way in which, during massive trauma, 'fiction, fantasy, and demonic art can become historical fact; this blurring of boundaries between reality and fantasy conjures up affect so violent that it exceeds the ego's capacity for regulation'; see 'Knowing and Not Knowing', 288.

[67] Wilkomirski associates the nightmare with a specific childhood memory involving his torment by the omnipresent biting lice and bugs of the camps; see *F* 41–2. For relevant papers on traumatic dreams and nightmares, and especially their screening function for prior events and existing internal object relations, see, for instance, Theodore Lidz, 'Nightmares and the Combat Neuroses', in Melvin R. Lansky (ed.), *Essential Papers on Dreams* (New York, 1992), 323–42; John Mack, 'Towards a Theory of Nightmares', ibid. 343–75; and Melvin R. Lansky, 'The Screening Function of Post-Traumatic Nightmares', ibid. 401–24.

A few years after his arrival in Switzerland, Binjamin is taken
on a group holiday to the alps. Here he meets a girl whom he
instantly recognizes as a fellow survivor. One day, the children
are taken skiing. Confronted by the huts that house the ski-lift
('an immense iron wheel . . . turning inside like some merciless,
indifferent mill', F 141) he sees, with a terrible sense of *déjà vu*,
'the death machine' of his nightmare and of Nazi engineering
(which came first, one wonders—the ski-lift or the dream?).[68] The
mechanics of Nazi destruction returns as a traumatically displaced
and disavowed memory. All the other children go up obediently,
two by two, into 'a huge yawning black hole that led right
through the house and into the mountain' (F 142). Binjamin looks
into the eyes of the girl ('eyes I remembered very well, of children who won't come back') and she says ' "The grave's inside
the mountain." . . . We were the only children who knew the truth'
(F 142–3). Hand in hand, the pair fall flat on their faces in the
snow rather than take their place on the ski-lift; they're sent back
to the children's home in disgrace as city kids. ' "They're all dead,"
said the girl, "we're the only ones who know the secret" ' (F 144).
Their misperception—ski-lift as death machine, ski-instructers
as potential executioners—would be comical, were it not for its
allegorical aptness. Beneath the charade of winter sports, the
children see the ever-present reality of the death camps, just as
Binjamin's foster home contains a Hansel-and-Gretel oven in the
basement waiting to be used again; they are lone witnesses to the
disavowed truth of the Holocaust in a postwar Europe preoccupied
with reconstruction rather than memory. The decayed helmet of
German imperialism, its rotten interior fed by railcars bearing
dead bodies, condenses the ideology and the technology of the
Holocaust into a single hideous image. But the killing machine
also doubles for the deadly and mechanical effects of traumatic
repetition. Ferenczi suggests that 'the sensation of *déjà vu* generally signifies the memory of an unconscious day dream'.[69] The

---

[68] See Jean-Claude Pressac and Robert-Jan van Pelt, 'The Machinery of Mass Murder
at Auschwitz', in Yisrael Gutman and Michael Berenbaum (eds.), *Anatomy of the
Auschwitz Death Camp* (Bloomington, Ind., and Indianapolis, 1994), 183–245.
[69] 'A Case of "Déjà Vu" ' (1912), *Final Contributions*, 320.

killing machine of the Holocaust endlessly reproduces the shared unconscious phantasy that Klein would locate at the period of an archaic oral drive. The Kleinian definition of trauma is the convergence of actual devastation or destruction in the external world with an unconscious phantasy of internal devastation and destruction; to the extent that they correspond—and in the deathly world of the camps, how could they not?—trauma results, not only for children but for adults.[70]

When Klein writes of the deflection on to the external world of aggression originally directed at the self and the maternal object, she locates the primitive superego as the site where the death drive announces itself most clearly. Klein's 1948 essay on 'The Theory of Anxiety and Guilt' links guilt to hate, invoking Ferenczi on 'a sort of physiological forerunner of the ego-ideal or super-ego' that he calls 'sphincter-morality'.[71] Significantly, this is also the period at which Anna Freud locates the defensive mechanism of identification with the aggressor.[72] In the camps, the parental demand that the child should gain control over his sphincter becomes a regime of savage reprisals that makes shitting in the wrong place punishable by death, while precluding the possibility

[70] See 'On the Theory of Anxiety and Guilt': 'if external danger is from the beginning linked with internal danger from the death instinct, no danger-situation arising from external sources could ever be experienced by the young child as a purely external and known danger. But it is not only the infant who cannot make such a clear differentiation: to some extent the interaction between external and internal danger-situations persists throughout life' (*Envy and Gratitude*, WMK iii. 39).

[71] Ibid. 33; the reference is to Ferenczi's 'Psycho-Analysis of Sexual Habits' (1925): 'a severe sphincter-morality is set up which can only be contravened at the cost of bitter self-reproaches and punishment by conscience' (*Further Contributions*, 267).

[72] See Anna Freud, *The Ego and the Mechanisms of Defense* (1936; repr. Madison, Conn. 1966), 109–21: 'By impersonating the aggressor, assuming his attributes or imitating his aggression, the child transforms himself from the person threatened into the person who makes the threat.' Anna Freud goes on to allude to *Beyond the Pleasure Principle* where Freud notes 'this change from the passive to the active role as a means of assimilating unpleasant or traumatic experiences in infancy' (ibid. 113). For an interesting discussion of this defence mechanism in children, see Joseph Sandler and Anna Freud, *The Analysis of Defense: The Ego and the Mechanisms of Defense Revisited* (New York, 1985), pp. 379–423. See also Dina Wardi, *Memorial Candles: Children of the Holocaust*, trans. Naomi Goldblum (London and New York, 1992), 114–49 for the internalized relations of aggressor and victim in camp survivors and their children.

of cleanliness.[73] Binjamin associates his overwhelming survivor guilt (a guilt compounded with terror) with a recollected episode involving an inexperienced new boy who arrives in the barracks. At night, the children are terrorized by a cruel block-warden and by their desperate need to relieve themselves. All they have is a single bucket; once full, it's taken away, and they know the penalty for transgressing. Many of the children are suffering from diarrhoea and dysentery, including the new boy. 'Help me! What should I do?', he screams, unfamiliar with the sanitary regime rigidly enforced in the children's barracks. Possessed by panic, fearful that the new boy's crying will attract attention from the guards and do for them all, Binjamin suddenly hears himself saying: 'Just go in the straw, right where you are' (F 63). These words ('I'd said right out loud, really loud, what I only thought I was thinking') prove, literally, lethal. In the morning, at roll call, a terrible roaring. The new boy shuffles forward. Pitiable, innocent, dangerously incompetent, he is doomed from the moment he steps out of line. After a pause, some discussion between the guards and the inspecting officer, the crack of bones. Meanwhile, Binjamin is choking with fear and guilt (will the new boy betray him? should he confess his own crime? where can he hide?). What hits Binjamin 'like a blow' in the aftermath of the brutal execution is the threat to his own life. He becomes the new boy's murderer; the other children in the barracks are his potential denouncers (for, as he knows, 'children's revenge can be terrible'). The only solution is not to speak at all—to become mute: 'I mustn't speak! Just keep absolutely silent. . . . I killed the new boy' (F 66). We know, of course, that whoever did the killing in the camps, it was not Binjamin. But the period of sphincter morality is also the period of childhood associated with the early formation of the superego in its cruellest and most primitive form. In Binjamin's confused internalization of the sadistic sanitary regime of the camps, we see him 'silencing' himself along with the new boy; involuntary loss of bowel control and inadvertently speaking out loud both

[73] Cf. the account of 'excremental assault' in Terence Des Pres, *The Survivor: An Anatomy of Life in the Death Camps* (New York, 1976), 53–71.

become crimes punishable by death. *Fragments* shows us how survivor guilt is the terrible by-product of both the superego and the Nazi killing machine.[74]

The Scene of Weeping

Among the most haunting and poignant images in *Fragments* is Binjamin's memory of two freezing bundles, tossed into the children's barracks at night. The bundles contain small children, who hold their blackened, frost-bitten hands dreamily in front of their eyes. They have their first teeth, but can't talk yet. Binjamin has never seen such small children. In the morning, he asks, 'what's that, Jankl—look—their hands!' when he sees their snow-white, stick-like fingers. 'Bones,' replies Jankl, his friend and teacher, 'just bones, that's what you look like inside, you have bones like that all over . . . That's what holds you together . . .' (F 71). Binjamin is anxious: ' "But—why are those two's bones outside? I've got skin holding me together. Are they ill?" . . . Something seemed to be not right.' Jankl explains to him that their sickness was called hunger: 'Sometime in the night they chewed their fingers down to the bone—but they're dead now' (F 71). On this occasion, Jankl, one of the unsung heroes of Binjamin's tale (like his oldest brother Mordecai, or the anonymous women who take care of him in the camps), breaks the law of camp survival and cries. Jankl's tears, holding Binjamin's memory together like a fragile envelope of skin, bind affect to representation in the midst of atrocity. Without them, *Fragments* would risk disintegrating into a kind of cannibalistic gnawing, a numbing catalogue of atrocities that exposes to view the bare bones of trauma. In place of the infant's total helplessness and disintegration (the broken skulls, the chewed

---

[74] For survivor guilt—the self-condemnation often experienced by those who survive trauma—see Robert Jay Lifton, *The Broken Connection: On Death and the Continuity of Life* (New York, 1983); Lifton sees survivor guilt, in all its harshness, as having an evolutionary function (see ibid. 172). See also Cathy Caruth for the ethical dimensions of 'this impossible demand at the heart of human consciousness' (*Unclaimed Experience*, 104).

bones), we register not defensive splitting or freezing—as so often
in Binjamin's memories—but the tenuous survival of affect. In the
same way, a primitive self is contained by the skin that functions
as a boundary for the ego ('I've got skin holding me together'),
providing the internal space for feeling and empathy.[75] The scene
of weeping recurs elsewhere, and we sense the deliberate placing
of the topos, when Binjamin tells his story—a child witnessing to
history—before the Rabbi and the Jewish elders of the Krakow
synagogue after the war:

> I suddenly began to talk in a way I'd never talked before. I heard myself
> talking, as if it was someone else inside me. I talked like a waterfall,
> but I have no idea any more what I said. But at some point it was enough,
> there was only a sick feeling in my throat, I stopped talking and every-
> thing inside me was quiet again, the way it was before. (F 114)

Afterwards, the two old men get up and go outside. When one
of them returns, 'he looked different, there were drops of water
still hanging in his beard and his face was a sort of gray green
color' (F 114). A stage direction to us, as readers responding to the
overwhelming effect of Binjamin's traumatic narrative? Surely. But
Wilkomirski provides a scene of weeping partly because the sick
feeling in his throat, and ours, must issue in tears; now it's safe
to cry. Without the listeners' tears, it would be difficult to distinguish a waterfall of words from the torrent of liquid abjection
that accompanied Binjamin's earlier birth scenes.

At the end of André Schwarz-Bart's Holocaust novel, *The Last
of the Just* (1959), as the narrator accompanies his hero into the
gas chamber itself, he remembers the legend of a Rabbi burned

---

[75] For the crucial psychic function of this skin container and the confusions
attending its failure, see Esther Bick, 'The Experience of the Skin in Early Object-
Relations' (1968): 'Until the containing functions have been introjected, the concept
of a space within the self cannot arise. Introjection, i.e. construction of an object
in an internal space, is therefore impaired. In its absence, the function of projective identification will necessarily continue unabated and all the confusions of
identity attending it will be manifest', in Elizabeth Bott Spillius (ed.), *Melanie Klein
Today* (London, 1988), i. 187. See also Didier Anzieu, *The Skin Ego* (New Haven
and London, 1989), for the importance of this primitive skin container or 'skin-ego'
and the traumatic effects of its breaching.

in the scrolls of the Torah. When asked by his pupils what he sees, the Rabbi replies: 'I see the parchment burning, but the letters are taking wing . . . *Ah, yes, surely, the letters are taking wing*, Ernie repeated'.[76] The words of the legend catch fire, repeat themselves, in another text, for other readers. Geoffrey Hartman refers to the phenomenon of textual contagion (the assumption 'that the materials being studied are contagious and that there will be a transference between teacher and student') as the condition of possibility for both teaching and the transmission of knowledge.[77] His example of textual contagion is a metaphorical conflagration. In Lacan's reading of the dream of the burning child from *The Interpretation of Dreams*, the child's dream-sentence (*'Father, can't you see I'm burning?'*) becomes—in Lacan's words—'a firebrand— of itself it brings fire where it falls'.[78] It's tempting to view this transfer from one text to another as a traumatic reading effect. Metaphor involves a transfer, a transformation, that makes both meaning and mourning possible, in us as readers and beyond the limits of the individual reading; we are changed by what we read. *The Last of the Just* rehearses the names of death camps in a blackly ironic prayer of remembrance—the negative poetry of the Holocaust—while explicitly refusing pious memorials or pilgrimages:

So this story will not finish with some tomb to be visited in pious memory. For the smoke that rises from crematoria obeys physical laws like any other: the particles come together and disperse according to the wind, which propels them. The only pilgrimage, dear reader, would be to look sadly at a stormy sky now and then.[79]

From this stormy sky, a single drop of pity falls. The raindrop— an imaginary weather effect—is at once material sign and meta- phorical reader effect, channelling the reader's response much as the elders' tears had done.

---

[76] *The Last of the Just*, trans. Stephen Becker (London, 1961), 408.
[77] 'On Traumatic Knowledge', 551.
[78] *The Four Fundamental Concepts of Psycho-Analysis*, 59.
[79] *The Last of the Just*, 408.

In 'Caesura', Wilfrid Bion uses the metaphor of psychic birth to point to the anxiety that accompanies all changes of state. Thoughts and feelings in transit—'part of a process from one thought or idea or position to another'—are the catastrophic stuff of psychoanalysis.[80] This (among other things) is what he means by the transitive–intransitive mood for which the trauma situation of birth provides a prototype. The same metaphor of transitive–intransitive crossing could be applied to reading, specifically to the way we're changed and enlarged as we read, or shift from intuition to understanding. In any event, an (ex)change of some sort takes place. At the end of 'Caesura', Bion imagines a scene of weeping in which the analyst is confronted by a suffering analysand:

Suppose the analysand begins, to all appearances, to weep. The analyst becomes aware of his own funds of compassion and is impelled to participate with caution lest his responses, like a chisel of tempered steel cutting into balsa wood, too easily fashion a pattern of which the effect could not be obliterated or corrected. The analyst is affected by the patient's tears which may trace out channels in his composure no less lasting than the excoriations which he has feared to produce in his patient. He must, therefore, be sensitive to the difference in real life— not in theory—between 'tears', and 'moisture' extruded from the bodily surface open to his inspection, both his own and the analysand's.

In this strangely impersonal, yet vividly elaborated chiasmic account of the necessity for, and pitfalls of, compassion, Bion suggests that there is all the difference in the world between merely enduring psychic pain and being able to suffer it; between moisture and tears (between raw, inchoate states and sensations and their transformation into thoughts and feelings).[81] Premature naming on the part of the analyst may prevent the transition from one state to another. In the literary encounter, the responsive reader runs a similar risk of permanently incising the balsa-wood text, just as the text risks tracing lasting channels in the reader. Both text

[80] *Two Papers: The Grid and Caesura*, 55–6.

[81] The distinction corresponds, in Bion's system, to the difference between beta-elements and alpha-elements; see Wilfred Bion, *Learning from Experience* (London, 1962).

and reader are liable to be changed by their potentially wounding encounter. Such mutually discomposing and excoriating effects are among the hazards of traumatic reading. If only for this reason, the exchange requires the palpable caution, sensitivity, restraint, and the all-important exercise of judgement evoked by Bion's hypothetical scene of weeping. But most of all, registering the difference between moisture extruded from the surface of the body and tears (like the movement from fragmentation and splitting to depressive anxiety and mourning; from torrents of abjection to weeping) requires the capacity to read metaphorically, to experience the carry-over from one state to another. Without this, there could be no scene of weeping, and—in its extended, metaphorical sense—no scene of reading either.

Postscript

Since this chapter was written, a controversy has emerged over the status and authenticity of *Fragments*, along with evidence that its author, whose real name is Bruno Doesseker, was born in Switzerland in 1941 and subsequently adopted. The issues raised by the controversy are troubling, not least in light of a revisionist movement that contests the facts of the Holocaust itself; fictional 'memoirs' may be used to discredit other Holocaust memoirs as well as the truth of the historical record. But what are the implications for Wilkomirski's 'Memories of a Wartime Childhood'? The author presents himself as a child survivor, rather than (for instance) as a spokesman for other child survivors, or as the author of a collective account. The controversy is complicated because *Fragments* turns out to be entangled with the 'recovered memory' movement. Wilkomirski describes his childhood story as having been reconstructed during therapy that involved the painstaking recovery of his fragmentary memories. His 'Afterword' states that he has taken steps to have his own 'imposed identity' annulled ('Legally accredited truth is one thing—the truth of a life another', *F* 154). To all intents and purposes, then, he has become 'Binjamin'. It is one thing to write and publish a Holocaust memoir knowing that it is fiction, while passing it off as fact; but it is another thing to write a Holocaust memoir believing that it is the truth of one's life.

The temptation exists to say that in so far as the text of *Fragments* is a work of imagination, its value as testimony remains unchanged. But the stakes are not simply extra-literary. Whatever has gone on in the reading encounter, and however alert the reader may be to the inevitably constructed nature of any auto-biographical memoir, reading involves an element of witnessing. Whether one witnesses to fact or fiction may amount to the same in the end. But in practice, the reader is likely to recoil from the idea that memories have been fabricated, emotions manipulated, sensibilities violated. If Binjamin is a fictional character, his trauma imagined or appropriated, what does that say about the reader's response? But perhaps, as Wilkomirski himself is quoted as saying in an interview, it is up to the reader to decide whether his book is fiction or memoir. After all, how could one ever represent the truth of a trauma that lies beyond the scope of memory, imagination, and (for most readers) experience? Perhaps only the worst nightmare could do justice, in the sense of providing an adequate representation, to what exceeds the bounds of the thinkable—to experiences that may none the less have psychic reality, as apparently they do for Wilkomirski. But the meaning of such psychic reality changes if it is thought of as psychological—as pertaining to the 'real' (fictive?) Bruno, as opposed to the 'fictive' (real?) Binjamin—rather than testifying to any individual, reconstructed, or collective historical experience of the Holocaust. The after-effects of trauma may make it hard to distinguish between what happened and what actually happened (or, for the reader, to distinguish between fiction, fantasy, and fact). There is, however, an important difference. For the Holocaust survivor, what actually happened—the event—was as bad as (worse than) anything that could happen in psychic reality. For this reason the question of authenticity doesn't only involve extra-literary considerations, since it brings both trauma theory and the historical record into question. A world of difference exists between events that really happened, whether to oneself or to others, and which should be addressed, redressed, or prevented, and events that did not.

An earlier version of this chapter contained a section on railway trauma. In one especially fragmented and hallucinatory episode, Binjamin survives a train-wreck unscathed (as often, apparently miraculously), only to succumb to the classic effects of trauma in the aftermath of the derailment—disorientation, depersonalization, and numbing. Freud's most famous instance of traumatic neurosis in *Beyond the Pleasure Principle*, repeated in *Moses and Monotheism* (1939), is that of a railway collision from which the survivor walks away, physically unhurt, but later develops a traumatic neurosis.[82] The episode prompted some reflections on my part about the possibility that the only way to testify to certain forms of trauma might be via the unreality of nightmare (some people—not me—might say, via 'recovered memory'). Here as elsewhere, *Fragments* recapitulates one of the familiar topoi of trauma theory. Dissatisfied with my own discussion of this end-of-line experience, I decided not to include it. In retrospect, my indecision seems telling. For all Binjamin's sense of unreality, the episode conforms to Freud's blueprint for the traumatic neurosis. My argument had been that no survivor's memoir could avoid reproducing the conventions of Holocaust writing, by now thoroughly mapped on to contemporary consciousness, along with psychoanalytic models for trauma which have gained wide currency today. (I might have argued that Wilkomirski's polemic is directed against the collective repression of the Holocaust in postwar Switzerland. His book is a critique of postwar amnesia as well as a work of 'recovered' memory—or rather, as I would prefer to call it, reconstructed memory. Fifty years on, such works of post-memory, or secondary Holocaust trauma, constitute a recognizable literary genre in their own right.)

I suggested at the end of my chapter that traumatic reading might be hazardous, risking the premature incising of meaning on both text and reader: 'Suppose', writes Bion, 'the analysand begins to all appearances, to weep.' Bion's hypothetical scene of weeping alludes not only to the analyst's funds of compassion, but to the dangers of premature knowing. Discriminating between

[82] See n. 48 above for the omitted episode.

'tears' and 'moisture extruded from the body', i.e. 'the difference in real life—not in theory' (which is not the same as the difference between real tears and fake tears), implies a corresponding willingness to entertain uncertainty. But this does not amount to saying that there is no difference. *Fragments* depends on Wilkomirski's strategic deployment of scenes of weeping to make bearable—to contain—scenes of extreme abjection. In the end, we may have to hold on to a difference that exists in real life (true or false?), while recognizing that there are some differences that can only be known in theory; and yet others that have to be addressed in the consulting room rather than by the literary critic. Whatever the outcome, the controversy over *Fragments* provides a timely reminder that trauma theory is more than just another branch of aesthetics. It may be hard, in the end, to distinguish between 'recovered memory' and reconstructed memory, or between tears and the appearance of tears—between memories and screen-memories. But just as trauma risks losing its specificity when it becomes a trope for figuration, Holocaust memory risks losing its historicity when it becomes a metaphor for object loss. To paraphrase Adorno, after Auschwitz there can be no metaphor untouched by the event.

PART THREE

Romantic Women

FIVE

Guilt that Wants a Name
Mary Shelley's Unreadability

Do analysts have an ear for *all* 'poems' and for *all* 'poets'?
Surely not. (Nicolas Abraham and Maria Torok, *The Shell
and the Kernel*)[1]

... books do much—but the living intercourse is the vital
heat, debarred from that how have I pined & died. (Mary
Shelley, *Journals*)[2]

WHAT does it mean to listen to a literary text that
speaks with such profound elisions that the listener
is unable to hear it? Does the failure lie in the 'poem'
or in the listener? Or, in the case of a literary text, does it lie in
the reader? This question opens Nicolas Abraham's and Maria
Torok's joint inquiry into a form of mourning they call 'The Lost
Object—Me'. Their account of the enigmatic poetics of pathological mourning brings psychoanalysis and poetry into the same
room with the phantom of analytic failure—the tormenting rift,
or mutilation, inflicted by a gap in the memory of patient or poem.
They suggest that this '*nescience*' or unrecognized knowledge—
perhaps the bearer of a buried parental secret—creates a formation
in the unconscious of the listener that mimes a mutilation in the

[1] Nicolas Abraham and Maria Torok, *The Shell and the Kernel: Renewals of Psychoanalysis*, ed. and trans. Nicholas T. Rand (Chicago, 1994), 140; this essay first appeared
in English in 1984 under the title 'Poetics of Psychoanalysis: "The Lost Object—Me"'.
[2] *The Journals of Mary Shelley 1814–1844*, ed. Paula R. Feldman and Diana Scott-
Kilvert (2 vols., Oxford, 1987), ii. 556 (cited hereafter as *Journals*).

text.[3] A similar rift preoccupies me here, along with the poetics of
buried memory, forgotten mourning, and a form of trauma, to
paraphrase Abraham, 'that can befall any work of art (be it a text
or a life)—the trauma of its being cut off from itself'.[4] Abraham is
referring specifically to the trauma of translation. In what follows,
however, I will be focusing on the different but related disjunction
involved in literary transmission. My example will be Mary Shelley's
melancholic and (in literary terms) incestuous incest-novel, *Matilda*.

To the current interest in the relations between trauma, memory, and history, I want to add an interest in the relation between
trauma and literary transmission.[5] Mary Shelley's tale of suicidal
despair can be read as a traumatized text (one that is cut off or
dissociated from itself) as well as a narrative that deals with incest-
trauma. Father–daughter incest—Shelley's ostensible subject—
seems both to cover over and to discover other losses that are
both more traumatic and more unspeakable. I will be suggesting that trauma in *Matilda* is not only manifested at the level
of narrative but associated specifically with problems involving
the transmission of prior texts, and that psychoanalysis may have
something to say about why this is so. Not surprisingly, *Matilda*
has proved an especially fertile site for psychoanalytic readings.
Interpreted as a seduction phantasy, for instance, it conforms to
the lines of the Freudian scenario sketched by Marie Bonaparte's
'L'identification d'une fille à sa mère morte'.[6] In this classically
Oedipal reading, *Matilda* is assimilated to the psycho-biographical

[3] See *The Shell and the Kernel*, 140 n.: 'Should a child have parents with "secrets", . . .
the child will receive from them a gap in the unconscious, an unknown, unrecognized
knowledge—a *nescience*—subjected to a form of "repression" before the fact.'

[4] Nicolas T. Rand and Maria Torok, 'Paradeictic: Translation, Psychoanalysis, and
the Work of Art in the Writings of Nicolas Abraham', *Rhythms: On the Work, Translation, and Psychoanalysis*, trans. Benjamin Thigpen and Nicholas T. Rand (Stanford,
Calif., 1995), 151.

[5] See, for instance, Cathy Caruth, *Unclaimed Experience: Trauma, Narrative, and History*
(Baltimore and London, 1996); Cathy Caruth (ed.), *Trauma: Explorations in Memory*
(Baltimore and London, 1995); and Shoshana Felman and Dori Laub, *Testimony: Crises
of Witnessing in Literature, Psychoanalysis, and History* (New York and London, 1992).

[6] See Terence Harpold, ' "Did you get Mathilda from Papa?": Seduction Fantasy
and the Circulation of Mary Shelley's *Matilda*', *Studies in Romanticism*, 28 (1989), 49–67.
As Harpold puts it (ibid. 52), Shelley 'remembered a history of forbidden desire and
death to repair a loss at the origin of that history'.

circuit structuring literary transmission between the daughter of a famous, dead feminist mother (Mary Wollstonecraft) and her chronically debt-ridden radical-philosopher father (William Godwin).[7] Biographical concerns will necessarily have a place in my own reading. But what follows has more to do with the poetics of unreadability, or what I'm tempted to call 'the unreadability effect' of Mary Shelley's novella. My point of departure is Tilottama Rajan's suggestive Kristevan account of *Matilda* as a 'textual abject', that is, neither narrative nor lyric but a mix of both.[8] Associating its melancholy with 'a form in which the writer submerges in some trauma or affect from which she will not separate', Rajan reads *Matilda* as the symptomatic outcast of the political economy of Godwin's and Percy Shelley's Romanticism. But she also goes beyond Romantic politics to define Mary Shelley's novella as a text resistant to the economy of reading itself.

Rajan speculates that what she refers to as *Matilda*'s 'unusable negativity' and 'resistance to productive reading' (whether formalist or political) is the source of its current fascination.[9] But, for her, *Matilda*'s resistance and negativity ultimately remain just that: unproductive and unusable. This negation—in Freud's sense, 'a way of taking cognizance of what has been repressed'—has interesting effects on her own reading.[10] Observing that Shelley's

[7] For Mary Shelley's 'excessive & romantic' attachment to Godwin, see *The Letters of Mary Wollstonecraft Shelley*, ed. Betty T. Bennett (2 vols., Baltimore and London, 1980–3), ii. 215. See also Anne K. Mellor, *Mary Shelley: Her Life, Her Fiction, Her Monsters* (New York and London, 1988), 191–201 for a reading of *Matilda* in relation to Godwin, male and female gothic, and the incestuous bourgeois family.

[8] See Tilottama Rajan, 'Mary Shelley's *Mathilda*: Melancholy and the Political Economy of Romanticism', *Studies in the Novel*, 26 (1994), 43–68. For Rajan's critique of Harpold, see ibid. 49–50. I am indebted to Rajan's suggestive and far-reaching discussion of *Matilda* for drawing my attention to the difficulties presented by its negativity. See also Judith Barbour, ' "The Meaning of the Tree": The Tale of Mirra in Mary Shelley's *Mathilda*', in Syndy M. Conger, Frederick S. Frank, and Gregory O'Dea (eds.), *Iconoclastic Departures: Mary Shelley After Frankenstein* (Totowa, NJ, 1997), 98–114, for an exploration of the 'patriarchal' and 'maternal' plots enfolded in the Dantean allusions of Shelley's novella.

[9] See Rajan, 'Mary Shelley's *Mathilda*', 44–7, 61.

[10] See Freud's 1923 paper, 'Negation' (*SE* xix. 235–9): 'Thus the content of a repressed image or idea can make its way into consciousness, on condition that it is *negated*. Negation is a way of taking cognizance of what is repressed; indeed, it is already a lifting of the repression, though not, of course, an acceptance of what is repressed' (*SE* xix. 235–6).

'borderline' novella tends not to impress readers (as she puts it) 'committed to an ideology of the aesthetic', Rajan notes that the 'traces' of Dante and Wordsworth fail to make its narrative beautiful.[11] To the extent that *Matilda* strikes most readers as both depressed and depressing, and its quotations from other poets strangely out of context, even wooden, she is right.[12] Along the same lines, Rajan also notes that 'echoes of Dante remain, but . . . survive only on the level of affect, where they protect a desire for idealization'.[13] It is just this 'survival on the level of affect' that interests me, however. A striking feature of *Matilda*'s use of poetic quotation is the way it functions not only as the trace of buried affect or protective idealization, but as the mark of disjunction itself. For Rajan, these traces and echoes of earlier poetry are the symptoms of *Matilda*'s borderline condition; at one point, in fact, she equates its failure as lyric with lyric as a sign of failure or lack, as such ('it lacks lyric's ability to idealize mood . . . *Matilda*'s lyricism . . . is less a positive identity than a subtraction from narrative').[14] I want to ask what kind of reading might lend an ear to this peculiar form of subtractive lyricism—a lyricism that Rajan appropriately associates with the Wordsworthian aesthetic of *Lyrical Ballads* (i.e. bare, affective narratives of trauma). My argument will be that reading Mary Shelley's failed lyricism as the sign of trauma may, paradoxically, allow us to hear *Matilda*'s missing poetry.

The reading that follows tries to explore *Matilda*'s negativity via the complicated relations between trauma and forgetting, trauma and attempted reparation, and trauma as the misreading, mis-application, misremembering, or dismembering of prior literary

---

[11] Rajan, 'Mary Shelley's *Mathilda*', 47.

[12] For a Kleinian reading of the aesthetic questions involved in 'beauty' and 'ugliness' in the work of art, see Hanna Segal, 'A Psychoanalytic Approach to Aesthetics', *The Work of Hanna Segal: A Kleinian Approach to Clinical Practice* (Northvale, NJ, and London, 1981), 185–206. Arguing in her classic paper that 'a satisfactory work of art is achieved by a realization and sublimation of the depressive position', Segal sees ugliness and destruction as the expression of the death instinct; failure to use symbols results, for her, from an 'inability to accept and use [the] death instinct and to acknowledge death' (ibid. 203).

[13] Rajan, 'Mary Shelley's *Mathilda*', 46.   [14] Ibid. 47.

texts. For Mary Shelley, the literary past was inextricably tied to the writings of her parents, and hence to the interconnected questions of literary and generational transmission. One could argue that this form of trauma is endemic in any attempt to grapple with the literary impingements of the past; incestuous repetition and radical discontinuity continually threaten both generational difference and the line of literary descent. This is why literary transmission can look like another chapter in the theory of translation (or, for that matter, melancholia). But to traumatize literary transmission as such risks evacuating the meaning of trauma altogether (as I have argued elsewhere, apropos of theories of literary language, subjectivity, and Holocaust writing).[15] If trauma is to retain its specificity, the psychic structures activated in the face of overwhelming catastrophe must retain their link to the event (whether this event is understood as external or internal, historical or 'structural', i.e. universal). The theory of trauma handed down by Freud includes, as is well known, a vexed temporal dimension (*Nachträglichkeit* or deferred action—Laplanche's 'afterwardsness').[16] An event may be traumatic in retrospectively transforming the meaning of the past, or, alternatively, traumatic in reactivating a prior trauma (or both); hence the ideas of a missed meaning or an unnarratable 'beyond' that often accompany the writing of, and writing about, trauma. But the damaging impingement of the environment on the individual—the collapse of inner and outer —remains an inescapable component for the so-called survivor. Shelley's incest-narrative makes it possible to explore the problematic relations of event to structure which arise when competing historical and trans-historical accounts of trauma are set in opposition to one another. It also enacts in literary ways some of the forms of cut-offness that may befall both texts and lives in the wake of psychic catastrophe. What is it, one finds oneself asking, that *Matilda* does transmit, if it fails to transmit 'beauty', and what is the nature of Mary Shelley's engagement with prior literary texts?

[15] See Ch. 4 above.
[16] For 'afterwardsness', see *Jean Laplanche: Seduction, Translation and the Drives*, ed. John Fletcher and Martin Stanton (London, 1992), 217–23.

Oedipus Is About To Die

Matilda opens with a chilling description which is also an extended form of pathetic fallacy. Mary Shelley's writing is luminously super-real in its attempt to record the feverish affective life belied by the wintry scene:

It is only four o'clock; but it is winter and the sun has already set: there are no clouds in the clear, frosty sky to reflect its slant beams, but the air itself is tinged with a slight roseate colour which is again reflected on the snow that covers the ground . . . no voice of life reaches me. I see the desolate plain covered with white . . . a few birds are pecking at the hard ice that covers the pools—for the frost has been of long continuance.

I am in a strange state of mind. I am alone—quite alone—in the world . . . I know that I am about to die and I feel happy—joyous. —I feel my pulse; it beats fast . . . there is a slight, quick spirit within me which is now emitting its last spark. I shall never see the snows of another winter—I do believe that I shall never again feel the vivifying warmth of another summer sun; and it is in this persuasion that I begin to write my tragic history. (*M* 151)[17]

Where have we heard such hectic quickening of affect in the face of impending death? Those familiar with Wordsworth's *Lyrical Ballads* will immediately recognize 'The Complaint of a Forsaken Indian Woman', whose refrain Shelley later makes her heroine convert into a prayer of her own, 'repeat[ing] with the poet—"Before I see another day | Oh, let this body die away!"'[18] Wordsworth's lyrical ballad imagines the wintry North American landscape as the setting for 'the last struggles of a human being at the approach of death, cleaving in solitude to life and society' (1800 'Preface' to *Lyrical Ballads*)—a gloss that would certainly have been known to Mary Shelley, along with Wordsworth's

---

[17] Cited hereafter as *M*. All references are to the text of *Matilda* included in Mary Wollstonecraft, *Mary* and *Maria*, and Mary Shelley, *Matilda*, ed. Janet Todd (Harmondsworth, 1991). The MS of *Matilda* remained unpublished until it was edited by Elizabeth Nitchie as *Mathilda* in a special issue of *Studies in Philology*, Extra Series, No. 3 (Chapel Hill, NC, 1959).

[18] 'Before I see another day, | Oh let my body die away!' ('The Complaint of a Forsaken Indian Woman', ll. 1–2, 9–10).

ethnographic headnote about the Indian custom of abandoning the sick on their travels.[19] Like the Indian woman, Shelley's first-person narrator survives in a condition of near death, and her prose is infused by the plaintive rhythms of Wordsworthian penultimacy ('I shall never see the snows of another winter— . . . I shall never again feel . . . the warmth of another summer sun', M 151).

But there is another, less audible echo. Wordsworth's 'Complaint' touches indirectly on the autobiographical situation that Mary Shelley has excised from her narrative—not just the Indian woman's unbearable solitude and longing for the tribe that has left her behind to die, but the loss of her child, handed over for survival to a surrogate mother: 'My poor forsaken Child! if I | For once could have thee close to me, | With happy heart I then would die . . .' (ll. 65–7). The wish involved in this literary allusion (the mother knows she is going to die, but the child will live) is reminiscent of Freud's 'Dream of the Burning Child', which Freud reads as fulfilling the father's wish to prolong by a few moments the illusion that his child is still alive.[20] This mother prolongs her attenuated sense of life by the life-sustaining wish that her child could be close to her. Tracking Mary Shelley's incest-narrative into the northern snows of Wordsworth's lyrical ballad may tell us something about why her lyric speaker is on the point of death, longs to die, and (above all) feels that she deserves to die. When Mary Shelley sent the manuscript of Matilda to her father (who dragged his feet over publication, and found its theme 'disgusting and detestable'),[21] she removed the original frame-narrative which had situated her tale of incest in its autobiographical context. This context was the death in Rome of her 3-year-old son William, in June 1819; her year-old daughter Clara had died

---

[19] Wordsworth's source is Herne's *Journey from . . . Hudson's Bay to the Northern Ocean* (1795).

[20] See *The Interpretation of Dreams* (1900), *SE* v. 509–11. For a Lacanian reading of this dream in relation to trauma, see Caruth, *Unclaimed Experience*, 91–112.

[21] See Harpold, 'Seduction Fantasy', 63: 'The subject [Godwin] says is disgusting and detestable, and there ought to be, at least if [it] is ever published, a preface to prepare the minds of the readers, and to prevent them being tormented by the apprehension . . . of the fall of the heroine'; see *Maria Gisborne & Edward E. Williams, Shelley's Friends: Their Journals and Letters*, ed. F. L. Jones (Norman, Okla., 1951), 44.

the previous year.[22] The death of a child must always be tragic, although not necessarily traumatic. But a child who dies before the parent can also be thought of in terms of a reversal of the natural order that puts in question the capacity for transmission from generation to generation. For the parents, the death may even appear as the sign of their own incapacity or failure to keep the child alive.[23] Whatever the meaning of her small son's death to Mary Shelley herself, I want to suggest that her repression of maternal mourning in *Matilda* constitutes an obvious, first-level gap in the text—although not (I think) the only one, since *Matilda* inevitably invokes another and older, but ultimately unknowable, experience of trauma: the death of Mary Shelley's own mother at her birth. In other words, this novella has something submerged to say about the loss of the child to the mother and the loss of the mother to the child.

The submerged relations between *Matilda*'s unreadable melancholia and identification with a lost object—as well as the relation between trauma and the death drive (manifested as the separation of representation from affect)—can be read in this single, telling repression.[24] In 'Analysis Terminable and Interminable'

---

[22] William was the last of the Shelleys' three children to die, and the second in one year; Mary Shelley was already pregnant with her fourth and only surviving child, Percy Florence, born in November after she had been childless 'for 5 hateful months'; see *The Letters of Mary Wollstonecraft Shelley*, i. 99–100, 114, and *Journals*, i. 291–302, for this period, which is also narrated by Emily W. Sunstein, *Mary Shelley: Romance and Reality* (Baltimore, 1989), 168–76. See also Margaret Davenport Garrett, 'Writing and Re-writing Incest in Mary Shelley's *Mathilda*', *Keats-Shelley Journal*, 45 (1996), 44–60, for an account of Mary Shelley's writing of her incest-narrative, and its literary sources, in the face of maternal bereavement.

[23] See Louise J. Kaplan's moving study of parental and childhood bereavement, *No Voice is Ever Wholly Lost* (New York, 1995), 10: 'The death of a child is an extraordinary blow to a parent's entire being, his or her sense of self-worth and self-esteem. This reversal of the natural order of things, wherein a child is meant to outlive the parents, brings into question a parent's capacity for generational transmission. A parent who loses a child interprets the unborn or dead child as a sign of his or her own degeneration. Very often the parents are consumed by a never-ending grief.'

[24] Declining the pathos of 'The Dream of the Burning Child' (along with the presence of death in its manifest content as the manifestation of the death drive), Laplanche locates the death drive instead in 'the destructuration tendencies in the psychic apparatus; especially repression . . . that is putting a representation apart from its affect and de-binding it'; see *Jean Laplanche: Seduction, Translation and the Drives*, 28.

(1937), writing of the mingling and defusion of life and death instincts, Freud alludes to the death drive as 'a force which is defending itself by every possible means against recovery and which is absolutely resolved to hold on to illness and suffering'. In a literary context, one could gloss this defence against 'recovery' not just as the melancholy that pervades *Matilda*, but as a failure of 'symbolization'—the failure to find adequate forms of literary representation for the affect that underlies it. Recognizing 'one portion of this force . . . as the sense of guilt and need for punishment', Freud also insists on 'unmistakable indications of the presence of a power in mental life which we call the instinct of aggression or of destruction'.[25] Such destructiveness might well work to undermine the links on which effective symbolization depends in a literary context. On a narrative level, we can already glimpse Freud's 'sense of guilt' at work in Matilda's self-announced (and entirely inappropriate) identification with Oedipus: 'While life was strong within me I thought indeed that there was a sacred horror in my tale that rendered it unfit for utterance, and now that I am about to die I pollute its mystic terrors. . . . Oedipus is about to die' (*M* 151). Matilda's breach of silence, her polluting 'utterance', repeats the chronologically earlier moment when her father pollutingly broaches the secret of incest at Matilda's own insistence. Just as 'a feeling that [she] cannot define leads [her] on' to tell her story, so she is 'led by passion' (*M* 172) in the compulsive rhythms of the climactic scene when she extorts the secret of her father's guilty passion. By making her heroine announce her 'tragic history' as that of the dying Oedipus

---

[25] *SE* xxiii. 242–3. See also Herbert Rosenfeld's Kleinian account of phenomena associated with the death instinct: 'they create something mysterious, hidden, unspeakable, and yet incredibly powerful and dangerous, against which it is impossible to fight' (*Impasse and Interpretation* (London and New York, 1987), 267–8). Rosenfeld is elaborating on Freud's description of a death instinct 'that remains mute and hidden but opposes the patient's desire to get better' as employed by both Freud and Klein to understand, among other things, 'masochism, the unconscious sense of guilt, negative therapeutic reactions, and resistance to treatment' (ibid. 107–8); with some relevance to *Matilda*, Rosenfeld redefines 'the wish to die or to withdraw into a state of nothingness or deadness' as active destructiveness directed not only against objects but against parts of the self—as 'destructive narcissism'—rather than as a primary drive towards death (ibid. 109).

(led to Colonus by his daughter), Mary Shelley accentuates Matilda's overwhelming identification with the guilt of her dead father, as well as with his unhappy daughter (Antigone).[26] To paraphrase Laplanche, culpability finds the Oedipal story to bind it ('the feeling of culpability is more primary than the elaboration in the complex')—confronted, as it were, with something even more awful than killing the father.[27] What Matilda and Oedipus have in common is not so much incest as their 'feeling of culpability', a guilt that is incommensurate with any actual crime committed, and which strictly speaking precedes it.

   Matilda's Oedipal thematics make it possible to sketch the link between trauma and the death drive, aesthetic failure and literary transmission. In particular, *Matilda* confronts us with the unbinding of affect (Freud's 'defusion') rather than its channelling into an adequate narrative structure. The adoption of an incestuous pseudo-narrative prevents both Matilda and Mary Shelley from narrating their stories in a way that has any relation to reality. Matilda's tragedy is not just her father's guilty passion for her, nor is it her paralysing, idealizing, and finally murderous love for her father. It is the fact that her father's story becomes hers (he is actually the one who has loved his mother in Oedipal fashion, and who sinks into mute despair when his wife dies). Incest is structured in *Matilda* as the intergenerational repetition of a prior romance and as an always prior trauma; the second generation takes on the burden of this past. Like Mary Shelley's mother, Matilda's mother has died giving birth to her. Identifying with the grief of the surviving parent makes her father's

---

[26] Shelley refers specifically to 'the wood of the Eumenides [which] none but the dying may enter' (*M* 151); for an interesting Kleinian reading of Oedipus' omnipotence and self-righteousness in the face of death, see John Steiner, *Psychic Retreats: Pathological Organizations in Psychotic, Neurotic, and Borderline Patients* (London and New York, 1993), 125–30.

[27] 'I said once that Oedipus was the first criminal through the feeling of culpability—that is, the feeling of culpability is more primary than the elaboration in the complex. And as Freud sometimes attributed to Klein: "You are not guilty because you killed your father; you killed your father because you were primarily guilty", that is, confronted with something even more awful than killing your father. The Oedipus is a way among others . . . in our civilization, to bind' (*Jean Laplanche: Seduction, Translation, and the Drives*, 31).

mourning the only form of mourning available to the daughter.[28] The trauma that *Matilda* can never fully mourn, yet must continually relive, is not only this loss of the child to the mother (or even the loss of an unreliable, disillusioning father), but this unmourned and unmournable loss of the mother to the child. The mother's death is *Matilda*'s missed event, its buried and unknowable 'beyond' —displaced, however, on to the imaginary loss of an infant 'Me' to the father who also abandons her in his grief. The incestuous substitute narrative at once occupies and obliterates the site of a founding (but unnarratable) loss.

For Mary Shelley, one might speculate, the death of a child may have reactivated the infantile trauma of not being able to mourn.[29] But the literary elaboration of this traumatic 'beyond' could also be read as an attempt at literary self-cure. We know from her own testimony that Mary Shelley wanted to die after William's death ('I feel that I am no[t] fit for any thing & therefore not fit to live').[30] Matilda's 'hatred of life' (*M* 185) seems to have been Mary Shelley's during the following months. She was unreachable by her husband, Percy Shelley, while Godwin tormented her with financial begging letters, attempting to rally her out of her depression with peculiar insensitivity and abrasive rationality.[31] After the death of her father, Matilda too is 'changed to stone', 'silent to all around [her]', lamenting (with Job), 'Where

[28] For the intensity of Godwin's mourning, see his *Memoirs of the Author of a Vindication of the Rights of Woman* (1798), written immediately after Wollstonecraft's death, and Mary Shelley's major source of information about her mother. See also Mitzi Myers, 'Godwin's *Memoirs* of Wollstonecraft: The Shaping of Self and Subject', *Studies in Romanticism*, 20 (1981), 299–316.

[29] Writing of the connections between trauma and creativity in a woman, Joyce McDougall also speculates on the role of fantasies of destructiveness directed at the mother; see *The Many Faces of Eros* (New York and London, 1995), 93–113.

[30] 'I never know one moment's ease from the wretchedness & despair that possesses me . . . I feel that I am no[t] fit for any thing & therefore not fit to live but how must that heart be moulded which would not be broken by what I have suffered' (*The Letters of Mary Wollstonecraft Shelley*, i. 101–2); 'I ought to have died on the 7th of June last', she told Leigh Hunt in September (ibid. i. 108).

[31] See *The Letters of Percy Bysshe Shelley*, ed. F. L. Jones (2 vols., Oxford, 1964), ii. 109. Godwin wrote: 'you have all the goods of fortune, all the means of being useful to others . . . But . . . all is nothing, because a child of three years old is dead'; see also *Journals*, i. 291 for her distress.

is now my hope? For my hope who shall see it? | They shall go down together to the bars of the pit, when our rest together is in the dust' (M 184, 185).[32] These words speak from the hopeless core of *Matilda* and, presumably, Mary Shelley. Yet for Shelley herself, the composition of her novella during the late summer and early autumn of 1819 apparently brought consolation. Why? Constrasting her situation after Percy Shelley's death, she recalled in her journal, 'when I wrote Matilda, miserable as I was, the *inspiration* was sufficient to quell my wretchedness temporarily'.[33] The emphasis on '*inspiration*' offers a clue to the consolation of writing. *Matilda* may quell the angry revolt masked by melancholia with a compensatory fantasy (roughly speaking, 'my father will come back to me, changed for the better'). But it also transforms the stoney state of the inconsolable mother into the possibility of phantasmal reunion with a lost parent. *Matilda*'s attempt to recover (or reform) this lost parent takes the form of projecting the ruptured temporality of the past into a Dantean future in which error could be converted into wisdom, division healed as reunion, and love freed from its inevitable ambivalence and confusion. The nevermore of loss becomes the evermore of imaginary repossession.

The model for Mary Shelley's 'inspiration' in *Matilda* is purgatorial narrative, a form of selective Dantean forgetting and remembering. Shelley transforms a psychic economy predicated on the convergence of parental prehistory and literary origins into a model of redemption through literary rememoration. Or, in the injunction that rings through the *Purgatorio*—'Ricorditi, ricorditi' ('Remember, remember'). Remembering keeps something alive. As Virgil enjoins the Pilgrim in Canto XXVII, 'here may be torment but not death'.[34] Dante can appeal to the redemptive

---

[32] The quotation is from Job 17: 15–16; cf. also *Matilda*: 'Often amid apparent calm I was visited by despair and melancholy; gloom that nought could dissipate or overcome . . .' (M 189).

[33] *Journals*, ii. 442.

[34] All references are to *The Divine Comedy*, trans. and commentary Charles Singleton (6 vols., Princeton, 1970–5). La Pia, who also appeals to memory earlier in the *Purgatorio*—'ricorditi di me' (v. 133)—will be one of those spirits saved at the last moment of life.

possibilities of memory since by this point in the *Purgatorio* the temporal journey is subject to renegotiation—in contrast to the *Inferno*, where memory can only be a source of despair—and may lead beyond memory to paradisal re-envisioning.[35] Mary Shelley had originally introduced Matilda's story by way of a Dantean frame-narrative where a consolatory figure named 'Fantasia' enables the recovery of imagination and memory as wisdom, here personified by Diotima (named after Socrates' instructress in Plato's *Symposium*).[36] Purgatorial retelling allows her story of father–daughter incest to be recuperated for the purposes of maternal instruction. It also effects a longed-for reunion with this imaginary literary and philosophic fore-mother. But Shelley's attempt to repair familial history remains uneasily suspended between the traumatic repetitions of seduction phantasy and the purgatorial re-envisioning of spiritual reality.[37] The symbolic elaboration involved in mourning—in Kleinian theory, typically located in the intra- and inter-psychic space of the psychoanalytic process—corresponds to the purgatorial realm of Dantean re-membering (at once the realm of process and of symbolization) where Diotima encourages Matilda to retell her story and so be free of it. Where seduction phantasy provides a figure for traumatic repetition, the Dantean scheme gestures towards the possibility of integration—but in *Matilda*, as I hope to show, under the sign of negativity. Resuming her journal two months after William's death, Mary Shelley wrote: 'to have won & then cruelly have lost the associations of four years is not an accident to which the human mind can bend without much suffering.'[38]

[35] For Francesca, for instance, in *Inferno*, v. 121–3, 'Nesun maggior dolore | che ricordarsi del tempo felice | ne la miseria' ('There is no greater sorrow than to recall, in wretchedness, the happy time').

[36] For 'The Fields of Fancy', see Nitchie, *Mathilda*, 90–101, and, for Mary Shelley's and Percy Shelley's use of Plato's *Symposium*, ibid. 103–4 nn.

[37] For a contemporary account of trauma, as opposed to what he calls 'psychic genera', see Christopher Bollas, *On Being a Character: Psychoanalysis and Self Experience* (London, 1993), 69–70; while 'the effect of trauma is to sponsor symbolic repetition not symbolic elaboration', Bollas writes, 'psychic genera' involve the re-envisioning of reality. Although an Independent rather than a Kleinian, Bollas associates trauma with the death drive.

[38] *Journals*, i. 293.

Matilda bears the marks of this suffering. Some traumas, some accidents, may be beyond repair.

My Daughter, I Love Thee!

What has seduction phantasy to do with literary transmission? Drawing on Ferenczi's 1933 essay, 'Confusion of Tongues between Adults and the Child', where the 'language of passion' —sexualized adult language—is traumatic because it conveys unknown meanings, Laplanche revises the theory of seduction to shift the emphasis from the primal scene, or overt parental seduction, to what he calls 'enigmatic signifiers'.[39] Such signifiers are opaque both to the adult and to the child. For Laplanche, sexuality is organized by prior, unconscious parental desires that are communicated to the child; by definition, it becomes a traumatic impingement from outside. Relocating seduction in the enigmatic communication itself, Laplanche suggests that a mother's attentions or a father's aggression become seductive because they set symbolization an impossible task. These unmasterable sexual messages or 'enigmatic signifiers' may even be coextensive with a gap or silence in language. The secrets of incest are linguistically transmitted, yet they remain paradoxically 'unspeakable'. *Matilda* thematizes just such repeated, enigmatic effects of language and unspeakability. If seduction phantasy can be redefined as traumatic communication, it may also be the case—as Laplanche speculates—that 'even when we think we are creating, we are always being worked by foreign messages'.[40] Literary creation, then, contains a potential for trauma as Laplanche defines it.

---

[39] See Jean Laplanche, *New Foundations for Psychoanalysis*, trans. David Macey (Oxford, 1989), ch. 3, esp. 125–9. For Sándor Ferenczi's essay, 'Confusion of Tongues between Adults and the Child' (1933), see *Final Contributions to the Problems and Methods of Psychoanalysis* (London, 1955), 156–67.

[40] *Jean Laplanche: Seduction, Translation, and the Drives*, 33. Laplanche is also speaking about the traumatic impingement of someone else's (Ferenczi's) ideas on him when he writes 'we have to find a way between seduction and trauma . . . It makes me think of the messages you don't want to receive because you hate to agree' (ibid. 33).

Shelley's heroine refers to incestuous passion as 'guilt that wants a name' ('so horrible to my own solitary thoughts did this form, this voice, and all this wretched self appear; for had it not been the source of *guilt that wants a name?*', M 204; my italics). The 'secret' which Matilda insists on prising out of her father serves to implicate her in her father's nameless guilt (hence her Oedipal self-accusation); his adult language of passion retrospectively colours her girlhood tenderness for him. From the first, her father's secret has been a love experienced as precociously sexual. For instance, we are told that he loves his childhood playmate as a sweetheart: 'At eleven years of age Diana was his favorite playmate but he already talked the language of love' (M 153). Later, as a young man, Matilda's spoilt and wilful father has 'one secret . . . a secret he had nurtured from his earliest years . . . *He loved*' (M 153; my italics— note the intransitive, objectless form of the verb 'to love'). This precociously sexualized childhood love, whose ostensible object is Matilda's virginal mother (aptly named Diana), is the secret that he transmits to his daughter. Structurally, Matilda comes to occupy the position of lost love while simultaneously identifying with her father's loss—at once effacing generational difference, and encrypting another's mourning as her own. After Diana's death in childbirth, Matilda's father goes abroad, refusing to see his infant daughter—nor, in fact, will he ever be able to see her as anything but the reincarnation of his dead childhood sweetheart, whose resemblance he finds on his return, sixteen years later. Matilda ('the offspring of the deepest love', M 157) becomes the enigmatic signifier—the carrier—for these prior and already incestuous parental passions.

In Mary Shelley's novella, Matilda is a figure for both poetry and seduction. Left unparented, she seeks the Wordsworthian consolations of passionate, focused, but indiscriminate attachment to the inanimate world ('I cannot say with what passion I loved every thing, even the inanimate objects that surrounded me. I believe that I bore an individual attachment to every tree', M 157). The scene of this solitary childhood, enlivened only by its animistic feeling for nature, is a northern landscape of lakes, mountains, and waterfalls. Predictably, then, Matilda is compared to a Lucy figure whom 'there were none to praise | And very few to love' (*M* 157–8)—an allusion to Wordsworth's lyrical ballad 'She dwelt among th'untrodden ways' (ll. 1–4). Matilda is at once the signifier of primal loss, and the symbol of Wordsworth's association of Lucy, nature poetry, and elegy ('But she is in her Grave, and Oh! | The difference to me', ll. 11–12). In this attenuated natural object-world, 'the place of human intercourse' is supplied by Matilda's 'only friend', a harp, or Romantic poetry in its responsive mode ('I could pour forth to it all my hopes and loves, and fancied that its sweet accents answered me', *M* 158–9).[41] Matilda is a poet in the making who 'wandered from the fancies of others and formed affections and intimacies with the aerial creatures of [her] own brain' (*M* 159). Clinging to the memory of her parents, and especially to the memory of 'the unhappy, wandering father' who becomes 'the idol of [her] imagination' (*M* 159), she models her day-dreams on the wandering, parentless heroines of Shakespearian and Miltonic romances ('I brought Rosalind and Miranda and the lady of Comus to life to be my companions'). These imaginary quest narratives have one common feature ('I imaged [it] in my mind a thousand and a thousand times, perpetually varying the circumstances', *M* 159)—the longed-for meeting in which, dressed like a boy, and displaying his miniature on her breast, she is reunited with her long-lost father: 'his first words constantly were: "My daughter, I love thee!"' (*M* 159).[42] These words are to have immense proleptic significance in Shelley's incest narrative.

Abraham and Torok allude not only to a 'buried speech of the parent' but to the buried memory of an illicit idyll, 'experienced with a valued object and yet for some reason unspeakable'. This secret is itself the trauma (as for Laplanche the enigma is

---

[41] I am grateful to Carol Jacobs for drawing my attention to the harp and to the complex of allusions to poetry submerged both here and elsewhere in *Matilda*, particularly the (Percy) Shelleyan 'poetry' of Woodville's 'Hymn to Intellectual Beauty'.

[42] For the 'family romances' ubiquitous in children who have lost a father or mother in early childhood, see Edith Jacobson, 'The Return of the Lost Parent', in Rita V. Frankiel (ed.), *Essential Papers on Object Loss* (New York and London, 1994), 232–50. See also John Bowlby's classic paper, 'Pathological Mourning and Childhood Mourning' (1963), ibid. 183–221.

the seduction), involving as it does a moment of loss which is 'untellable and therefore inaccessible to the gradual, assimilative work of mourning'. Because the illegitimate idyll can be neither owned nor let go, what they call 'a sealed-off psychic place', or crypt, is permanently established in the ego.[43] Abraham's and Torok's term for this buried identification with another's mourning is 'endocryptic identification' ('and Oh! | The difference to him'). Matilda's romantic quest for her father is based on just such a phantasy; she mourns herself as 'The Lost Object—Me!' (in the words of Abraham's and Torok's title)—'exchanging [her] own identity for a fantasmic identification with the "life"—beyond the grave—of an object of love'.[44] In this construction, 'the "I" is understood as the lost object's fantasied ego', staging 'the words, gestures, and feelings . . . of the lover who mourns for his forever "dead" object'.[45] The language surrounding Matilda's secret iden-tification is appropriately all-consuming and incorporatory. When her father writes to announce his return, the 16-year-old Matilda 'read his words with devouring eyes', exclaiming with rapturous anticipation: 'He will love me!' (M 186). After their reunion, we are told that she 'hung with delight on his words'. Her eyes devour the words she hangs on; instead of introjecting them, she imag-ines swallowing them (the distinction is Abraham's and Torok's), making them her lifeline.[46] Her father, in turn, identifies Matilda with his dead childhood sweetheart in the same literal fashion; Matilda is not 'like' her mother, but rather, she is—or ought to be—her mother ('In my madness I dared to say to myself—Diana died to give her birth; her mother's spirit was transferred into her frame, and she ought to be as Diana to me', M 179). His equation

---

[43] The Shell and the Kernel, 141.   [44] Ibid. 142.

[45] Ibid. 148. As Abraham and Torok put it, apropos of this case, 'she lived entirely on the concealed fantasy that she was herself her father, weeping over her, suffer-ing because he was bereft of her; the father who, forever disconsolate, accuses himself of the worst of crimes, since he had to be subjected to the punishment of losing her' (ibid. 147).

[46] See 'Mourning or Melancholia: Introjection versus Incorporation' (ibid. 126–7); the distinction goes back to Ferenczi's early papers on introjection; see, for instance, Ferenczi, 'Introjection and Transference' (1909), First Contributions to Psycho-Analysis (1952; repr. London, 1994), 30–79.

of mother and daughter refuses both death and figurativeness, attacking metaphor as well as generational difference with the weapon of what Abraham and Torok call 'anti-metaphor'.[47]

In Mary Shelley's *Matilda*, the enigmatic signifier of this unrecoverable and illicit idyll is the word 'love'. Locating father and daughter in the force field of a precocious and unspeakable sexuality, love is defined both by its literalization and by its destructiveness. When the father–daughter idyll turns to misery, Matilda perceives in her father a silent melancholia, 'an unknown horror that now he could master but which at times threatened to overturn his reason' (*M* 165). Using the tropes of gothic narrative, Matilda refers repeatedly to 'a horror which will not bear many words', a misery 'beyond all words'. This unknown, unverbalizable horror threatens to overturn not only reason, but language itself. What it leaves in its place is silence, the most extreme language of anti-metaphor. Confronted by the mysterious change in her father, Matilda tries to win his secret with 'persuasive words'— 'Alas! You have a secret grief that destroys us both: but you must permit me to win this secret from you' (*M* 171). Matilda wins his secret only to lose her 'nescience', the (saving) gap constituted by her previous determined refusal to know: 'I gained his secret and we were both lost for ever' (*M* 169). In this scene of traumatic loss, the reciprocal dynamics of mutual seduction are driven by the daughter's 'frantic curiosity' and the transport of violent emotion it triggers in her father. Matilda's father cautions her, to no avail: 'One word I might speak and then you would be implicated in my destruction' (*M* 172). This destructive and implicating word is 'love'. 'Led by passion', Matilda demands: 'Speak that word. . . . Yes, speak, and we shall be happy . . . speak that word' (*M* 172). And finally: 'I demand that dreadful word . . . speak it.' Stung by her accusation of what she calls 'an unnatural passion', by which she means the reverse of love ('you hate me!' *M* 172), Matilda's father finally acknowledges the destructiveness of what he calls love ('Yes, yes, I hate you!'), and then divulges his damaging and 'unnatural' passion.

---

[47] For incorporation as anti-metaphor, see *The Shell and the Kernel*, 131.

The words he uses return to Matilda, with their meaning utterly transformed, the 'constant' words of her girlhood quest-romance: 'My daughter, I love you!' (M 173). As Matilda puts it, 'In one sentence I have passed from the idea of unspeakable happiness to that of unspeakable grief' (M 166). Unspeakable happiness becomes a grief that dare not speak its name. The instantaneousness of Matilda's response (she sinks to the ground and covers her face) signals her recognition that her girlhood day-dream has become an incestuous phantasy, at once originating from outside as an impingement, and lodged within her as something guiltily known. Through the double and deferred structure of trauma, an earlier, imaginary moment of speech ('My daughter, I love thee!', M 159) takes on new significance in both past and present. This retrospective sexualization, and the damaging realization that accompanies it, correspond to the temporal structure of traumatic seduction as Laplanche describes it. A prior event that was experienced as neither inherently sexual nor necessarily traumatic (a girl's longing for her absent father) becomes traumatic in its re-presentation and re-enactment.[48] The incestuous overture impinges from outside, yet the 'event' is already an internal state or wish; event and unconscious phantasy coincide. One might ask what makes possible Matilda's deferred understanding of the meaning of her own earlier day-dream. A previous episode offers a clue. Baffled by her father's 'incomprehensible' state of mind when a prospective suitor presents himself, Matilda had 'chanced to say that [she] thought Myrrha the best of Alfieri's tragedies' (M 165)—an allusion by which her father is visibly disturbed, as well he might be. In Alfieri's Myrrha, a tragedy of father–daughter incest which Mary Shelley herself had begun to translate in 1818, the daughter's secret love for her father motivates her mysterious refusal to marry: 'Thou thyself, by dint of force, from out my heart . . . didst wrest . . . | The horrid secret'—so Myrrha accuses her horrified parents as she commits

---

[48] See the discussion of the concept of *Nachträglichkeit* in John Fletcher, 'The Letter in the Unconscious: The Enigmatic Signifier in the Work of Jean Laplanche', *Jean Laplanche: Seduction, Translation and the Drives*, 93–120, especially 105.

suicide at the end of the play.[49] Even before her father's incestuous disclosure, therefore, Matilda had read the illicit idyll encrypted in her unconscious girlhood phantasy; it becomes traumatic in the light of a subsequent moment of understanding, when the secret forced from her father becomes a secret forced into her. At once extrinsic and invasive, it inhabits her as intimately as the expression of her father's eyes, 'convuls[ing] every nerve and member of [her] frame' (M 173) with terror and shame.[50] Matilda is possessed by a concrete event (a word, a look) where once there had been an ordinary Oedipal phantasy. This, rather than any attempt at physical seduction, turns out to be Mary Shelley's definition of incest trauma and its wretched after-effects.

Shelley's narrative posits reading as a mode of compulsory re-enactment; the scene of incest trauma enforces her hysterical identification with her father. The 'dreadful word' (love = hate) binds daughter and father in a paroxysm of shared bodily excitement: 'I shivered in every limb', Mary Shelley writes. The affects of gothic fiction 'convulse' Matilda's body and create a fever of arousal in that of her father—'My blood riots through my veins' (M 173). 'Surely', he exclaims rapturously, 'this is death that is coming . . . let me die in your arms!' (M 173). As Matilda recognizes, it is indeed death that is 'coming' here. Shelley makes us witness something very like a hysterical attack in Matilda's rapid alternations of love and hate ('at one moment . . . I would have

[49] 'Tu stresso, a viva forza, l'orrido arcano . . . dal cor . . . mi strappasti' (Mirra, v. ii. 194–5). Mary Shelley might have known Charles Lloyd's translation of 1815; this translation comes from The Tragedies of Vittorio Alfieri, ed. Edgar Alfred Bowring (2 vols., London, 1876), ii. 363. See Journals, i. 226 and n. 4, and The Letters of Percy Bysshe Shelley, ii. 39. Urged on by Percy Shelley, Mary Shelley herself had begun to translate Alfieri's Myrrha in 1818. Myrrha also appears in Dante's Inferno, xxx. 37–41; her sin is not only that she 'became loving of her father beyond rightful love', but counterfeited the form of another. Mary Shelley's reading list for 1818 included the tragedies of Alfieri and the Vita di Vittorio Alfieri alongside the Inferno; see Journals, i. 267. Byron saw a performance of Alfieri's play in Bologna in Aug. 1819 and recorded 'the agony of reluctant tears' it produced in him; see Byron's Letters and Journals, ed. Leslie Marchand (13 vols., Cambridge, 1973–82), vi. 206.

[50] See John Fletcher, in Jean Laplanche: Seduction, Translation and the Drives, 105–6, for the ways in which this formulation by Laplanche displaces the dualism of inner and outer, constitution and event, in trauma and seduction theory.

clasped my father in my arms; and then starting back with horror I spurned him with my foot', M 173).[51] The textual solution to this impasse is to preserve love in the form of hate, which involves killing off Matilda's father. Weeping over his insensible body, Matilda imagines him already dead and therefore once again lovable ('I felt for a moment as if he with white hairs were laid in his coffin and I . . . were weeping at his timely dissolution', M 174). This murderous and primitive manœuvre (the splitting, destruction, and idealization of a loved object) gets rid of the hateful seducer, leaving Matilda to mourn a father transformed and aestheticized by age and death. Her curse, for such it is ('a daughter's curse'), is to wish that he will grow old and return, purified, to 'thy Matilda, thy child, who may then be clasped in thy loved arms, while thy heart beats with sinless emotion' (M 175). Such a sinless and forgiven father can only, of course, be dead. In a prophetic dream, Matilda sees him 'deadly pale and clothed in flowing garments of white' (M 176), fleeing from her until he comes to a cliff at the edge of the sea and plunges over it; his death is prefigured as a tree symbolically split by lightning. Incest trauma leaves in its wake this simultaneously death-dealing and idealizing phantasy. The phantasy extends to *Matilda* itself, where its heroine's eloquence—sustained precariously between the poles of depression and exaltation, violence and resignation—also seems to demand the tribute of posthumous idealization on the part of the reader.

The Eloquence of Despair

The scene of Matilda's insertion into a prior romance becomes explicitly literary when her father asks her to take up reading Dante to him—in his words—'where [her mother] left off'. But he corrects himself hastily: 'No, that must not be; you must not read

---

[51] Cf. Freud's description, in his short papers on 'Hysterical Fantasies' and 'Hysterical Attacks' (1908), of a woman patient 'simultaneously playing both parts in the underlying sexual fantasy' by 'press[ing] her dress up against her body with one hand (as the woman), while she tried to tear it off with the other (as the man)' (*SE* ix. 166; cf. *SE* ix. 230).

Dante. Do you choose a book' (M 167).[52] Dante stands for the lost
earthly paradise he once shared with Diana. Matilda chooses to
read Spenser instead, settling on 'the descent of Sir Guyon to the
halls of Avarice'. Her choice of allegory is significant, involving
as it does a descent into Pluto's underworld (not to mention the
possibility of an oblique reference to Godwin's financial demands).[53]
But, one wonders, where did her mother's reading leave off?
Perhaps with Canto XXVIII of the *Purgatorio*, which Mary Shelley
was again reading in August 1819 as she worked on *Matilda*, and
which Percy Shelley translated not long afterward.[54] This is the
canto in which the Pilgrim-poet first sights Matelda in the Earthly
Paradise, where she appears to him across the Lethean and
Eunoëan streams as a singing and dancing maiden, but also as a
figure pre-emptively marked by loss. In Percy Shelley's translation,

> like Proserpine, in Enna's glen,
> Thou seemest to my fancy, singing here
> And gathering flowers, as that fair maiden when
> She lost the spring and Ceres her . . . more dear. (ll. 48–51)[55]

Dante's Matelda, seen through the veil of Ovidian literary reference, belongs as much to elegy as to exquisitely wrought pastoral;
she is the daughter lost to her mother, and perhaps even a lost

[52] See Jean de Palacio, *Mary Shelley dans son œuvre* (Paris, 1969), 36–47, for Mary
Shelley's debt to Dante in *Matilda*; Palacio focuses particularly on the theme of the
terrestrial Paradise and on the relation between Matilda, Matelda, and the figure of
Proserpine. See also Arlene Bowen, ' "Colui da cu'io tolsi | Lo bello stilo": Dante's
Presence in Mary Shelley's *Mathilda*', *Italian Culture*, 12 (1994), 59–84. I am grateful
to Marilyn Migiel for the opportunity to discuss readings of Dante and particularly
questions involving memory and the figure of Matelda in both the *Commedia* and
Shelley's novella.

[53] *Faerie Queene*, II. vii (Mammon's attempt to seduce Sir Guyon with wealth).

[54] Timothy Webb, *The Violet in the Crucible: Shelley and Translation* (Oxford, 1976),
314 n., dates the translation to Aug. 1820, a year after the composition of *Matilda*.
But see also Jean de Palacio, 'Shelley traducteur de Dante: le chant XXVIII du
Purgatoire', *Revue de Littéraire Comparée*, 36 (1962), 571–8, who argues for 1819 on the
grounds of the use of the Matelda episode in *Matilda*. My quotations from Shelley's
translation are drawn from the text established by Webb from Bodleian MS Shelley
adds. e. 6, fos. 339–42, and printed in *The Violet in the Crucible*, 313–14.

[55] Ibid. 314. 'You make me recall where and what Proserpine was at the time her
mother lost her, and she the spring' (*Purgatorio*, xxviii. 49–51).

poetics as it would have appeared before sin—the personification of the spirit or 'inspiration' of love that breathes in Dante's poem, moving with the very melody of the Canzone.[56] In Mary Shelley's novella, Matilda similarly compares herself to 'Proserpine, who was gaily and heedlessly gathering flowers on the sweet plain of Enna, when the King of Hell snatched her away to the abodes of death and misery' (M 164). The wintry landscape she inhabits in the opening scene is the same winter that is brought on by Pluto's rape of Proserpine.

A precursor for Beatrice, Dante's Matelda is the female intercessor who will explain the conditions of existence and redemption prior to the Pilgrim-poet's reunion with a lost but now paradisal love. Later, she will dunk him in the Lethean waters and make him drink the Eunoean stream—washing away the memory of sin while restoring the memory of every good deed. She is a psalmist who purges pagan romance by singing the inspiration of divine love, conducting the Pilgrim-poet beyond the literature of earthly love. But hers is the unheard music of paradise. The *Purgatorio* delineates the space of the Pilgrim-poet as one in which it is not yet possible either fully to forget the past or hear the paradisal poetry of the future. Ovidian allusion becomes a form of literary memory from which the Pilgrim-poet can never be entirely free, at least on the earthly side of the paradisal divide; Matelda is compared to Venus, and can easily be mistaken for her, framed as she is by the perspective of distance and desire.[57] In her own way, she

---

[56] For the suggestion that, in this comparison of Matelda to Proserpine, Dante is drawing not so much on Ovid's account in *Metamorphoses* as on the elegiac formulation of the *Fasti* (where Ceres cries out 'Persephone' and 'daughter' by turns—'sed neque Persephone Cererem nec filia matrem | audit'), see Patrizia Grimaldi Pizzorno, 'Matelda's Dance and the Smile of the Poets', *Dante Studies*, 112 (1994), 115–32, esp. 120–2. Challenging the traditional reading of the Matelda episode in terms of the *pastorella*, Pizzorno argues persuasively for the association of Matelda with the Canzone itself.

[57] 'Non credo che splendesse tanto lume | sotto le ciglia a Venere . . .' ('I do not believe that so great a light shone forth under the eyelids of Venus . . .', *Purgatorio*, xxvii. 64–5). See Peter S. Hawkins, 'Watching Matelda', in Rachel Jacoff and Jeffrey T. Schnapp (eds.), *The Poetry of Allusion: Virgil and Ovid in Dante's Commedia* (Stanford, Calif., 1991), 181–201, for the complex Ovidian allusions in the Matelda episode and for the ways in which Matelda can be thought of as educating the Pilgrim-poet in how to 'read' her.

too is an 'enigmatic signifier', the bearer of unspoken passions. Although Dante's *Purgatorio* simultaneously evokes and revises prior tragic or erotic narratives, the possibility of confusing Matelda with an earthly lover makes the episode pregnant with longing as well as potential misunderstanding. Matelda figures the seductive delights of poetry, on which Dante's allegory after all depends; in the face of such remembered pleasure, the transformations of paradise are all the more remote to human understanding. Matelda's already ambiguous meaning allows Mary Shelley to read Dantean literary sublimation (in which something must actually be given up) as mere nostalgia—as the restoration of what has been and continues to be desired. Her references to Canto XXVIII of the *Purgatorio* focus on the initial moment of specularity which frames Matelda as a lost object of desire, using the Earthly Paradise as the setting for Matilda's imaginary restoration of the past.

In Percy Shelley's translation of the beautiful passage in which the Pilgrim-poet first catches sight of her, Matelda appears as 'A solitary woman, and she went | Singing and gathering flower after flower | With which her way was painted and besprent' (ll. 40–2).[58] Mary Shelley quotes Dante's words to narrate Matilda's innocence as if from the perspective of her absent father's astonished and delighted gaze: 'I wandered for ever about these lovely solitudes, gathering flower after flower "Ond' era pinta tuta la mia [sua] via"' (*M* 158). Later, Matilda's father will elide Matelda and Beatrice when his suicide letter compares Matilda's eyes to those that 'shone on me as did those of Beatrice on Dante, and well might I say with him yet with what different feelings "E quasi mi perdei gli occhi chini"' (*M* 178; 'and almost lost myself, with downcast eyes').[59] The reference here is to the deeply moving moment of self-loss at the end of Canto IV of the *Paradiso* when Beatrice gives the Pilgrim-poet a look of such divine love that he turns away.[60] Dwelling on his first sight of Matilda as 'a nymph

---

[58] Webb, *The Violet in the Crucible*, 314: 'a lady all alone, who went singing and culling flower from flower, with which all her path was painted' (*Purgatorio*, xxviii. 40–2).

[59] *Paradiso*, iv. 139–41.

[60] Significantly, Dante has just been asking whether it is possible for those who break their vows to compensate with good deeds.

of the woods', her father sees her as 'the ministering Angel of a
Paradise to which . . . you admitted only me' (M 178). The same
idealization colours Matilda's culminating picture of the after-death
paradise where she imagines being reunited with her father:
'I pictured to myself a lovely river such as that on whose banks
Dante describes Matilda [sic] gathering flowers, which ever
flows—bruna, bruna, | Sotto l'ombra perpetua, che mai | Raggiar
non lascia sole ivi, nè Luna' (M 205).[61] This time it is her father
who plays Beatrice's part, arriving in his car of light: 'And then I
repeated to myself all that lovely passage that relates the entrance
of Dante into the terrestrial paradise; and thought it would be
sweet when I wandered on those lovely banks to see the car of
light descend with my long lost parent to be restored to me' (M 205).
Absorbed in her reverie, Matilda tries to gather a flower, waking
from her day-dream to find herself 'on that bleak plain where no
flower grew' (M 206) and catch her death of cold.

In 'Analysis Terminable and Interminable', Freud writes of the
psychoanalytic reader who 'is "stimulated" only by those passages
which he feels apply to himself' ('Everything else leaves him cold').[62]
Matilda offers an object-lesson, not so much about the refusal of
psychoanalytic enlightenment as about a form of resistance that
may be involved in all reading, given that we are bound to mis-
apply what we read when we apply it to ourselves. Mary Shelley
was surely right to read both reunion and the reform of love as
overarching themes in Dante's Purgatorio.[63] But in reading Dante
with all the selectivity of Matilda's own wish to restore the status
quo ante, what she mis-took from it was the longing for paradisal

---

[61] In Percy Shelley's translation, a river 'Dark, dark [yet] clear moved under the
obscure | Eternal shades, whose interwoving . . . [glooms] | The rays of moon or
sunlight ne'er endure' (ll. 31–3); see Webb, The Violet in the Crucible, 314 ('. . . it flows
quite dark under the perpetual shade, which never lets sun or moon beam enter
there', Purgatorio, xxviii. 31–3).

[62] See SE xxiii. 233.

[63] See Jeffrey T. Schnapp, 'Introduction to Purgatorio', in Rachel Jacoff (ed.),
The Cambridge Companion to Dante (Cambridge, 1993), 192–207: 'Reunion is one of
Purgatorio's great themes. Not only the reuniting of individuals with their Creator,
but also the reconvening of broken families and dispersed communities, whether
political, spiritual, moral, or linguistic' (197).

reunion rather than the difficult impetus towards transformation. In *Matilda*, this longing takes the form of a fantasized resumption of the father–daughter idyll, purged of incestuous passion in a Dantean exchange of loving looks: 'Then the mark of misery would have faded from my brow, and I should raise my eyes fearlessly to meet his, which ever beamed with the soft lustre of innocent love' (*M* 205). The turning back of the clock to childhood is signalled when Mary Shelley makes Matilda transpose Dante's paradisal river into the words of an old sentimental song: 'I thought how . . . I would sing *"sul margine d'un rio"*, my father's favorite song, and that my voice gliding through the windless air would announce to him . . . that his daughter was come' (*M* 205). 'Sul margine d'un rio' has been identified as an anonymous air published in about 1800.[64] This would make Mary Shelley herself (born in 1797) a small child, singing a very different tune from the post-prelapsarian poetics of Matelda's paradisal Canzone. Rehearsing Baudelaire's green paradise of infantine loves ('le vert paradis des amours enfantines, | L'innocent paradis, plein de plaisirs furtifs . . .'), Matilda imagines death as the return of a time prior to what Hanna Segal refers to, in the context of literary creation, as 'the havoc of the depressive position'.[65]

Mary Shelley's greatest eloquence, however, is reserved not for nostalgia but for despair—the melancholic entity first decisively conjured up as a third in the incestuous encounter. At the crisis of his disclosure, her father misinterprets Matilda's words of attempted consolation ('no more grief, tears or despair; were not those the words you uttered', *M* 173), making her stand apotropaically between him and despair. As he sinks to earth in a faint, she 'nearly as lifeless, gazed on him in despair'. It is at this moment that she depicts herself as 'seized' by a phantom named despair: 'Yes it was despair I felt; for the first time that phantom

---

[64] See Nitchie, 88 n. 77.

[65] Charles Baudelaire, *Les Fleurs du mal*, poem 64, ll. 25–6; trans. Richard Howard (Boston, 1982). Hanna Segal invokes Baudelaire's paradise in connection with her speculation that literary creation may include a longing to re-create an ideal state 'before what is felt as the havoc of the depressive position'; see 'Art and the Depressive Position', *Dream, Phantasy and Art* (London, 1991), 98.

seized me' (M 173). The insistent doubling suggests that for both father and daughter the 'seizure' is the same; they are both in the grip of their phantasmal identification with a personification, or allegory, named Despair, the same fanged phantom who attends the father's declaration of incestuous love ('After the first moments of speechless agony I felt her fangs on my heart', M 173). This is the spirit of the dead mother whom the deluded father believes to have migrated into his daughter's frame: 'Better have loved despair, & safer kissed her' (M 179), he laments. In Mary Shelley's autobiographical frame-narrative, the narrator's own profound despondency was to have been mediated by the figure of 'Fantasia' whose lovely appearance may recall the portrait of Mary Wollstonecraft by Opie that hung in Godwin's study.[66] As the phantom despair seizes Matilda, so Fantasia is similarly said to 'seize' the unhappy narrator, transporting her from Rome to the fields of Elysium (the fields of fancy) where she finds Matilda telling her story, instructed and encouraged by Diotima—perhaps Wollstonecraft re-imagined as a mature female philosopher. But the lovely spirit Fantasia also doubles disquietingly with a split-off version of this ideal mother, appearing, beyond idealization, as an object that bites and seizes, destroys and lays waste.

The recurrent form of despair surfaces in Matilda as the fantasy of suicide, a force tending at once to self-destruction and silence. After her father's suicide by drowning, Matilda—'the sole depository of [her] own secret' (M 185)—fakes her death in imitation of his (perhaps modelling it also on the suicide of Fanny Imlay, Mary Wollstonecraft's older daughter and Mary Shelley's half-sister).[67] Practising a duplicitous passivity ('I with my dove's look and fox's heart', M 186), she constructs a new

---

[66] For the resemblance, see Harpold, 'Seduction Fantasy', 60 n. Harpold points out that Mary Shelley seems likely to have completed the novel around 10 Sept. 1819, the twenty-second anniversary of Mary Wollstonecraft's death; see ibid., 51 n.

[67] For the relations between incest and suicide, see Janet Todd's edition of Mary, Maria, and Matilda, pp. xxii–xxiv. It was, of course, Godwin who had referred to Mary Wollstonecraft herself as a female Werther (a Romantic suicide) in his Memoirs. For Fanny Imlay's suicide, see Sunstein, Mary Shelley: Romance and Reality, 127, and William St Clair, The Godwins and the Shelleys: The Biography of a Family (New York, 1989), 411–12.

but radically impoverished identity predicated on a retreat into
solitude and nun-like seclusion. Even the longing for sympathy
and friendship that motivates Shelleyan object-relations *in extremis*
ends in disaster (the yearning of Frankenstein's monster for
intercourse with a sympathetic being has a similarly destructive
outcome). Chance throws in Matilda's way an Orphean poet
named Woodville, an obvious idealization of Percy Shelley ('poetry
. . . seemed to hang upon his lips and to make the very air mute
to listen to him', *M* 195). Mourning a dead love of his own in the
language of Percy Shelley's 'Hymn to Intellectual Beauty' ('the
brightest vision that ever came upon the earth', *M* 196), Woodville
attempts to console the peevish and frantic Matilda with the
effects of his 'living pity'—turning his eyes on her, in another
loving but ineffectual exchange of Dantean looks, 'Gli occhi
drizzo ver me con quel sembiante | Che madre fa sopra figliuol
deliro' (*M* 198: 'with the expression of a mother who looks at her
delirious child').[68] Matilda counters his attempted consolations
by proposing a double suicide, deliberately quoting the eloquent
and quietistic words with which Spenser's Despair attempts to
seduce Spenser's Red Cross Knight in *The Faerie Queene*:

> 'What if some litle paine the passage have
> That makes fraile flesh to feare the bitter wave?
> Is not short paine well borne that brings long ease,
> And lays the soul to sleep in quiet grave?'
>
> (*M* 201; *Faerie Queene*, I. ix. 40)

'Mark my words', she tells him, 'I have learned the language of
despair: I have it all by heart, for I am Despair: and a strange being
am I, joyous, triumphant Despair' (*M* 201). The opiate she offers
him is Spenserian poetry in its most seductive guise.

Matilda is at once the Freudian reader ('stimulated' only by
those passages which she feels apply to herself), and the Romantic
reader for whom Spenser was primarily the poet of day-dream
and an idealized past. In this triumphant moment of ventriloquism,
we can hear 'the overbearing eloquence of despair' (so Woodville
characterizes it) as a form of linguistic identification with the

---

[68] *Paradiso*, i. 101–2.

languorous rhythms and half-rhymes of Spenserian verse. Personification gives Matilda a voice, but it also implies the threat of muteness.[69] Woodville plays the part of Una in this Spenserian script, urging Matilda to resist her longing for death ('Come, as you have played Despair with me I will play the part of Una with you and bring you hurtless from [death's] dark cavern', M 202). But Matilda is prepossessed by what Kristeva calls 'the delights of reunion that a regressive daydream promises itself through the nuptials of suicide'.[70] One could put it in more literary terms and say that Mary Shelley re-enacts the delights of reunion promised by the language of the past. She places the sign of father–daughter incest over this moment of linguistic regress, but the subtext of her narrative implicates Kristeva's archaic maternal Thing in Matilda's (and the novella's) suicidal trajectory. Not for nothing does Matilda quote to Woodville a phrase that would have echoed from beyond the grave, where it was closely identified with Mary Wollstonecraft's life and writings: 'A little patience, and all will be over' (M 201).[71] Italicized by Mary Shelley, these words link the transmission—the traces—of affect to a maternal origin. The same words were attributed by Mary Wollstonecraft to her own mother at the point of death, given to the heroine's mother in Wollstonecraft's posthumously published novel, Maria, or The Wrongs of Woman, and finally, in Godwin's Memoirs, attributed to Mary Wollstonecraft herself as she lay dying. Bearing in mind their transmission to the next generation, from mother to daughter, we could paraphrase Laplanche by saying that quotation itself is a form of traumatic seduction that comes from elsewhere, and that 'even when we think we are creating, we are always being worked by foreign messages'.[72]

---

[69] Cf. the De Manian discussion of personification and prosopopoeia in Benjamin by Ian Balfour, 'Reversal, Quotation (Benjamin's History)', Modern Language Notes, 106 (1991), 622–47, esp. 644–5. For Benjamin's comparison of quotations to armed robbers, see ibid. 638 and n.

[70] Julia Kristeva, Black Sun: Depression and Melancholia, trans. Leon Roudiez (New York and Oxford, 1987), 14.

[71] Janet Todd points out the echo of Mary Shelley's dying words to Godwin; see Mary, Maria, and Matilda, p. xix.

[72] See Jean Laplanche: Seduction, Translation and the Drives, 33.

I Am a Tragedy

Mary Wollstonecraft's allegorical legacy to *Matilda* is a scene of instruction. The scheme of Wollstonecraft's fragmentary 'The Cave of Fancy' (1787) includes the cautionary retelling of her story by a melancholy victim of sensibility.[73] This tale of female unhappiness is intimately connected with sensibility's ambiguous relation to the rehearsal of suffering, as it is passed on from one generation to another.[74] The device of the instructional story links 'The Cave of Fancy' to Mary Shelley's 'The Fields of Fancy', in which another victim of sensibility tells her story, this time for the author's benefit. When Fantasia promises to lead the desponding narrator to the Elysian Fields (where she is promised consolation but not tat she will recover her lost loved ones), the narrator rejects her offer, preferring to remain self-enclosed in her grief and tormenting memories. Later, however, she is transported unawares in a dream to the Elysian Fields, where she finds herself in the company of a group of seekers after knowledge and virtue. Among them are those 'whose hearts although active in virtue have been shut through suffering from knowledge'.[75] At the centre of the group, Diotima discourses to her listeners in a vein of radical scepticism ('the great secret of the universe' is '*I can know nothing*') which is echoed within *Matilda* by the (Percy) Shelleyan Woodville. Confronting the problem of the coexistence of good and evil in the world, Diotima concludes that the 'end' (i.e. purpose) of

---

[73] See Syndy McMillen Conger, *Mary Wollstonecraft and the Language of Sensibility* (London and Toronto, 1994), 61–8. Noting that Wollstonecraft's fragment 'is written with such intensity, such obvious emotional participation, that it seems more like a lyric poem than a tale', Conger points to an ambivalence in 'The Cave of Fancy': 'Sensibility is otherworldly and silent to the point of extreme antisociability; its insights are bought at the price of self-isolation, its affective experience at the cost of suffering. Most alarming is its intimate alliance in this narrative with death: some of those who died had it; those still alive who have it are drawn themselves to the dead, to silence, and to the state of death' (ibid. 67–8).

[74] As Rajan points out of these inherited narratives, 'Stories are passed on from generation to generation here, but the model of transmission remains one of passive absorption'; see Tilottama Rajan, 'Wollstonecraft and Godwin: Reading The Secrets of the Political Novel', *Studies in Romanticism*, 27 (1988), 227.

[75] Nitchie, 93.

being is 'knowledge of itself', or self-knowledge, along with a proper appreciation of love and beauty. Admitting that her 'self-concentrated misery & narrow selfish feeling' have 'shut all love & all images of beauty from [her] soul',[76] Matilda—prompted by Diotima—now tells her melancholic story as a lesson in the unproductive uses of despair.

The original interpretive structure of Mary Shelley's novella had attempted to dedicate its negativity to the work of self-knowledge; its failure to be beautiful could (at a stretch) be read as reflecting Matilda's failure to respond to the images of beauty, along with her inability to confront the pain and guilt of mourning. Given these multiple perspectives, a more complex narrative emerges. Within the frameless novella as Mary Shelley reconstituted it, Woodville becomes the therapeutic spokesperson for Diotima's point of view ('if you can give one other person only one hour of joy ought you not live to do it?', M 202); in other words, he has to take on the role of wise mother as well as Una. Mary Shelley may have dropped the frame-narrative because she wanted to make the purgatorial process internal to Matilda's story.[77] But the shift underlines a problematic literary transaction enacted in, and by, the text of *Matilda*. One of the unfounded suspicions Matilda harbours about Woodville is connected precisely with his idealization as 'a Poet' who 'seemed . . . to make the very air mute to listen to him' (M 195). Matilda, like the air, also becomes 'mute' in the vicinity of his eloquence; muteness, indeed, is her refuge—one might almost say, an expression of her will.[78] Refusing

[76] Ibid. 98, 99.

[77] Nitchie suggests as another reason for dropping her original frame the fact that Percy Shelley had already translated the passages from the *Symposium* on which she drew for Diotima's wisdom (see ibid. 104 n.). Shelley was translating the *Symposium* in July 1818, a year before the composition of *Matilda*; see *The Letters of Percy Byshe Shelley*, ii. 22. For the importance of the *Symposium* to Shelley in relation to his reading of Dante, see also Webb, *The Violet in the Crucible*, 299–300.

[78] See Barbara Johnson, 'Muteness Envy', *The Feminist Difference: Literature, Psychoanalysis, Race, and Gender* (Cambridge, Mass., 1998), 129–53, for an acute discussion of feminine 'muteness' (with particular reference to Jane Campion's film, *The Piano*); Johnson argues that the idealization of women's silence about both their pleasure and their violation—and a corresponding mistrust of women's expressiveness—is helpful to (literary) culture.

to speak, she shuts herself off from Woodville's consolation and
the voice of life he represents ('No voice of life reaches me',
M 151). Described as 'younger, less worn, more passionless' than
Matilda's father, Woodville occupies an ambiguous position in
relation to this drama of speech and silence (or so Matilda feels
in her darker moments) because she suspects him of planning
to appropriate her tragedy for his own poetry—making her a
'figure' or personification of tragedy itself:

I am, I thought, a tragedy; a character that he comes to see act: now
and then he gives me my cue that I may make a speech more to his
purpose: perhaps he is already planning a poem in which I am to figure.
I am a farce and play to him, but to me this is all dreary reality: he
takes all the profit and I bear all the burthen. (M 199)

This has the ring of an authentic marital complaint. The tragic
character for which Mary Shelley herself provided the model was,
of course, that of Beatrice in The Cenci—not 'a farce' at all, but
the lyric tragedy about incest that Percy Shelley was writing at
the time, drawing on Mary Shelley's earlier translation of the Cenci
story to create his own politicized version of father–daughter incest
and parricidal murder.[79]

In the light of her suspicion that she is once more to play
a part in someone else's tragedy, the scene of Matilda's suicide
invitation to Woodville starts to look like a cunning attempt to
upstage him ('I . . . decorated the last scene of my tragedy
with the nicest care', M 200). In the final phase of her narrative,
Matilda again refers to 'the last scene of [her] tragedy' (M 206),
observing: 'if the world is a stage and I merely an actor on it my
part has been strange, and, alas! tragical.' Her main complaint is
that, for most of her life, 'The earth was to me a magic lantern
and I a gazer, and a listener but no actor.' As a performer in her
own right, Matilda becomes the lyric monodramatist of despair,
practising the heady form of literary excitement associated with
the poetry of near-death: 'This was the drama of my life which

---

[79] See Sunstein, Mary Shelley: Romance and Reality, 164, 173.

I have now depicted upon paper . . . the last that I shall perform'
(M 209). *Matilda* suggests that the problem of playing a part in
someone else's tragedy might be addressed by writing one's own
version of the story. But it also tends to project poetic eloquence
on to someone else—typically, Woodville, along with the poet-
ical canon he represents (a canon to which both Mary Shelley and
Matilda have remained marginal until recently). The poetry of loss
becomes a poetry lost to the self—and lost also to readers who
mistakenly equate Matilda's own sense of poetic depletion with
Mary Shelley's fraught, exalted, demanding, but, in its own way,
unremittingly 'poetic' text. The unreadability effect of *Matilda*
is a measure of its readers' surrender to this negative deployment
of empathy; its poetic failure can be redefined as Mary Shelley's
failure to own—take credit for—the strained and overwrought
poetry of her 'lyrical' prose.[80] Instead, poetry is given an ideal
form and vested in the figure of Woodville (anticipating Mary
Shelley's later devotion to editing and preserving Percy Shelley's
poetic *œuvre* after his death)—or else located in the 'elsewhere'
of quotation from Dante, Spenser, and Wordsworth.

I want to end by reflecting on the effects of trauma as they
emerge in Mary Shelley's literary uses of canonical poets such as
Spenser, Dante, and Wordsworth (not to mention Percy Shelley).
These effects could be glossed as the trauma of being cut off
from a productive relation to the poetry of the past. The 'voices
of life' that fail to reach Matilda represent not only the voices by
which a writer is constituted, but the means by which a writer
becomes audible to others. As it happens, Spenser's Cave of
Despair had already played a central part in Percy Shelley's writing, especially in *Prometheus Unbound*. Percy Shelley's revisionary
drama of psychic integration and regeneration is both a political
manifesto and a psychic allegory. It can also be read as staging
a successful negotiation of his relation to literary precursors,
including Spenser (significantly, *The Faerie Queene* had been recommended to Percy Shelley as essential reading by none other

---

[80] For the idea of projective identification as the negative deployment of empathy,
see Steiner, *Psychic Retreats*, 6, 54–61.

than William Godwin).[81] But Mary Shelley—and *Matilda* too—stages
this drama in a different and less assimilable form. Both the Cave
of Despair and the Cave of Mammon disrupt her narrative with
the intrusion of something like an unmanageable archaic underworld; these passages, indeed, seem to figure a problematically
literal relation to the poetry of the past. Spenserian eloquence
becomes the ruse by which Matilda tries to seduce Woodville from
his Platonic role, while she responds to her father's attempt to
make her read Dante with a seduction scene of her own involving the repulsively powerful figure of the Money God (perhaps
a displaced figure for the financially demanding Godwin). The
allegorical landscape of this psychic hinterland is inhabited by a
veritable phantasmagoria of the Passions: pain, strife, revenge,
despight, treason, hate, jealousy, sorrow, shame, horror, and the
like. Such passages gesture towards a poetics of (self-)hatred which
the purgatorial process is finally unable to transform. Ripped from
their context, pieced together to produce a roughly sutured text,
they represent (no less than *Frankenstein*'s creature) what Rajan
aptly terms a literary concretion of trauma.[82] Quotation becomes
a figure for melancholic and incorporatory acts of reading; these
texts impinge from the past with an unsymbolizable message
because they have been 'devoured' in piecemeal fashion.

The same could be said of Mary Shelley's use of Dante. The
Purgatorio is traditionally read as the mediating and idealizing
literary articulation of the past, where earlier poets are enlisted as
guides and previous narratives melded into a transcendent literary and spiritual project (the *Commedia* too is an allegory of the
passions—just as the celebration of love unfettered by earthly
limits can equally be found in Spenser's poem). But in *Matilda*, the
Purgatorio becomes a figure, not so much for literary transmission

---

[81] See Greg Kucich, *Keats, Shelley, and Romantic Spenserianism* (Philadelphia, 1991),
302–11. For the significance of the Despair episode, especially in relation to *Prometheus
Unbound*, see esp. ibid. 257–60. The Shelleys were reading *The Faerie Queene* in 1814,
1815, and 1817: see *Journals*, ii. 677.

[82] Equating 'the abject' with 'a concretion of trauma', Rajan observes that 'the
creature in *Frankenstein* is associated with monstrosity and filth' (Rajan, 'Mary
Shelley's *Mathilda*', 45).

as for memory misapplied—for memory that surfaces in the wrong place, abused rather than used. Matilda's father interprets the possibilities of reunion beyond death as permitting the resumption of a literal reading of Dante, with Matilda in the role of Beatrice; while Matilda, in turn, fantasizes a return to the past as a post-purgatorial idyll in which the father has grown older and the daughter has become a little girl again. Despite the reassertion of generational difference as the condition for non-incestuous father–daughter relations, *Matilda* wishfully implies that death is merely an interruption before returning to paradisal childhood. This is not quite the kind of forgetting that Dante intends to take place in the waters of Lethe. It is, of course, Spenser himself who refers most concretely to the potential for damage in the time-bound processes of literary transmission, when he writes that the work of Time 'that all good thoughts doth waste' leaves the (Chaucerian) literary monument 'quite defaste':

> How may these rimes, so rude as doth appeare,
> Hope to endure, sith workes of heavenly wits
> Are quite devourd, and brought to nought by little bits?

> (*Faerie Queene*, iv. ii. 33)

Contrast Dante's optimism in the opening words of the *Purgatorio* as the poetry of the past revives: 'Ma qui la morta poesì resurga' ('But here let dead Poetry rise again', *Purgatorio*, i. 7). Against Percy Shelley, for whom death made it possible to liberate poets from the errors of history, Mary Shelley suggests that literary transmission is complicit in the defacement and consumption of 'little bits' of prior texts.[83]

In the melancholic work of literature, poetry is consumed, devoured, and destroyed as part-objects—the meal made, as it were, by the paranoid-schizoid infant in Melanie Klein's epic psychomachia. *Matilda*'s tragic performance, its performativity, points beyond the narrative of incest trauma to the scene of

---

[83] Compare Benjamin: 'Quotations in my work are like robbers on the highway who ambush the idler and deprive him of his convictions'; see Balfour, 'Reversal, Quotation (Benjamin's History)', 638 and n.

literary transmission as the place where, in the very process of
attempted repair, the trauma is re-enacted. To think oneself a
tragedy ('I am, I thought, a tragedy') is to refuse the exit line offered
by the literary as the representation rather than repetition of affect.
Matilda's closing pages dwell insistently on the insensate condition of a longed-for, consummatory death; the keyword here is
'destruction' (*M* 207). Identified with a Lucy figure not only in
her solitary childhood but also in her dying—'Rolled round in
earth's diurnal course | With rocks, and stones, and trees' (*M* 207;
a quotation from 'A Slumber Did My Spirit Seal', ll. 7–8)—
Matilda herself becomes the literary concretion of a lost object,
rather than a symbol for Wordsworth's poetry of loss.[84] By reading Shelley's novella as a text of trauma, however, I don't mean
to claim that psychoanalysis has the status of a master discourse,
or to give a post-Kleinian account of creativity the last word on
the feelings, aesthetics, or histories that complicate its writing.
But as a discourse that has something to say about negativity
and destructiveness, psychoanalysis offers a way, not so much to
'economize' what would otherwise remain unusable in *Matilda*,
as to hear its lost poetry. One should, of course, be wary of
substituting too legible a figure of literary transmission for the
unreadability of trauma, or allowing a too lurid figure of secret
destructiveness (a.k.a. the death drive) to usurp the 'event' of
incestuous seduction. None the less, putting pyschoanalysis in a
productive relation to literary criticism helps to remind us that the
effect of unreadability is produced by reading. In Mary Shelley's
allusion to Alfieri's *Myrrha*, Dante's *Purgatorio*, Spenser's *Faerie
Queene*, and Wordsworth's *Lyrical Ballads*, we can see how moments
of missed meaning and traumatic understanding, or misreading,
might even be thought of as constitutive of meaning. Considered
as a form of literary transmission, reading comprises both an
event and a structure of temporal deferral or 'afterwardsness'. But
I would prefer to define *Matilda*'s peculiar unreadability effect

---

[84] The fact that Shelley had Wordsworth's poetry in mind as she concluded
her MS can be seen from her use of Wordsworth's 'A Night Piece' to indicate the
mood and setting at the end of her novella; see Nitchie, *Mathilda*, 88 n., where the
quotation is incorrectly attributed to Mary Shelley herself.

as a difficulty endemic in 'hearing' trauma—as an allegory of reading only so far as it involves a text or a life traumatically cut off from itself.

Matilda's disjunction from the socio-political issues associated with the writings of Mary Wollstonecraft or William Godwin is a residual but significant aspect of its marginality.[85] That incest trauma in *Matilda* deflects mainline political and feminist critiques can be read as a specific instance of what it means for a text or a life to be cut off from itself and its past. In this sense, psycho-analytic reading bears on the political reading it is sometimes thought to exclude. Twenty years after writing *Matilda*, recalling her parents' and her husband's 'passion for reforming the world' from the perspective of the liberal ferment of the late 1830s, Mary Shelley used the privacy of her journal for a tortured inquiry into her support for 'the "good Cause"—the cause of the advancement of freedom & knowledge'. Apropos of her precarious situation as a woman writer negotiating the straitened public and private (and economic) spaces then available to her, she concluded: 'If I have never written to vindicate the Rights of women, I have ever befriended women when oppressed—at every risk I have defended & supported victims to the social system.' She goes on: 'And as I grow older I grow more fearless for myself—I become firmer in my opinions.'[86] Mary Shelley does not vindicate the rights of women in *Matilda*; nor were the unhappy circumstances of its writing conducive to the airing of such opinions as she may have had as a bereaved mother of scarcely 22.[87] But her novella addresses forms of female misery that are among the most intractable as well as the least susceptible to social and political reform. Questioning the category of the unreadable in *Matilda* makes it possible to hear Mary Shelley's silence along with her poetry. Unreadability is the trace of the unrepresentable, or 'guilt that wants a name'.

---

[85] See Rajan, 'Mary Shelley's *Mathilda*', 52–8, for an intertextual reading of *Matilda* which triangulates it with Godwin's and Wollstonecraft's writings.

[86] 21 Oct. 1838, *Journals*, ii. 553, 557.

[87] 'I am not a person of Opinions' (ibid. ii. 553).

SIX

Traces of an Accusing Spirit
Mary Hays and the Vehicular State

And only think if one could get hold of this physical
equivalent of the psychical act! It would seem to me that
psycho-analysis, by inserting the unconscious between
what is physical and what was previously called 'psychical',
has paved the way for the assumption of such processes as
telepathy. If only one accustoms oneself to the idea of
telepathy, one can accomplish a great deal with it—for the
time being, it is true, only in imagination. (Sigmund Freud)[1]

'I wish we were in the vehicular state, and that you understood the sentient language; you might then comprehend
the whole of what I mean to express, but find too delicate
for *words*.' (Mary Hays)[2]

WITH this remarkable speculation, Freud 'accustoms'
his startled readers to the novel idea that telepathy
might turn out to be as valid a form of communication as the telephone. He goes on to suggest that telepathy may
once have been 'the original, archaic method of communication between individuals' before being replaced by more direct
methods of conveying information. His thinking about telepathy
has unexpected antecedents in earlier notions about the ability of
one mind to communicate directly with another. It also anticipates

---

[1] Sigmund Freud, 'Dreams and Occultism', in *New Introductory Lectures on
Psycho-Analysis* (1933), *SE* xxii. 55.
[2] Mary Hays, *Memoirs of Emma Courtney* (1796), ed. Eleanor Ty (Oxford, 1996),
89; subsequently cited as *EC*.

contemporary psychoanalytic concepts involving unconscious communication between analyst and analysand, or, for that matter, unconscious intersubjective exchanges between reader and text. Surprisingly, these ideas about thought-transference also turn out to haunt the margins of at least one influential theory that connects the origins of the eighteenth-century novel with letters, emphasizing the role of autobiographical memoirs or epistolary fiction in creating a shared subjectivity. Too easily, perhaps, we tend to claim that such epistolary novels or memoirs are 'psychologically' realistic, when what we really mean is that they create in us the very forms of subjectivity which we think of ourselves as sharing. The same hypothesis holds good for letters— a less archaic form of communication than telepathy, but older than the telephone. Letters may create an equivalent sense of self in the reader to whom they are addressed; while for the writer, they may be associated with conscious or unconscious phantasies of unmediated communication—the illusion that letters not only convey the immediacy of unspoken wishes and desires, but constitute a form of thought-transference. I want to explore some of the interrelated questions that link memoirs, epistolary fiction, and letters to the emergence of the 'literary'—a form of writing equated neither with communicativeness as such, nor with unconscious phantasy, while necessarily containing elements of both.

My example will be Mary Hays's epistolary novel, *Memoirs of Emma Courtney* (1796), which participates in the Enlightenment project of rational investigation into the human mind, while simultaneously entertaining a playful fantasy about the ideal form of communication that Hays refers to as 'the vehicular state'. Hays's novel is usually read as a *roman-à-clef*—a disguised autobiography based on Hays's triangular epistolary relationship with Godwin and the Cambridge radical, activist, and Unitarian, William Frend.[3] Adopting the mode of the memoir, Hays's

[3] For an interesting reading that considers *Memoirs of Emma Courtney* as 'autonarration' (neither fiction nor autobiography), see Tilottama Rajan, 'Autonarration and Genotext in Mary Hays' *Memoirs of Emma Courtney*', *Studies in Romanticism*, 32 (Summer 1993), 149–76. See also Vivien Jones, ' "The Tyranny of the Passions": Feminism and Heterosexuality in the Fiction of Wollstonecraft and Hays', in Sally

novel, no less than Godwin's account of Mary Wollstonecraft in *Memoirs of the Author of the Vindication of the Rights of Woman* (1798), helped to fuel conservative and anti-Jacobin delineations of Godwinian women as the deluded victims of their own misplaced or transgressive desires.[4] But Hays's *Memoirs* can also be read as an attempt to theorize—to 'philosophize'—the realm of passion, drawing 'the universal sentiment' of love into the public domain, and making it a subject for enlightened inquiry. Hays's preface announces boldly that 'The philosopher . . . may . . . discover in these Memoirs traces of reflection, and of some attention to the phaenomena of the human mind' (*EC* 4). Her claim is not new (she cites Helvétius), but the radical scepticism of her preface would have been immediately recognizable as both contemporary and Godwinian: 'Free thinking, and free speaking, are the virtue and the characteristics of a rational being . . . every principle must be doubted, before it will be examined and proved.'[5] But her free-thinking and free-speaking memoirs narrate the failure of what Hays calls a 'hazardous experiment'. This was an experiment in love, but equally an experiment in letter-writing, 'calculated' (so she tells us) 'to operate as a *warning* rather than as an example'. Like Godwin's *Memoirs* of Wollstonecraft, *Memoirs of Emma Courtney* portrays 'vigorous powers' producing 'fatal mistakes and pernicious exertions'.[6] Using much the same language

Ledger, Josephine McDonagh, and Jane Spencer (eds.), *Political Gender: Texts and Contexts* (Brighton, 1994), 173–89. For an account of Hays and her writing in the context of the politics and 'cultural revolution' of the 1790s, see Gary Kelly, *Women, Writing, and Revolution 1790–1827* (Oxford, 1993), 80–125.

[4] For anti-Jacobin attacks provoked by Wollstonecraft's *Vindication* and Godwin's *Memoirs*, see R. M. James, 'On the Reception of Mary Wollstonecraft's *A Vindication of the Rights of Woman*', *Journal of the History of Ideas*, 39 (1978), 293–302.

[5] For Helvétius, Godwin, and the importance of the passions, see *EC* 198–9 n.; Ty's notes provide detailed information about Hays's debt to Godwin's writings.

[6] Cf. the terms used by Hays to describe Wollstonecraft in her own 'Memoirs of Mary Wollstonecraft' for the *Annual Necrology for 1797–8*, which emphasise her 'intrepid spirit'—'a spirit of enterprise, a passion for experiment, a liberal curiosity' which sometimes 'betrayed [her] into false conclusions' but always 'awaken sympathy and seize irresistibly upon the heart'; see *Annual Necrology for 1797–8* (London, 1800), 411–12. Hays, who attended Wollstonecraft during her protracted post-partum illness, also wrote the obituary of Wollstonecraft that appeared in the

as Godwin, Hays takes pains to remind us that 'The errors of [her] heroine were the offspring of sensibility'. Although Emma is 'enslaved by passion', the author appeals to her readers to 'look into their own hearts' and find the same record there, 'traced by an accusing spirit' (*EC* 4). Emma's passionate enslavement, already inscribed in the hearts of Hays's readers, accuses them of the same amatory and epistolary obsession.

The Godwinian project of rational enlightenment is continuous with contemporary accounts of an eighteenth-century public sphere based on the production of a shared subjectivity and conceived as a community of critical reflection. Jürgen Habermas, arguing that 'The eighteenth century became the century of the letter', and that 'through letter writing the individual unfolded himself in his subjectivity', proposes a public sphere predicated on the peculiar forms of intimacy 'whose vehicle was the written word'—an intimacy generated by the privatization of the bourgeois family:

From the beginning, the psychological interest increased in the dual relation to both one's self and the other: self-observation entered a union partly curious, partly sympathetic with the emotional stirrings of the other I. The diary became a letter addressed to the sender, and the first-person narrative became a conversation with oneself addressed to another person. They were experiments with the subjectivity discovered in the close relationships of the conjugal family.[7]

For Habermas, not only did such experiments create the characteristic forms of Enlightenment intimacy, but (more strangely) the psychological realism of the epistolary novel encouraged its readers to substitute a literary reality for their own. Just such a substitution allows Hays to represent *Memoirs of Emma Courtney* as 'philosophic' (i.e. self-observation united with 'the emotional stirrings of the other I'), while simultaneously conducting her own

Monthly Magazine, 4 (Sept. 1797), 232–3. See Nicola J. Watson, *Revolution and the Form of the British Novel, 1790–1825* (Oxford, 1994), 62, for Hays's representation of Wollstonecraft, and cf. Janet Todd, *The Sign of Angelica: Women, Writing and Fiction 1660–1800* (London, 1989), 237, on Wollstonecraft and Hays as two authors in whom autobiography and fiction are intertwined.

[7] See Jürgen Habermas, *The Structural Transformation of the Public Sphere*, trans. Thomas Burger (Boston, 1991), 48–9.

hazardous experiment in epistolary intimacy. Like the Godwinian philosopher who may discover 'traces of . . . the phaenomena of the human mind' in her novel, Hays sets out to 'trac[e] the character of [her] heroine from her birth' (*EC* 5). But the ideal of Enlightenment rationality has tended to be both ungendered and disembodied, not to say classless and affectless.[8] Hays's feminist philosophy allows her to level an accusation at the idealization of the Enlightenment subject, no longer portrayed as the subject of Godwinian reason, but as the subject of social constraints and incomprehensible passions.

Hays's definition of psychic causality (at once 'traces' of the universal human mind, and the 'trace' of individual character) introduces a troubling equivocation relating to gender. Does Emma's story warn us against the slavery of passion, or against unavoidable (gendered) accidents? Is Hays's overdetermined narrative dictated by Emma's social circumstances and defective upbringing, or does the passion of love necessarily take the form of enslavement?[9] In telling what she calls her 'simple story', Hays prides herself on scrupulous regard to 'the more minute, delicate, and connecting links of the chain' (*EC* 5, 4). This allusion to a well-known proto-feminist precursor, Elizabeth Inchbald's *A Simple Story* (1791), argues for reading *Memoirs of Emma Courtney* as another feminist account of the mis-education of women and its transgenerational effects. But Hays's regard for the connecting links of the chain turns out to be lined with a contradictory anxiety involving what she calls 'repetition and prolixity' (*EC* 4). Emma's story is one of 'extravagance and eccentricity'—not simple at all,

[8] For contemporary discussion and critique of Habermas in relation to feminist concerns, see, for instance, Nancy Fraser, 'What's Critical about Critical Theory', in Johanna Meehan (ed.), *Feminists Read Habermas: Gendering the Subject of Discourse* (New York and London, 1995), 21–56, and Joan Landes, 'The Public and the Private Sphere: A Feminist Reconsideration', ibid. 91–116. For a related argument about Habermas and letters in connection with Mary Wollstonecraft's *Letters to Imlay*, see my 'Intimate Connections: Scandalous Memoirs and Epistolary Indiscretion', in Charlotte Grant and Elizabeth Eger (eds.), *Women and the Public Sphere: Writing and Representation 1700–1830* (Cambridge, forthcoming).

[9] See Freud's 'The Disposition to Obsessional Neurosis' (1913), where the problem of 'choice of neurosis' raises a similar question about 'the constitutional and the accidental' (see *SE* xii. 317).

but strange and unaccountable. *Memoirs of Emma Courtney* warns us against the extravagance of repetition, the eccentricity of passion. The 'traces' that make up Hays's narrative (traces which are also 'connecting links of the chain') point to what is disconnected as well as contingent; they become the sign of an incomprehensible and mechanical compulsion to repeat. Taking Godwin's rationalist philosophy as her point of departure, Hays ends by discovering its limits. But she also goes beyond feminist social critique to hint at something that (in the wake of Freud) it is tempting to refer to as the death drive. At the same time, she puts a question mark over Habermas's thesis that the letter novel contributed to the formation of a rationally communicative and critically reflective public—a reading public that lacks an unconscious as well as a gender.

What kind of history could trace both the human mind and the character of its heroine from her birth, as Hays's novel sets out to do? Presumably, a history in which the author appeals to a recognizable theory of mind with its own internal consistency. One thinks inevitably of Freud in his case-histories of women, attempting to trace the aetiology of hysteria or homosexuality 'with complete certainty and almost without a gap', only to find that something eludes his grasp, forcing him to turn back and add a disclaimer, a revision, or a retrospective admission of oversight.[10] Hays's *Memoirs of Emma Courtney* can also be read as an Enlightenment case-history—an attempt to understand recalcitrant forms of female passion from the perspective of Godwinian philosophy. As a feminist, she refuses to relegate women's extravagant passions to the realm of eccentricity, offering an explicit critique of the gender arrangements imposed by her society, and depicting alternative forms of intimacy between men and women (and between women themselves). But just as Godwin's *Memoirs* trace the actual disjunction between Wollstonecraft's rational feminism and the vicissitudes of her personal life, so Mary Hays traces the

[10] See 'The Psychogenesis of a Case of Homosexuality in a Woman' (1920), *SE* xix. 147. But cf. 'Psycho-Analysis and Telepathy' (1921), where Freud writes of analysts having to be 'content with fragmentary pieces of knowledge and with basic hypotheses lacking preciseness and ever open to revision' (*SE* xviii. 179).

failure of Godwinian philosophy to account for her heroine's passionate self-enslavement, or even the vicissitudes of writing. Like Godwin's *Memoirs*, her novel reveals an unaccountable resistance to reform, not only on the part of the conjugal family, but on the part of the female psyche.[11] In addition, Hays suggests that the letter is not so much a means of overcoming separation (as it is, for instance, for the lovers in Rousseau's *La Nouvelle Héloïse*), as an imaginary form of thought-transference capable of abolishing difference altogether. This may be why Hays can imagine Emma's story as a text already 'traced with an accusing spirit' in the very hearts of her readers. Freud's provocative remark that one can accomplish a great deal with telepathy (but 'for the time being, it is true, only in imagination') applies also to the Enlightenment ideal of shared intimacy and transparent communication. Fiction depends for its accomplishments on a similar collective madness that takes literally, for the time being, what is true only in imagination. And perhaps—as André Green writes apropos of psychoanalysis, a modern philosophy of the mind that also has its origins in the Enlightenment—writing itself is a form of private madness that one can only get rid of by writing about the private madness of others.[12]

A Never-Ending Romance

Memoirs of Emma Courtney tells the story of a rejection in love and letters that had its autobiographical basis in Hays's own experience. In October 1794, Hays—by this time, a feminist and minor author in her own right—wrote to Godwin asking for the loan

[11] See Jacqueline Rose, 'Where Does the Misery Come From?—Psychoanalysis, Feminism and the Event', in *Why War?—Psychoanalysis, Politics, and the Return to Melanie Klein* (Oxford, 1993), 89–109.

[12] Cf. André Green, *On Private Madness* (Madison, Conn., 1986), 16, on the role of the analyst's writing: 'When colleagues get together, they agree: "What a mad profession!" Perhaps writing is part of the analyst's private madness. He can rid himself of it, in part, only by writing of others' private madness: that of his analysands, to whom the psychoanalyst consecrates one of the most precious parts of himself in the inter-subjective exchange of the unconscious.'

of *Political Justice* (1793), informing him that it had been recommended to her by 'a respected friend, Mr Wlm Frend late of Cambridge' (the punning coincidence of 'friend' and 'Frend' will recur insistently in her novel).[13] Identifying herself as a political sympathizer and an admirer of Godwin's own psychological and political novel, *Caleb Williams* (1794), Hays embarked on a philosophical correspondence which rapidly turned into a confessional monologue about her unrequited passion for Frend. Hays's heady, transferential, and melancholic letters to Godwin between late 1794 and mid-1796—at times written almost weekly—underscore the link between Godwinian philosophy and an Enlightenment practice of self-analysis.[14] Arguably, her epistolary friendship with Godwin (the man she regarded as the greatest living philosopher of her time) constituted an enabling form of intellectual exchange. More importantly, it also gave rise to a fictional account of her relations to Godwin and Frend, and to an arduous attempt to understand them. Tilottama Rajan has emphasized the transgressive political implications of Hays's use of the letters she actually wrote to Godwin and Frend as the basis for her novel: 'As the site of a crossing between actual and possible worlds', she writes, 'the intimate letter also transgresses the boundary between public and personal space.'[15] Hays uses

[13] William Frend would have been known to Godwin for the Cambridge fracas over his public Unitarianism and for his political activism; see Frida Knight, *University Rebel: The Life of William Frend (1757–1841)* (London, 1971), 198–213, for his friendships with Godwin and Hays; he was also a friend of Lamb, Dyer, and Coleridge, whose tutor he had been at Cambridge, hence allied with the radical circles to which Godwin and Hays both belonged.

[14] Hays's correspondence with Godwin, at the Carl Pforzheimer Library, New York, is currently being edited by Marilyn Brooks in *Selected Letters of Mary Hays: 1779–1843* (forthcoming). See also Gina M. Luria, 'Mary Hays's Letters and Manuscripts', *Signs*, 3 (1977), 524–30. A relevant selection of Hays's letters is also included in Marilyn Brooks (ed.), *Memoirs of Emma Courtney* (Peterborough, Ontario, 1999). I am grateful to the Carl Pforzheimer Collection of the New York Public Library for permission to quote from Mary Hays's letters to Godwin.

[15] See Rajan, 'Autonarration and Genotext', 171 and n. For the view that the expressiveness of women's fictional letters are inherently transgressive or political, see Peggy Kamuf, *Fictions of Feminine Desire: Disclosures of Héloise* (Lincoln, Neb., and London, 1982), and Linda S. Kauffman, *Discourses of Desire: Gender, Genre, and Epistolary*

the space of the intimate letter, not only to cross the boundary between private and public worlds, but to articulate the intellectual and amatory ambitions of a fictionally elaborated female self. Interestingly, Rajan goes on to suggest that in what she calls Hays's 'autonarrative', her desires are transposed into the world of history, and hence acquire political agency by way of their transfer to the reader. In other words, we too harbour thwarted ambitions and unrequited passions: 'Emma Courtney, c'est nous.' But just what kind of transposition does this epistolary and novelistic transfer involve? Adopting the in-between form of the memoir and the letter-novel, *Memoirs of Emma Courtney* redefines the relation between actual and possible worlds as the space of the literary. This is a space of unpredictable accidents and unchecked imagination.

D. W. Winnicott makes just such an in-between world or 'intermediate state' the paradoxical location of shared illusions and of culture, but one that bears 'the hallmark of madness when an adult puts too powerful a claim on the credulity of others, forcing them to acknowledge a sharing of illusion that is not their own'.[16] Habermas, as we have seen, argues that the epistolary novel not only 'threw a veil over the difference between reality and illusion' but allowed its readers to become *sujets de fiction*, engaging in a collective form of literary madness that might seem to have little to do with rational enlightenment.[17] Hays's letters remind us that the subject is always the *sujet* of her own fictions, even before the epistolary novel—perhaps even before the letter. In her correspondence with Godwin, she approaches him, respectfully

Fiction (Ithaca, NY, and London, 1986). For a recent discussion of women, politics, and epistolarity during the Romantic period, see especially Mary Favret, *Romantic Correspondence: Women, Politics, and the Fiction of Letters* (Cambridge, 1993). See also Ruth Perry, *Women, Letters, and the Novel* (New York, 1980), and, for epistolary narrative in general, Elizabeth J. MacArthur, *Closure and Dynamics in the Epistolary Form* (Princeton, 1990).

[16] See 'Transitional Objects and Transitional Phenomena' (1953), in *Playing and Reality* (1971; repr. New York and London, 1982), 3, and 'The Location of Cultural Experience' (1967), ibid. 95–103.

[17] See Habermas, *The Structural Transformation of the Public Sphere*, 50.

but forcefully, in the guise of a female philosopher committed to discussion, debate, and the expression of doubt.[18] Initially, she tells him, she responded with excitement to the austere and abstract reasoning of *Political Justice*. But, like other contemporary readers, she was shocked at Godwin's drastic views on 'private affections' ('I started at the idea of their annihilation', 7 December 1794). Man, she argues, is a feeling as well as a rational animal—and does virtue automatically produce happiness, as Godwin had argued? Rather, for her the passionate unhappiness that tends to accompany mental strength produces virtue: 'Strong passions . . . are said to accompany strong mental powers. . . . The rock must be *convulsed* ere it produced the diamond.' Wishfully, Hays proceeds to construct Godwin as just such a man of convulsive feeling ('Symptoms of such convulsion I think I can trace even in the calm philosophic principles of political justice!'), and confides in him her own struggle to overcome a 'too exquisite sensibility— fostered by the delicacy of female education, & the habits of privacy and retirement' (7 December 1794). Would Godwin perhaps be willing to engage in frank conversation with her? ('From you I shall expect truth'). Her next letter, hailing the 'benevolence and wisdom' of the conclusion to *Political Justice*, repeats the suggestion that Godwin, like Hays herself, has a mind ' "roused" & strengthen'd by adversity' (1 January 1795). Surely, he too must have suffered. Taking issue with Godwin's central tenet (perfectibility, or 'the future triumph of mind'), Hays uses philosophic disputation as a stalking-horse for the project of her self-analysis, which depends on the assumption that every equivalent self has been similarly '*convulsed*'.

Godwin—a busy man who had to earn his living by writing of a different kind—tactfully regretted 'that the nature of [his]

[18] Cf. Freud in 'The Disposition to Obsessional Neurosis' on the relation between the instincts for knowledge, mastery, and the role of doubt : '. . . we often gain an impression that the instinct for knowledge can actually take the place of sadism in the mechanism of obsessional neurosis. Indeed it is at bottom a sublimated off-shoot of the instinct of mastery exalted into something intellectual, and its repudiation in the form of doubt plays a large part in the picture of obsessional neurosis' (*SE* xii. 324).

avocations restrain[ed him] from entering into regular discussions
in the epistolary mode' (7 May 1795). But he playfully encouraged
Hays to write to him from a distance when she felt like it ('when
your mind is bursting with thought, at random as you would to
your genius in the moon'). In response, Hays—more seriously—
proposed that '[her] bewildered mind shall seek from [Godwin]
. . . a solution to the difficulties which oppress it' (10 May 1795).
These difficulties become the theme of their one-sided correspondence. Hays's letters to Godwin thus resemble the psychoanalytic
encounter, in which the analyst's reticence and self-control make
possible the analysand's self-disclosure and potential self-realization.
Confessing to 'seasons of despondency' (6 May 1795), Hays tries
to unravel the obscure tangle of difficulties that beset her—the
'thousand wayward, contradictory, ideas & emotions, which I am
myself unable to disentangle' (28 July 1795). In part, she attributes this tangle to her circumstances as a woman. Her novel,
which re-uses the first two pages of this eloquently crafted letter,
makes Emma express the same confused complaint about her
'solitary, inactive situation as a woman' (*EC* 85). As Hays herself
writes to Godwin, 'Hemmed in, on every side, by the constitutions of society . . . I perceive, indignantly perceive, the magic
circle, without knowing how to dissolve the spell' (28 July 1795;
cf. *EC* 85).[19] But the very terms she uses suggest that her confines are not, or not only, societal, but illusory. 'Hence,' she
continues (again using the words of her own letter to Godwin
to justify the erotic obsession of her high-minded heroine) 'the
eccentricities of conduct with which women of superior minds
have been accused!' (*EC* 85–6). Hays wrestles not only with 'the

---

[19] This passage, quoted as part of Emma's letter to Mr Francis, is also reworked
elsewhere: 'Cruel prejudices!—I exclaimed—hapless woman! why was I not educated for commerce, for a profession, for labour? Why have I been rendered feeble
and delicate by bodily restraint, and fastidious by artificial refinement? Why are we
bound, by the habits of society, as with an adamantine chain? Why do we suffer
ourselves to be confined within a magic circle, without daring, by a magnanimous
effort, to dissolve the barbarous spell?' (*EC* 32). Eleanor Ty notes that Wollstonecraft
uses the phrase 'magic circle' in her *Letters Written during a Short Residence in Sweden,
Norway, and Denmark* (1796) to refer to illusion; see ibid. 204 n.

constitutions of society'—with the political obstacles placed in the way of women—but with internal difficulties that can only manifest themselves as eccentric behaviour. She continues to insist that although she is passionately unhappy, she is empowered both by philosophy and by unhappiness itself: 'Philosophy, it is said, should regulate the feelings, but it has added fervour to mine— What are passions, but another name for powers?' This opinion, inspired by Helvétius, recycled in her novel, was later ridiculed in Elizabeth Hamilton's satire on the Godwinian novel, *Memoirs of Modern Philosophers* (1800).[20] Despite her Foucauldian attempt to discipline the impassioned subject through confessional discourse, Hays's letters testify to the failure of the Godwinian equation of philosophic knowledge with power over a well-regulated self.

Isolated, unhappy, self-absorbed, and agitated by inchoate desires ('with inexpressible yearnings, my spirit still pants for something higher', 28 July 1795), Hays's letters depict herself as bound to repetition by a mysterious chain of circumstances. She attributes her chronic melancholia to 'a shock' from which she will never recover—presumably the death of John Eccles, her fiancé, who died unexpectedly when she was only 19: 'a peculiar train of circumstances called these feelings into exercise, & privacy & retirement fixed the fatal, connected, chain.'[21] But while the nature of Hays's illness—the chain of association—is clear to

[20] See *EC* 86 and 209 n., and cf. *Memoirs of Modern Philosophers* (3 vols., London, 1800; repr. New York and London, 1974), i. 74. Hamilton's Godwinian anti-heroine, Bridgetina Botherim, perfectly catches the tone of intellectual grandiosity in Emma's letters to Augustus Harley: 'Why should I despair of arguing you into love? Do I want energy? Am I deficient in eloquence?—No. On you, therefore, beloved and ah! too cruel Henry, on you shall all my energy and all my eloquence be exerted . . . It is your mind I wish to conquer, and mind must yield to mind' (ibid. ii. 400); Bridgetina plans to publish her correspondence under the title *The Sweet Sensations of Sensibility, or the Force of Argument* (ibid. iii. 108).

[21] For the young Mary Hays's long correspondence with John Eccles, see *The Love-Letters of Mary Hays (1779–1780)*, ed. A. F. Wedd (London, 1925). Cf. the obsessional neurotic's refusal to get well in *The Ego and the Id* (1923) where Freud refers to the 'negative therapeutic reaction' as 'a sense of guilt, which is finding its satisfaction in the illness and refuses to give up the punishment of suffering' (*SE* xix. 49).

her, it is beyond her to find a cure: 'Like a skilful physician, I can retrace the causes, the symptoms, the progress, & thoroughly understand the nature of my mind's disorders, but the remedies are not within my power' (13 October 1795). Hence her appeal to Godwin, whom she calls 'my mind's physician' (11/18 January 1796). Her letters appeal to the Godwinian philosopher (presumably the same philosopher alluded to in her preface) to trace her mental disorder to its origin: 'It is because you are a philosopher that I can unfold my mind without reserve or apprehension: you are able to trace, & to investigate, the sources of its disorders & its mistakes' (13 October 1795). Like Breuer's Anna O, Hays invents her own cure in the course of her transferential relationship with Godwin—not 'the talking cure', however, but a writing cure: 'There are two sorts of writers, I am told, one who lives to write, the other, who writes to live; the former I cannot afford to do, the later I should despair of doing; something, I wish for, between them both' (13 October 1795).[22] This wished-for 'something . . . between them both'—between living to write and writing to live—is the compromise formation (satisfying both the instincts of mastery and the life instinct) that gives rise to *Memoirs of Emma Courtney*. In response to a suggestion by Godwin ('the plan which you hinted to me, when I last saw you', 5 November 1795), Hays turned to 'a more certainly productive literary undertaking'—a work, she says, written under his auspices, and one that Godwin 'should conceive not unworthy of being publickly addressed to [him]' (20 November 1795). This was to be a novel of letters based on her real-life correspondence. As she told Godwin, 'The epistolary form I conceived the most adapted to my style & habits of composition, but I could not please myself—fictitious correspondence affords me not the stimulus which I ever feel when addressing my friends.' Using letters originally addressed to her mentor and her supposed lover as a kind of pre-writing, the memoir-novel allowed her to rewrite the epistolary triangle

---

[22] See, however, Mikkel Borch-Jacobsen's revisionary *Remembering Anna O: A Century of Mystification*, trans. Kirby Olsen (New York and London, 1996) for a different perspective on Breuer's account of the talking cure in *Studies on Hysteria* (1895).

between herself, Godwin, and William Frend in the form of a political inquiry into the origin of female unhappiness. Throughout, however, Hays emphasizes the mysterious origin and progress of Emma's unrequited passion, and its ambiguous relation to the social affections.

Mr Francis, Emma's Godwinian mentor in the novel, calls Emma's love for the elusive hero, Augustus Harley, 'the unnatural and odious invention of a distempered civilization'. He insists, in thoroughly Godwinian fashion, that 'there is no topic that may not be subjected to the laws of investigation and reasoning' (*EC* 139, 138; here Mr Francis is apparently echoing Godwin's earlier admonitions to Hays). In response to an objection made by Godwin—that unrequited passion is a static and uninteresting subject for a novel—Hays replied, emphatically: 'I am by no means convinced, that a hopeless, persevering, & unrequited, attachment, is *in itself* uninteresting—it is a proof of a lively & strong imagination . . . It is strength, tho' ill directed' (? May 1796). Even unrequited love, she implies, brings narcissistic gains to the lover (since 'passions are but another name for powers'). Arguing, against Godwin, that 'the heart is not to be compelled' (*EC* 138), Hays develops a counter-discourse about the nature of individual attachment that contests the Godwinian rationality for which Mr Francis is the novel's official spokesman. Hays had already hinted at her differences of opinion with Godwin over the important matter of '*individual* attachments' and 'individual affections' (16 December 1795). Acting (in this instance) on a strictly Godwinian model of sincerity in personal relations, she brought matters to a head with Frend in a letter declaring her long-standing attachment. January 1796 finds her writing to Godwin—a letter redeployed in her novel (see *EC* 136–7)—in acute distress at Frend's long-awaited rejection:

a blow that has been suspended over my head, for days, weeks, months, years has at length descended—but 'still *I live*', & tho' my tears will flow, in spite of my struggles to suppress them, they are not tears of blood . . . my heart is pierced through & through & though it is not broken . . . a barbed & envenomed arrow rankles in my bosom—philosophy will not heal the festering wound. (11 January 1796)

'*I am exquisitely miserable!*' (11 January 1796), she tells Godwin. Con-cretizing the language of sensibility, her feeling heart—pierced by an envenomed arrow—becomes the festering wound that Godwinian philosophy can never heal.[23]

By now intimate with the broken-hearted and abandoned Mary Wollstonecraft (whose love-letters to her American lover, Gilbert Imlay, Godwin was to publish after her death), Hays con-tinued to hone her relentless self-analysis in long and repetitive letters to Godwin.[24] She refers to her capacity for 'attachments' with 'the narrowness & the tenacity of a savage' (11 January / 18 January 1796)—reminding us, along with Freud and Ferenczi, that obsessional neurosis and primitive thought have something in common.[25] The heroine of Hays's novel repeats the same lan-guage when she tries to account for the persistent self-wounding involved in her pursuit of her elusive and unsatisfactory lover: 'In my attachments, there is a kind of savage tenacity—they are of an elastic nature, and, being forced back, return with additional violence' (*EC* 131). The deflected violence of her attachments forms the underside of the pleasurable self-piercing involved in Hays's confessional correspondence. A similar deflection can be seen in the collisions and vehicular accidents which befall the reluctant hero of Hays's novel, not once, but twice (and even in the viol-ence which the heroine's jealous and self-destructive husband turns against himself when he commits suicide in the novel's

[23] The same language of piercing recurs when Emma quotes Pope's *Eloisa to Abelard*: 'unequal task, a passion to resign, | For hearts so touch'd, so pierc'd, so lost as mine' (*EC* 146); Hays's 'still I *live*' also alludes to Pope's Eloisa.

[24] See Godwin's *Posthumous Works of the Author of a Vindication of the Rights of Woman* (1798); see also *Collected Letters of Mary Wollstonecraft*, ed. Ralph Wardle (Ithaca, NY, 1979).

[25] See Sándor Ferenczi, 'Stages in the Development of the Sense of Reality' (1913), which refers to Freud finding 'in the mental life of the savage the characters of the obsessional neurosis', in connection with his discussion of the omnipotence (and fears) of obsessional neurosis: 'Obsessional patients . . . admit to us that they cannot help being convinced of the omnipotence of their thoughts, feelings, and wishes, good and bad. However enlightened they may be . . . they have the feeling that their wishes in some inexplicable way get realised. . . . Hence the inner discordance of the obsessional patient, the inexplicable occurrence of enlightenment and superstition side by side'; see *First Contributions to Psycho-Analysis*, trans. Ernest Jones (1952; repr. London, 1994), 236, 215–17. Freud cross-refers to Ferenczi's essay in his own essay of 1913 (*SE* xii. 325).

melodramatic finale).[26] In *Memoirs of Emma Courtney*, Emma and Augustus Harley are first thrown into each other's arms as the result of a carriage accident. The random vehicular collision that brings them together foretells the fatal accident which restores the dying Augustus to Emma's arms at the end of the novel, and entrusts her with the child of his secret marriage; this marriage is the convenient fiction that explains Augustus's otherwise inexplicable failure to respond to Emma's epistolary eloquence and powers of rational persuasion. In *The Ego and the Id* (1923), when Freud writes that the clamour of life proceeds both from and against Eros, he footnotes a telling reminder: 'it is through the agency of Eros that the destructive instincts that are directed towards the external world have been diverted from the self.'[27] Emma's love is dangerous to herself, but it also endangers the objects of her love, and proves fatal to Augustus.

When Godwin admonished Hays for having sacrificed at 'the shrine of illusion' rather than worshipping at 'the altar of reason', a criticism echoed by Mr Francis (*EC* 139), she replied with an elaborate and interesting defence of her passion for Frend:

—But, do you not perceive, that my reason was the auxiliary of my passion—or rather, my passion the generative principle of my reason? Had I not these contradictions, these oppositions, [to rouse] my mind into energy, I might have continued tamely domesticating [in] the lap of indolence & apathy. (6 February 1796; cf. *EC* 142)

Better to be hopelessly in love than to domesticate in the lap of indolence and apathy. Contradictions and oppositions become a source of energy and life ('the generative principle of [her] reason'), giving rise to undomestic savagery; her discontents (Hays seems to say) not only rouse her mind, but unsettle civilization.

[26] Despairing of Augustus Harley's love, Emma marries a long-time but unbalanced admirer, Mr Montague, whose latent jealousy is aroused when Augustus once more appears on the scene as the victim of a fatal accident and dies in Emma's arms; Montague kills himself after his subsequent seduction of a servant girl and murder of their infant; see *EC* 190–2.

[27] *SE* xix. 46. Cf. Freud's remark, in 'The Disposition to Obsessional Neurosis', that 'obsessional neurotics have to develop a super-morality in order to protect their object-love from the hostility lurking behind it' (*SE* xii. 325).

In the same letter, Hays boasts of 'the pleasurable madness which none but madmen know!', and concludes: 'I am at least a reasoning maniac—perhaps the most dangerous species of insanity' (6 February 1796). Is a reasoning maniac someone who is mad about reason, or someone who deploys the tools of modern philosophy in the service of a delusion? 'Mine', she writes to Godwin (with more than a touch of grandiosity), 'is almost a solitary madness in the 18th century.' In this solitary madness, Frend's indifference externalizes an inner obstacle, the 'indolence and apathy' of a woman denied the ordinary outlets of political action or public discourse available at the time to men, but permitted only to exceptional women (Hays knew at first hand the cost to Wollstonecraft). Attempting to rationalize her 'extravagant' fixation, Hays's letters to Godwin none the less represent something like an attempt at an epistolary working-through of the self-torments of amatory obsession—at one moment, suspecting Frend of pecuniary motives for 'ic[ing] his heart and stifl[ing] his humanity'; at another, finding grounds for hope in his ambiguous behaviour ('too inconsistent to be *entirely* the result of indifference', 6 February 1796). But in the end, it is her own feelings that baffle her rather than those of the enigmatic or indifferent Frend. For all her addiction to Godwinian philosophy, Hays confesses herself unable to solve the problem by rational inquiry: 'I deeply reason'd & philosophised upon the subject . . . [yet] the affair altogether, appears to me a sort of phenomenon which I am unable to solve' (6 February 1796). Why, she seems to ask, should passion seek its satisfaction in an indifferent or unfriendly object?

Describing the state of mind in which she communicated her passion to Frend (acting on strictly Godwinian notions of sincerity), Hays tells Godwin: 'I covered my paper with its emotions & transmitted them to him—I did it at length, mechanically, as the man, of whom it is related, that he whisper'd his secret into the earth to relieve the burden of uncommunicated sensation—' (6 February 1796; cf. *EC* 148). This mechanical compulsion 'to relieve the burden of uncommunicated sensation' conveys the same pressure to unburden herself felt in Hays's long and frequent

letters to Godwin. Such repetitive and obsessional communica-
tions might well feel like a mechanical compulsion (akin to the
compulsion to repeat that Freud associates with the death drive).[28]
By this time, however, Hays had made the decision to go public
in the form of a fictional narrative that approximated to the outlines of her own. Some way into the project of her memoir-novel,
she asked both Godwin and Frend for the return of her letters—
dismayed (so she tells Godwin) by Frend's continuing silence in
the face of her request. As she apparently explained to Frend,

I wish (said I), to employ myself in a work of fiction, to engage my mind,
to sluice off its impressions—a philosophical delineation of the errors of
passion, of the mischief of yielding to the illusions of the imagination
. . . nothing coolly written could express, with equal force, the feelings,
mistakes, & miseries, I mean to depict. (6 February 1796)

This hydraulic model ('sluicing off' the mind's impressions) turns
writing into a means of discharging what Freud refers to as
'the great reservoir' of displaceable libido.[29] Passion is diverted
from an instinctual object to a substitute—'I want a substitute,
for the mind must have an object', she writes (14–20 February
1796).[30] Hays recognizes that she had overvalued her love-object,
but without an object, she says (identifying herself with Othello),
her life is meaningless: 'Place then, *for a moment*, the object
out of the question, still I tell you, I am unhappy because "my
occupation's gone" . . . I sink into apathy, because I lose every thing
that endears life' (1 March 1796). Writing defends against apathy,
loss of meaning, and emptiness in the wake of erotic disillusion.
Forced to admit that her love for Frend was a fiction, Hays turns
to her fictional memoir: 'I shall write, to get rid of vacuity'
(1 March 1796). *Memoirs of Emma Courtney* is the substitute
'occupation' that fills the vacuum.

[28] See *Beyond the Pleasure Principle* (1920), SE xviii. 32–6.
[29] See the *Ego and the Id*, SE xix. 30 n., 45–6; for discussion of 'the great reservoir
of libido', see ibid., Appendix B (*SE* xix. 63).
[30] Or, as André Green puts it apropos of the need for an object, even a bad object
is better than none: 'The object is bad, but it is good that it exists even though it
does not exist as a good object'; see 'The Analyst, Symbolization and Absence in
the Analytic Setting', in *On Private Madness*, 55.

The Vehicular State

In her letters to Godwin, Hays plausibly attributes her tenacious passion and her self-absorption to isolation: 'It is the nature of strong passion, particularly in retirement, to be absorbed in its sensations' (11 May 1796). The 'Beastly Solitude' which she refers to in writing to Godwin (29 April–3 May 1796) had been constitutive of her obsession with Frend, just as absence had led her to idealize a distant object; 'absence magnified objects', she admits in due course (8 March 1796). Writing of the role of absence in the psychoanalytic situation, André Green invokes a 'narcissistic domain' which exists alongside object relations, calling it 'an encapsulated personal space . . . positively cathected in the silent self of being, or negatively cathected in the aspiration towards non-being. The dimension of absence,' he goes on, '. . . finds its place in the potential space between the self and the object.'[31] This 'dimension of absence' between the self and the object, which Green equates with the Winnicottian potential space or 'intermediate area of experiencing', is also the encapsulated space of epistolarity—for Hays, the narcissistic domain, whether positively or negatively cathected, which gave rise to *Memoirs of Emma Courtney*. Or rather, in the startling reversal proposed by Hays herself, literature (rather than a life of letter-writing) gives rise to her novel. Hays took as her epigraph Rousseau's apology for the obsessional passions and heightened perceptions of his lovers in *La Nouvelle Héloïse*, where retirement and solitude breed 'strange and false notions':

'The perceptions of persons in retirement are very different from those of people in the great world: their passions, being differently modified, are differently expressed; their imaginations, constantly impressed by the same objects, are more violently affected. The same small number of images continually return, mix with every idea, and create those strange and false notions, so remarkable in people who spend their lives in solitude.'[32]

---

[31] Ibid. 59.
[32] See *Eloisa: Or, A Series of Original Letters*, trans. William Kendrick (1803); *E* i, p. xxviii, and see *EC* 197 n. This was the standard translation of *La Nouvelle Héloïse* during the Romantic period; Mary Hays was reading Rousseau and quoting him at length in her correspondence in May 1796.

Emma, we are told, has always 'sighed for a romance that would never end' (*EC* 15)—a romance like that of Rousseau's Julie (Eloisa) —and she adopts 'the language of the tender Eloisa' (*EC* 150) to express her feelings for Augustus Harley. Hays even goes so far as to suggest that Emma's adolescent encounter with the early volumes of Rousseau's *La Nouvelle Héloïse* (reading, we're told, 'productive of a long chain of circumstances') is the source of her lifelong habit of unrequited love.[33]

But Hays's novel contains a still more startling implication: that prior even to reading Rousseau, 'a foundation is laid for the operations of our mind, years—nay, ages—previous to our birth' (*EC* 10). So far back her memoir does not go, although it projects its story of solitary passion forward into the next generation. None the less, the narrative foundation for the operations of Emma's mind is her mother's premature death at her birth. This first, unknowable loss is repeated by her later loss of a substitute breast at the time of weaning. Which comes first, literature or the loss of an object? *Memoirs of Emma Courtney* suggests that this question may prove to be an unanswerable 'both'. Adopted by her aunt as an infant, Emma finds a substitute mother while her-self replacing a dead child who has died shortly before: 'she received me, from the hands of my dying mother, as a substitute.— From these tender and affecting circumstances I was nursed and attended with peculiar care. . . . I hung at her breast' (*EC* 13). Hays predicates the conjugal family on the principle of substitution; the subject is marked by trauma at its origin. Like maternity, the bond of nursing ('I hung at her breast') is similarly liable to traumatic interruption. This severing of the bond between child and nurse prefigures Emma's subsequent affective relations:

---

[33] Hays quotes Rousseau himself on the lasting effects, not of first reading, but first love: ' "People, in general", says Rousseau, "do not sufficiently consider the influence which the first attachments, between man and woman, have over the re-mainder of their lives; they do not perceive, that an impression, so strong, and so lively, as that of love, is productive of a long chain of effects, which pass unobserved in a course of years, yet, nevertheless, continue to operate till the day of their deaths" ' (*EC* 60–1). The quotation is from *Emilius, or, An Essay on Education*, trans. Mr Nugent (2 vols., London, 1763), ii. 285 (see *EC* 207 n.).

At the age at which it was thought necessary to wean me, I was sent
from my tender nurse . . . My aunt dared not visit me during this short
separation, she was unable to bear my piercing cries of anguish at her
departure. If a momentary sensation, at that infantine period, deserve
the appellation, I might call this my first affectionate sorrow. I have fre-
quently thought that the tenderness of this worthy woman generated
in my infant disposition that susceptibility, that lively propensity to attachment, to which I have through life been a martyr. (*EC* 13–14)

'Separation . . . piercing cries of anguish . . . my first affectionate
sorrow . . . that lively propensity to attachment'—this is the story
of unrequited first love. Ostensibly, Hays protests against the
enslaving conditions of female dependence and social prejudice:
'Cruel prejudice! . . . —hapless woman! . . . Why are we bound,
by the habits of society, as with an adamantine chain?' (*EC* 32).
But the chains that bind women in her novel turn out not to be
social chains, but chains of contingency and traumatic loss. Emma
is 'hapless'—the victim or witness of serial accidents—because
she is bound to repetition by the chains of circumstance.

What Hays calls 'the magic circle' or 'the barbarous spell' that
binds both her and her heroine obtrudes mysteriously from time
to time into the narrative, along with 'the powerful enchantment'
or the 'train of overwhelming reflection, that is every moment
on the point of breaking [its] thread' (*EC* 27–8). As this insistent
doubling of language suggests, the story-line of Hays's novel is often
strained by repetition. More strikingly, a 'train of overwhelming
reflection'—in other words, obsessional thought—threatens to turn
the novel into a succession of linguistic accidents that underline
the uncanny recurrence of a proper name: 'I weep, (said I),
because I am *friendless*' (*EC* 40; Hays's italics). The word 'friend'
(and its variants—*'friendship'* and *'friendless'*), often with the textual
marker of italics, punctuates Hays's printed text. The want of a
friend—the want of William Frend—condenses into a single,
melancholy refrain the convergence of pre- (or over-)determined
object-relations, on one hand, and the accidents or sheer contingency of language, on the other. Hays's novel inadvertently
publishes its secret (the 'burden' or refrain of her unrequited
passion for Frend) in the form of this literal repetition. Hays kept
her lover's name out of the public domain, yet it appears in print

everywhere.[34] But Emma's story also displaces what can't be recalled (the infant's 'piercing cries of anguish') on to what can be told (a story of amorous rejection). Forgotten affect takes the form of a lost friend. At the close of her memoir, Emma reiterates her commitment to the bonds of the past: 'Friendship was the star, whose cheering influence I courted . . . The social affections were necessary to my existence, but they have been only inlets to sorrow—*yet, still, I bind them to my heart!*' (*EC* 195; Hays's italics). Social affections and the pursuit of friendship—the pursuit of Frend—provides an inlet for pre-existing sorrow. Emma's 'first affectionate sorrow' is the precursor for all other affectionate ties, whether social or self-destructive. Paradoxically, however, this binding of affective energies ('*yet still I bind them to my heart*') is what allows Hays to transform the atemporality of infantile sorrow into a temporal narrative of unrequited love. As André Green puts it, 'free (unbound) energy' that seeks release in condensation, displacement, and the coexistence of opposites transforms itself into 'bound energy whose release is postponed, restrained, and limited in conformity with the laws of logic and temporal succession'.[35] This is as much as to say that narrative not only comes to the rescue of amatory obsession, but may itself be an obsessional form. Energized by the oppositions and contradictions of passion, Hays's narrative is made possible by the binding of energy in conformity with the logic of temporality. But traces of primary process remain, and this, perhaps, is why the reader becomes the *sujet* of Hays's epistolary fiction, or what Green calls 'the *analyzed*' of her text.[36]

---

[34] Hays steadfastly refused to tell Godwin the name of the man she loved (who would have been personally known to him), although presumably she told Wollstonecraft, who defended Hays's passion in her letters to Godwin. Wollstonecraft may have been the woman friend who accompanied Hays on the visit to Frend during which she apologized for her pursuit of him and tried to make rational amends (see Hays's letter of 8 Mar. 1796).

[35] See Green, 'The Unbinding Process', in *On Private Madness*, 338.

[36] See ibid. 338: 'those traces [of primary process] always give themselves away, behind the logic-bound construction of the text . . . the reader's unconscious perceives and registers them. Whence the fact that the effect of every literary text . . . is to awaken both an idea and an affect in the reader. . . . the analyst reacts to the text as if it were a product of the unconscious. The analyst then becomes the *analyzed* of the text.'

When Godwin objected that Hays's self-absorbed heroine,
'interested only about herself, will find it difficult to interest
others for her', Hays replied, with some energy, that her manu-
script 'was not written *merely* for the public eye—another latent,
& perhaps stronger, motive lurked beneath . . . I intended this
book to be a memento of my own folly or madness' (11 May 1796).
But *Memoirs of Emma Courtney* is more than a memento to private
madness. One reading of Hays's correspondence with Godwin—at
times self-abasing, at times self-aggrandizing, but always relentlessly
analytic (even when she turns her attention to Godwin himself)—
is simply that it gave her something to do (providing her with
an 'occupation').[37] As she wrote, 'I am fond of analyzing my feelings' (6 June 1796; surely an understatement). This, after all, was
a 'philosophical romance'; for 'may there not be philosophical
romance?', she asks (9 February 1796). It could be argued that Hays's
identification with Godwinian philosophy gave her both an intellectual apprenticeship and a form of intellectual (self-)mastery.
Analogously, it has also been argued that the heroine of her novel
loves Augustus Harley less for himself than for the educational
and professional opportunities he represents (opportunities closed
to Emma herself).[38] Such readings speak to and of the erotics of
knowledge, and to the implied assumption that knowledge is
power, as well as to women's struggle for access to the public
spheres of education and politics during the Enlightenment period
that coincided with the French Revolution. Jessica Benjamin
explores the erotic dimensions of just such transferential relations
involving women as they are played out, not in the political realm,

[37] For Hays's attempts to analyse Godwin, see, for instance, her letter of 4 Apr.
1796, in which she writes of being convinced of his 'sensibility', or her letter of 29
Apr.–3 May 1796: 'You are, at once, kind & cruel, polite & rude, tender & savage,
candid & intolerant—I cannot describe, how paradoxical you appear to me.'

[38] See, for instance, Luria, 'Mary Hays's Letters and Manuscripts', 526, and
Rajan, 'Autonarration and Genotext', 156, for the suggestion that Hays's relation to
Godwin, and Emma's to Harley, provided simultaneous access to education and political discourse. But cf. Freud's telling suggestion in 'The Disposition to Obsessional
Neurosis' that 'the instinct for knowledge . . . is at bottom a sublimated off-shoot
of the instinct of mastery exalted into something intellectual' (*SE* xii. 324)—an equally
compelling reading of the case of Emma Courtney, if not of Hays herself.

but in the psychoanalytic setting.[39] Freud thought that the overcoming of transference love—giving up the pleasure principle
in order to identify with the analyst, and putting the analyst's
understanding in place of an ego ideal—produced 'that extra piece
of mental freedom that distinguishes conscious mental activity'.[40]
But Benjamin points out that the Freudian paradigm of instinctual self-mastery and regulated passion (the paradigm implicitly
offered by Godwin to Hays, and by Mr Francis to Emma) is based
on the model of the all-knowing male analyst to the female
analysand who sues for love.

What happens, by contrast, if the analyst is modelled not on
a father, but on a mother, whether literally or metaphorically
understood?—modelled, that is, on a symbolic figure capable
of a maternal function as well as a paternal one. The possibility
of transference involving the mother, or at any rate associated
with attributes culturally coded as maternal, shifts the emphasis
from mental activity as the pay-off for struggling against instinctual demands to something like the 'use' of an object (in its
Winnicottian sense).[41] Jessica Benjamin is appropriately wary about
the dangers of what she calls 'idealized notions of therapeutic
reparation, founded in magical beliefs about maternal power'—
just as Winnicott himself was irked by the idea of the analyst as
good breast.[42] Her aim is to displace the model of the paternal or
Lacanian analyst ('the one supposed to know') with an analyst
redefined as 'the one who knows *me*'. Associated with 'the idea
of holding or containing rather than penetrating with insight',
this 'maternal' analyst implies for Benjamin a relationship of
mutuality and recognition, along with the reciprocal satisfactions
of knowing and being known.[43] The mother may be many things

[39] See Jessica Benjamin, 'What Angel Would Hear Me?', in *Like Subjects, Love Objects* (New Haven, 1995), 143–74.

[40] See 'Observations on Transference Love' (1915), *SE* xii. 170.

[41] See D. W. Winnicott, 'The Use of an Object and Relating through Identifications' (1969), in *Playing and Reality*, 86–94.

[42] See Benjamin, *Like Subjects, Love Objects*, 157, and D. W. Winnicott, 'The
Depressive Position in Normal Development' (1954), in *Collected Papers: Through
Pediatrics to Psycho-Analysis* (London, 1958), 276.

[43] See *Like Subjects, Love Objects*, 169.

(including the father), and the father many things (including the mother). But Benjamin sets out to re-imagine Winnicott's 'space of being alone in the presence of the (m)other' in terms of women's experience—or would it be more accurate to say, imagining? —of a non-phallic erotics associated with the maternal body. The phallically penetrated heart (the wounded or pierced heart enshrined in the masochistic language of exquisite sensibility) gives way to a metaphor based on the pre-verbal dialogue of mother and infant. In *Memoirs of Emma Courtney*, Emma's first love is not, in fact, an idealized, indifferent, and ultimately dead Enlightenment man (Augustus Harley), but his kindly and cultivated mother, Mrs Harley: 'a strong sympathy united us, and we became almost inseparable. Every day I discovered . . . a new and indissoluble tie, that bound me to her' (*EC* 59). In a novel where the place-holder for the missing or distant father is Emma's Godwinian mentor, Mr Francis, Mrs Harley reoccupies the place of Emma's substitute mother, the aunt who had nursed her so tenderly in place of her own child.

In yet another of the novel's substitutions, Emma comes to occupy the space in Mrs Harley's heart vacated by her perennially absent son, Augustus; later, she herself becomes 'more than mother' to Augustus's son (Augustus junior)—the *'more than son'* for whose edification Emma's epistolary memoir is supposedly written, and to whom it is addressed (he in turn has become embroiled in a hopeless and self-destructive passion; her memoir is meant to serve as a warning to the next generation).[44] In this space of cultivated retirement, where an older and a younger woman talk, read, and walk in an uninterrupted intimacy that is defined by 'the *absence* of Augustus' (my italics), Emma falls in love, not with the son, but with the son's likeness in the form of a portrait. Augustus Harley's picture is oddly described as 'this resemblance of a man'. Hays's heroine, we are told, unconsciously transfers to it her feelings for his mother: 'Without being conscious of it myself, my grateful love for Mrs Harley had, already,

---

[44] Hays frames her story at start and end with letters addressing the younger Augustus Harley as 'Rash young man' and 'My Augustus, *my more than son*' (*EC* 7, 195).

by a transition easy to be traced by a philosophic mind, transferred itself to her son' (*EC* 59). In this 'easy transition' from mother to son, one could trace the normalizing substitution of a heterosexual love for an originally same-sex object. But a counter-reading inevitably presents itself. The heterosexual simulacrum ('this resemblance of a man') provides a substitute, not only for Emma's 'grateful love for Mrs Harley', but for Emma's 'first affectionate sorrow'—her propensity for attachment to a lost object. As gratitude to the mother turns into love for the son, Emma's feelings for Augustus become an obscure memorial to the long-lost mother who died at her birth and was lost again at the time of her weaning. Emma's fixation on Augustus (the 'solitary passion, that concentrates all our desires within one point', *EC* 61) focuses the diffuse and multiple yearning associated with her substitute mother(s) as unrequited love for a heterosexual object.[45] The word 'transferred' ('my grateful love for Mrs Harley ... transferred itself to her son') makes it plausible to invoke the form of transference love described by Benjamin, associated as it is with maternal erotics, and, in particular, with an unconscious phantasy of immersion in the maternal body.

Behind Hays's transferential correspondence with Godwin, with its formation of a precociously 'philosophic' self, lies the imaginary space of intersubjectivity represented by Mrs Harley's enfolding bosom:

I yearned to throw myself upon her bosom, to weep, to unfold to her the inmost recesses of my mind—that ingenuous mind, which languished for communication, and preyed upon itself. Dear and cruel friend, why did you transfix my heart with the barbed and envenomed arrow, and then refuse to administer the only healing balsam? (*EC* 61)

---

[45] Hays is quoting Helvétius, *A Treatise on Man, His Intellectual Faculties and His Education*, trans. W. Hooper (2 vols., London, 1777), ii. 42: 'The more desires I have (observes an acute, and profound French Philosopher), the less ardent they are. The torrents that divide themselves into many branches, are the least dangerous in their course. A strong passion is a solitary passion, that concentrates all our desires within one point' (see *EC* 61 and 207 n.).

Here the 'Dear and cruel friend' who punitively withholds the
cure for love is the mother not the son. Later, Mrs Harley is '[her]
maternal friend' (EC 71), and even—as Emma exclaims in an ecstatic
sickbed reunion—'My mother!' (EC 151). The 'healing balsam' for
Emma's wounded heart turns out not to be the prescriptions
of Godwinian philosophy, let alone Augustus's chilly love, but
this idealized form of maternal attachment. The intersubjective space figured by Mrs Harley's bosom corresponds to the
space of writing where what Habermas calls 'intimate mutual
relationships between privatized individuals' substitute for the
reality of relations between author, work, and public, leading to
the attainment of psychological insight, self-knowledge, and
empathy.[46] More controversially, Winnicott locates the origins of
cultural experience in what he calls the 'potential space between
the individual and the environment (originally the object)'—
a third area of experience 'contrasted with inner or personal
psychic reality and with the actual world in which the individual
lives'.[47] This third area has a more than generic resemblance to
the paradoxical in-between space of Hays's epistolary memoir-
novel. Significantly, Emma avows her feelings for Augustus in a
letter which ends, not with a demand for love (as one might have
expected), but simply with a heartfelt request to write to her:
'I relinquish my pen with reluctance. A melancholy satisfaction,
from what source I can scarcely define, diffuses itself through my
heart while I unfold to you its emotions.—Write to me' (EC 83).
The communication of emotions to another provides its own,
melancholy and diffusive satisfactions. Yet Emma's request ('Write
to me') asks for something more: not just for an acknowledgement of the receipt of her feelings, but for a response to her
private epistolary madness.

This is the subtext of Hays's intellectual correspondence with
Godwin. As we have seen, he was philanthropically willing to

---

[46] See The Structural Transformation of the Public Sphere, 50: 'The relations between
author, work, and public ... become intimate mutual relationships between
privatized individuals who were psychologically interested in what was "human",
in self-knowledge, and in empathy.'

[47] See 'The Location of Cultural Experience', Playing and Reality, 100, 102–3.

receive, if not understand, the communication of her feelings
—perhaps all he really needed to do—but the correspondence
remained largely one-sided. He was too reasonable to be either
a lover or a madman (too reasonable for her, anyway).[48] In the
last resort, both Hays and her heroine seem to be in search of
an outlet (an inlet?) for 'tender affections' which her memoir-novel
relocates, not in any affective or erotic experience with Augustus
Harley (a cold fish who has problems of his own), let alone in
Godwin's intellectual mentorship, but in the intimacy associated
with his mother and with letters. One condition for such intimacy
is a shared response to literature, as we see when Hays writes:
'To feel these affections in a supreme degree, a mind enriched
by literature and expanded by fancy and reflection, is necessary—'
(EC 89). For Habermas, the ideal form of this enriched and expans-
ive literary interchange would be a public created by just such a
union of private individuals through critical reflection on their
reading.[49] Habermas's notion of the public sphere has been crit-
icized as both an idealization and an abstraction—as a 'phantom
public sphere'.[50] For Hays, the ideal form of this union would
be a form of communication in which words (whether spoken
or written) become redundant altogether. Emma writes wishfully
to Augustus, 'I wish we were in the vehicular state, and that you
understood the sentient language; you might then comprehend the
whole of what I mean to express, but find too delicate for *words*'
(EC 89). The same letter ends, startlingly: 'it is your mind, only,
I desire to read' (EC 91)—anticipating Freud's fanciful exclamation,
'And only think if one could get hold of this physical equivalent

---

[48] See Hays's letter of 10 Mar. 1796, in which she wishes Godwin had been in
love himself: 'I do wish you had been in love (but not, as I have, tasted only its
bitterness) & then you would always understand me, which you are yet, I doubt
not, notwithstanding your delicacy & sensibility, too wise & too reasonable to do.'

[49] See *The Structural Transformation of the Public Sphere*, 51: 'The privatized individuals coming together to form a public also reflected critically and in public on
what they had read, thus contributing to the process of enlightenment which they
together promoted.'

[50] See Bruce Robbins (ed.), *The Phantom Public Sphere* (Minneapolis and London,
1993), especially Bruce Robbins, 'Introduction: The Public as Phantom', pp. vii–xxvi.

of the psychical act!' (*SE* xxii. 55). Hays's novel clarifies Emma's playful, but at the same time serious, reference to 'the vehicular state' with a footnote citing Edward Search's late eighteenth-century work of speculative philosophy, *The Light of Nature Pursued* (1768).

Search anticipates Freud's speculation about telepathy by developing an elaborate fantasy of non-vocal or 'sentient' communication, capable of exciting in the other 'the same ideas that gave rise to them in ourselves, making him as it were feel our thoughts. This is a much completer way of conversing, being not liable to misapprehension . . .'[51] This is also nothing more nor less than thought-transference. Search's 'vehicle', a kind of muscle or fibre imperceptible to the eye, resembles Freud's imaginary prototype for the transformation of mental states into physical states and back again—a prototype lost, he suspects, in the process of phylogenetic evolution.[52] The 'vehicular state' (so called by Search himself) is the imaginary of letter-writing—a transparent form of communication that would make the letter obsolete, uniting two bodies as one. Thought-transference satisfies the wish to know another's mind and be known without ever having to undertake the 'hazardous experiment' of letters (or even conversation). Where Habermas envisages a public sphere predicated on private acts of written or spoken intimacy, Freud, as we have seen, develops the argument that telepathic communication might have been 'the original, archaic method of communication between individuals' (and even excited mobs). Search's 'completer way of conversing' ultimately depends on the intimate bodily connection between mother and child, where the exchange of unconscious phantasies and feelings can be imagined as taking place without words, and the movements of nursing and sucking keep time to the reciprocal rhythms of reverie and reception,

---

[51] See *EC* 210 n. and cf. *The Light of Nature Pursued* (5 vols., London, 1768), ii. 135–6.

[52] See 'Dreams and Occultism', *SE* xxii. 55. Cf. also Freud's tentative explorations of 'telepathic' phenomena in 'Psychoanalysis and Telepathy' (1921) and 'Dreams and Telepathy' (1922), as well as his 'lost' essay, *A Phylogenetic Fantasy: Overview of the Transference Neuroses*, ed. Ilse Grubrich-Simitis, trans. Axel Hoffer and Peter T. Hoffer (Cambridge, Mass., 1987).

fullness and emptiness.[53] This is not to privilege silence over speech, or thought-transference over writing—let alone (as Benjamin warns) to attribute magical powers to maternal reparation, or (as Freud feared) occult power to unconscious wishes. Rather, what Hays's allusion to Search allows us to glimpse is the invisible assumption that informs the Habermasian equation of subjectivity with the 'intimateness whose vehicle was the written word'.[54] Some version of Search's 'vehicular' fantasy underlies both Habermas's model of epistolary subjectivity, in which a letter serves as a transparent 'vehicle' for intimacy, and Freud's startling speculation about the physical basis of telepathy.

In his more recent theory of communicative action, Habermas moves to speech-act theory in order to differentiate between a bourgeois public sphere predicated on the existence of a reading public, on the one hand, and the fragmented public of mass communication and mass culture on the other. He none the less tends to assume the primacy and continuity of an idealized speech-event which he sometimes refers to as 'conversation' and sometimes as 'the written word'.[55] Predicated as it is on non-presence, the letter lends itself to an alternative model, that of writing conceived as mechanically iterable, independent of an actual author or sender, and subject to the mechanical markings of repression, repetition,

[53] Cf. also Ferenczi's account of the omnipotence of the infant's 'hallucinatory re-occupation of the satisfying situation that is missed, the untroubled existence in the warm, tranquil body of the mother. The first wish-impulse of the child . . . cannot be other than to regain this situation' ('Stages in the Development of the Sense of Reality', *First Contributions to Psycho-Analysis*, 221). Ferenczi also refers to the ministrations of nurses: 'by rocking the child and crooning to him monotonously rhythmical lullabies . . . reproduce the slight and monotonously rhythmical stimuli that the child is not spared even in utero (the swaying movements of the mother when walking, the maternal heart-beats, the deadened noise from without that manages to penetrate to the interior of the body)' (ibid. 221). For a different account of the role of the mother as container of the infant's unconscious projective identifications in relation to omnipotence, see, for instance, W. R. Bion, 'A Theory of Thinking' (1962), *Second Thoughts* (1967; repr. London, 1984), 110–19.

[54] *The Structural Transformation of the Public Sphere*, 49.

[55] For Habermas's implicit assumption that subjectivity is transparent and that public print culture exists in an unbroken relation to speech, see Neil Saccamano, 'The Consolations of Ambivalence: Habermas and the Public Sphere', *Modern Language Notes*, 106 (1991), 685–98.

and the materiality of print culture. The irreducibility of text to conversation—the incommensurability of what Habermas calls 'the ordinary practice of normal speech' and the 'extraordinary spheres' of literature and philosophy—allows an expanded, Derridian understanding of textuality to displace a communicative one founded on the analogy with speech.[56] The 'extraordinary spheres' of literature and philosophy become the type of writing. But letters—the paradigmatic site for the emergence of the literary —demand with particular insistence to be relocated in what André Green (estranging the Winnicottian transitional object from its nursery setting) refers to as 'this no-man's-land . . . this site of a trans-narcissistic communication where the author's and reader's doubles—ghosts which never reveal themselves—communicate through the writing'.[57] If one hazard of epistolarity lies in its secret adherence to a phantasy of intimate bodily connection (presence), the other hazard that lines it is Green's contrastingly *dis*embodied written communication between two ghosts (radical absence). The persistence of such contradictory ways of thinking about letters emerges from the way we imagine them as a no man's land of wishing and hallucination, self-creation and literary illusion; as both a substitute for knowledge about others or ourselves and a burdensome form of mechanical repetition. Considered not as therapy, but as private madness, writing may even produce the extra-literary losses it attempts to repair.

But perhaps there is another way to think about it. According to Freud, the most truly 'psychoanalytic' form of communication occurs between one unconscious and another; 'everyone', he writes, 'possesses in his own unconscious an instrument with which he can interpret the utterances of the unconscious in other

---

[56] For the lines of the Derridian critique and the three-cornered argument between Habermas, Derrida, and Searle, see, for instance, Benjamin Lee, 'Textuality, Mediation, and Public Discourse', in Craig Calhoun (ed.), *Habermas and the Public Sphere* (Cambridge, Mass., 1996), 402–18, esp. 410–11.

[57] *On Private Madness*, 322. For Green's redefinition of the *'potential space'* of literature as 'a metaphorical locus . . . within which the field of illusion is constituted as the celebration of a transitional trans-narcissistic object', see ibid. 347.

people.'⁵⁸ Imagined as a potential object relation—an object relation observable also in the transferential and counter-transferential dimensions of the analytic relation—the intimacy of letters draws attention, not so much to an audience (as Habermas would have it do) as to the existence of the unconscious; as Freud puts it, 'inserting the unconscious between what is physical and what was previously called "psychical" '. In positing the identificatory basis of empathy, letters also draw attention to what Freud calls 'the mechanism by means of which we are enabled to take up any attitude at all towards another mental life' (a mechanism inadequately paraphrased by Habermas as 'the dual relation to both one's self and the other').⁵⁹ As the quintessential site for this identificatory and empathetic substitution, the letter also marks the emergence of what Habermas calls the literary, or what Winnicott sees as the space of collective illusion. Transitional phenomena, according to Winnicott's account of this intermediate area of experience, is a no man's land in the sense of being unclaimed territory (neither private nor public), but an area that defines the interrelation between inner and outer: 'It is an area that is not challenged, because no claim is made on its behalf except that it shall exist as a resting place for the individual engaged in the perpetual human task of keeping inner and outer reality separate yet inter-related.'⁶⁰ But the 'hazardous experiment' of letters (Green's no

⁵⁸ See 'The Disposition to Obsessional Neurosis', *SE* xii. 320. For the extensive literature on counter-transference as a mode of unconscious communication, from the 1950s on, see, for instance, Paula Heimann, 'On Counter-Transference' (1950), in Margaret Tonnesmann (ed.), *About Children and Children-No-Longer* (London and New York, 1989), 73–9; Margaret Little, 'Counter-Transference and the Patient's Response to it', *IJP-A* 32 (1951), 32–40; Heinrich Racker, 'The Meanings and Uses of Countertransference' (1957), in *Transference and Countertransference* (New York, 1968), 127–73; and, more recently, Christopher Bollas, 'Expressive Uses of the Counter-transference' and 'Self Analysis and the Countertransference', in *The Shadow of the Object: Psychoanalysis of the Unthought Known* (London, 1987), 200–35, 236–55.

⁵⁹ *The Structural Transformation of the Public Sphere*, 49. Cf. Freud's speculation that 'a path leads from identification by way of imitation to empathy, that is, to the comprehension of the mechanism by means of which we are enabled to take up any attitude at all towards another mental life' in ch. vii of 'Group Psychology and the Analysis of the Ego' (1921), *SE* xviii. 110 n.

⁶⁰ *Playing and Reality*, 2.

man's land where author's and reader's doubles communicate through writing) testifies to something stranger—to forms of interrelatedness which, like Freud's fantasy of telepathic communication, exist 'only in imagination'.[61] It is this strange territory that is perpetually being renegotiated in the intersubjective exchange that characterizes both psychoanalysis and the scene of reading.

[61] For Freud's 'conversion' to telepathy, see also *The Complete Correspondence of Sigmund Freud and Ernest Jones 1908–1939*, ed. R. Andrew Paskauskas, intro. Riccardo Steiner (Cambridge, Mass., 1993), 596–7.

Index